REASON
TO REJOICE

Books by Ray C. Stedman

Adventuring Through the Bible
Authentic Christianity
Body Life
The Fight of Faith
For Such a Time as This
Friend of God
God's Final Word
God's Loving Word
God's Unfinished Book
Is This All There Is to Life?
Let God Be God
Letters to a Troubled Church
Our Riches in Christ
The Power of His Presence
Psalms: Folk Songs of Faith
Spiritual Warfare
Talking with My Father
Waiting for the Second Coming
The Way to Wholeness
What on Earth Is Happening

DISCOVERY HOUSE
PUBLISHERS®

Ray C. Stedman

REASON TO REJOICE

Love, Grace, and Forgiveness in Paul's Letter to the Romans

Discovery House Publishers is affiliated with
RBC Ministries, Grand Rapids, Michigan 49501.

Requests for permission to quote from this book should be directed to:
Permissions Department, Discovery House Publishers, P. O. Box 3566,
Grand Rapids, MI 49501, or contact us by e-mail at
permissionsdept@dhp.org

Interior Design by Sherri L. Hoffman

Library of Congress Cataloging-in-Publication Data

Stedman, Ray C.
    (From guilt to glory)
    Reason to rejoice: love, grace, and forgiveness in Paul's letter to the
    Romans / by Ray C. Stedman
        p. cm.
    Originally published: From guilt to glory, Waco, Tex: Word Books,
    ©1978.
    Includes bibliographical references.
        ISBN 1-57293-091-8
    1. Bible. N.T. Romans—Criticism, interpretation, etc. I. Title.
    BS2665.52.S74 2003
    227'.107—dc22
    2003015684

Printed in the United States of America
Second printing in 2012

CONTENTS

EDITORS' PREFACE

Ray Stedman (1917–1992) served as pastor of the Peninsula Bible Church from 1950 to 1990. He was known and loved as a man of outstanding Bible knowledge and wisdom coupled with a depth of Christian integrity, love, and humility. Born in Temvik, North Dakota, Ray grew up on the rugged landscape of Montana. When he was a small child, his mother became ill and his father, a railroad man, abandoned the family, so Ray grew up on his aunt's Montana farm from the time he was six. He came to know the Lord at a Methodist revival meeting at age ten.

As a young man he tried different jobs, working in Chicago, Denver, Hawaii, and elsewhere. He enlisted in the Navy during World War II, where he often led Bible studies for civilians and Navy personnel, and even preached on local radio in Hawaii. At the close of the war, Ray was married in Honolulu, though he and his wife Elaine had first met in Great Falls, Montana. They returned to the mainland in 1946, and Ray graduated from Dallas Theological Seminary in l950. After two seminary summers interning under the widely regarded Bible teacher, Dr. J. Vernon McGee, Ray traveled for several months with another renowned Bible teacher, Dr. H. A. Ironside, pastor of Moody Church in Chicago.

In 1950, Ray was called by the two-year-old Peninsula Bible Fellowship in Palo Alto, California, to serve as its first pastor. Peninsula Bible Fellowship later became Peninsula Bible Church, and Ray eventually served a forty-year tenure there, retiring on April 30, 1990. During those years, Ray Stedman authored a number of life-changing Christian books, including the classic work on the meaning and mission of the church, *Body Life*. He entered into the presence of his Lord on October 7, 1992.

This book, *Reason to Rejoice*, is derived from two sermon series Ray Stedman preached on the book of Romans.[1] In Romans 12:1, Paul challenges Christians to "offer your bodies as living sacrifices, holy and pleasing to God." Though the book of Romans is rich in wisdom and practical instruction on many themes, from justification by faith to our struggle against sin to authentic Christian love, the theme of presenting ourselves to God as "living sacrifices" is a good summation of what Romans is all about.

In these pages, you'll be inspired and instructed as Ray shares powerful insights into the apostle Paul's most famous New Testament letter. Like all of Ray Stedman's writings, *Reason to Rejoice* is lively, conversational, and avoids technical jargon. Ray's personal warmth and humor shine through, making this an enjoyable book to read—and reread. Most important of all, you'll be challenged and encouraged to apply these life-changing truths in your everyday life.

The journey through Paul's letter to the Romans is the journey of a lifetime. So turn the page and enrich *your* adventure of faith in Christ!

—THE EDITORS

CHAPTER 1

FROM GUILT TO GLORY

Romans 1:1–17

Saint Augustine of Hippo was a great church leader of the fourth century. But as a young man before his conversion to Christianity, Augustine struggled with God and with the temptation to sin. He tried to live a morally upright life in his own strength, but he would inevitably fail.

In his autobiography, *The Confessions*, he wrote that on one occasion he felt such so much guilt, shame, and condemnation for his sins that he flung himself down under a fig tree and wept a flood of tears. "God, why can't I live a righteous life?" he prayed. "I want to stop sinning, but I can't!"

Just then, he heard a child, chanting in a sing-song voice, "Take up and read, take up and read!" He interpreted those words as a message from God.

But what did the message mean—"take up and read"? Read what? Then Augustine remembered the scroll he had left with his close friend, Alypius—a scroll of Paul's letter to the Christians at Rome.

Augustine jumped up, went to his friend, and found the scroll. He decided to read the first passage his eyes fell upon:

> Let us behave decently, as in the daytime, not in orgies and drunkenness, not in sexual immorality and debauchery, not in dissension and jealousy. Rather, clothe yourselves with the Lord Jesus Christ, and do not think about how to gratify the desires of the sinful nature. (Romans 13:13–14)

Instantly, a sense of peace came over him. His struggle with God was over. Though he could not resist temptation in his own power, he could "clothe [himself] with the Lord Jesus Christ" and allow the Lord live through him. At that moment, Augustine was a changed man. His transformation had begun with two sentences from the book of Romans.

Paul's letter to the Romans is his greatest. In fact, I believe it is the most powerful document ever written. Of all the New Testament letters, Romans is the broadest in scope and deepest in insight. No other document has affected and transformed more human lives. Here are just a few stories of lives it has changed:

Eleven centuries after St. Augustine, a German theologian named Martin Luther was meditating on this great phrase from Romans 1:17: "The righteous will live by faith." As he contemplated those words, Luther realized that he had completely missed the point of the Christian gospel! True Christianity is not a matter of rites and rituals and ceremonies. The essence of Christianity is *faith*, not works! Those words from the book of Romans lit a fire in Luther's soul, a fire that would become the great Protestant Reformation.

The seventeenth-century Puritan preacher John Bunyan spent twelve years in jail in Bedford, England. His crime? He left the Church of England and sought to worship God according to his own conscience. While studying Romans in his jail cell, Bunyan was inspired by the themes of Romans to write an allegorical novel, *The Pilgrim's Progress*. Today, that novel—which illustrates how Christians should relate to God and the world around them—is still a widely read classic.

Another whose life was transformed by the message of Romans was a young Anglican minister, John Wesley. In 1735, Wesley went to America, where he had served a brief stint as a pastor to British colonists in Savannah, Georgia. There he was spurned by the woman he loved and rejected by his congregation. He returned to England in February 1738, embittered and dejected, feeling like a complete failure.

For the next few weeks, Wesley tried to live a righteous life, but he continually battled temptation. "I was indeed fighting continually, but not conquering," he later recalled. "I fell and rose, and fell again." During this time, he often doubted God and his own faith.

On May 14 of that year, Wesley went to a meeting on Aldersgate Street in London. There, a man was reading to the congregation from Martin Luther's preface to the book of Romans. Wesley wrote in his journal that as he listened, "I felt my heart strangely warmed. I felt I did trust in Christ alone for salvation."

As a result of his encounter with the book of Romans, John Wesley's life was transformed. He became one of the leaders of the Great Evangelical Awakening that brought thousands of people to faith in Jesus Christ.

That is the power of this amazing book. Embedded in the pages of Paul's letter to the Romans is the power to change individual lives and entire societies. It is a power that we all long to experience as followers of Jesus Christ.

Every Christian should study and master the book of Romans. I hope that, by the time you have completed this study, you will be able to outline the great themes of Romans from memory. I pray that you will develop such a love for this life-changing New Testament letter that you will return to it again and again, and that you will live daily in its truths. If you do, I guarantee that it will change your life, just as it has changed thousands of lives through the centuries.

The Central Truth of Romans: Jesus Is Lord

The theme of Romans could be expressed as "From Guilt to Glory." In other words, this letter deals with how God, through Jesus Christ, has enabled human beings to move from a place of condemnation and sin to a place of reconciliation and righteousness. The sixteen chapters of Romans divide into three main sections with a number of subsections (see "The Structure of Romans" on page 13).

Paul's letter to the Romans was written around AD 56 to 58 while he was in the Greek city of Corinth on his third missionary journey. As you read this letter, you can catch glimpses of the social and spiritual condition of Corinth at that time. Corinth was located at the crossroads of trade in the Roman Empire, much like New York or San Francisco in our own time. And like those modern cities, Corinth was notorious for its godlessness and its atmosphere of bold, blatant immorality. Paul characterizes that godlessness in his letter to the Romans.

Paul wrote less than thirty years after the crucifixion and resurrection of the Lord Jesus. The impact of the life of Jesus was sharply etched in the minds of Christians throughout the Roman Empire. Paul wrote Romans to instruct them and remind them of these profound events that had shaken the first-century world.

The first seventeen verses of Romans are an introduction to the great themes of the letter. In those opening verses, Paul lays out the themes he will return to repeatedly. There is a logical, literary order to them that leads us to a central theme: *Jesus is Lord.* We see it in the first seven verses:

> Paul, a servant of Christ Jesus, called to be an apostle and set apart for the gospel of God—the gospel he promised beforehand through his prophets in the Holy Scriptures regarding his Son, who as to his human nature was a descendant of David, and who through the Spirit of holiness was declared with power to be the Son of God by his resurrection from the dead: Jesus Christ our Lord. Through him and for his name's sake, we received grace and apostleship to call people from among all the Gentiles to the obedience that comes from faith. And you also are among those who are called to belong to Jesus Christ.
>
> To all in Rome who are loved by God and called to be saints:
>
> Grace and peace to you from God our Father and from the Lord Jesus Christ. (Romans 1:1–7)

The STRUCTURE of ROMANS

PART 1: Reconciliation and Righteousness EXPLAINED by Paul

Romans 1:1–17	Paul's introductory remarks to the Christians in Rome
Romans 1:18–32	God's diagnosis of the human condition; the wrath of God
Romans 2	The guilt problem: why rites, rituals, and religion fail
Romans 3	The world is dead in sin—*but now* a righteousness from God is revealed
Romans 4	Abraham illustrates God's grace; he was justified by faith, not works
Romans 5	Rejoicing in our hope, in our suffering, in God our Friend
Romans 6	How to live by grace instead of law; slaves to righteousness, not sin
Romans 7	Our struggle against "the flesh" (our sinful nature)
Romans 8:1–17	There is now no condemnation for believers
Romans 8:18–39	The privilege of suffering for Christ; God works all things together for good

PART 2: Reconciliation and Righteousness EXHIBITED in the History of the Nation of Israel

Romans 9	God's sovereignty demonstrated in the life of Israel
Romans 10	How to be saved—and what about those who have never heard the gospel?
Romans 11	The hope of Israel and the hope of the church

PART 3: Reconciliation and Righteousness EXPERIENCED in Everyday Living

Romans 12	Our identity as living sacrifices; spiritual gifts; Christian love
Romans 13:1–7	Our Christian duty toward the government
Romans 13:8–14	How to authentically love one another
Romans 14:1– 15:13	Christian liberty; building up and accepting one another in the church
Romans 15:14– 16:27	Paul's postscript: Greetings and concluding remarks

The heart of Paul's argument is Jesus Himself. As he wrote in Colossians 1:27, "Christ in you, the hope of glory" is the one great truth from which all others flow. Other profound truths, such as *justification by faith* and *sanctification* (solving the sin problem) are certainly important, but the great central theme of the New Testament is the astonishing fact of *our union with Jesus Christ, God's Son.* That's why the person of the Lord Jesus is central to Paul's thinking, just as it is central to God's program for humanity. We do not simply believe in a creed or follow a philosopher. Our lives are *joined* to the life of the Savior, the Redeemer, the Lord.

Another major theme of Paul's introduction is that Jesus is the promised Messiah whose coming was predicted throughout the Old Testament. The good news of salvation was promised through the "prophets in the Holy Scriptures regarding his Son." The Christian faith was not invented in the first century AD; rather, it was the culmination of centuries of Jewish teachings, Jewish prophecies, and Jewish anticipation throughout Old Testament times.

In John 5:39, Jesus told the scribes and Pharisees, "You diligently study the [Old Testament] Scriptures because you think that by them you possess eternal life. These are the Scriptures that testify about me." Later, after His death and resurrection, Jesus met two discouraged disciples on the road to Emmaus. They didn't recognize Him, nor did they understand that His death and resurrection had been predicted many times in the Old Testament Scriptures. So Luke 24:27 tells us, "beginning at Moses and all the prophets, he [Jesus] expounded unto them in all the scriptures the things concerning himself" (KJV).

The great messianic passages of the Old Testament point unerringly to Jesus. When reading the Old Testament, we are gripped by the feeling that Someone is coming! All the prophets speak of Him, all the sacrifices point to Him, all the longings of humanity are focused on the coming Person who will one day arrive and solve the great crises of history. When the Old Testament closes, it is clear that He has not yet arrived—but He is expected.

And when the New Testament opens, the first story we read is of angels appearing to shepherds near Bethlehem. They sing a song of hope: "For unto you is born this day in the city of David a Saviour, which is Christ the Lord" (Luke 2:11 KJV). The Promised One has come!

These resounding truths are echoed in Paul's introduction to Romans as he points to Jesus as the One who was promised beforehand. Paul presents Jesus to us in two unique ways:

First, Paul speaks of His human nature. In Romans 1:3, Paul tells us that Jesus "was made of the seed of David according to the flesh."

Second, Paul tells us that there was more to Jesus than mere humanity. Linked with His humanness is the profound deity of the Creator God. In verse 4, Paul writes that Jesus was "declared to be the Son of God with power, according to the spirit of holiness, by the resurrection from the dead" (KJV). That phrase, "the Son of God," unmistakably declares the deity of our Lord. He was God. Paul emphasizes this fact many times throughout his letter to the Romans.

Yet, as we see in Romans and other letters of Paul, Jesus set aside His deity when He came in human form. He didn't come to act as God; rather, He came to act as a man *filled* by God. Jesus set an example for us, because Christians must live the same way, seeking to do God's will by being filled with God's Spirit. You and I can't be God, but we can be *possessed* by God, so that He can fill us and use us to accomplish His good and perfect will.

In verse 4, Paul notes three signs of the deity of Jesus, saying that He was declared to be the Son of God (1) with power, (2) according to the spirit of holiness, (3) by the resurrection from the dead.

First, the phrase "with power" speaks of the miracles Jesus did—the healings, the deliverance of people from demons, the miraculous feedings, and many more signs of His authority as the Son of God.

Second, Jesus came by "the spirit of holiness." Understand, this word *holiness* does not refer to putting on religious or sanctimonious airs. The word *holiness* actually comes from the same root as the word *wholeness*, and that is a good clue as to what holiness means. Paul is telling us that Jesus came as a whole person. He demonstrated a complete and fully integrated human personality. He showed us what it means to be a whole person living in a world of brokenness. When we look at Jesus, we see what He is calling us to become as whole and holy human beings. That is good news for us all.

Third, the deity of Jesus is authenticated in His resurrection from the dead. That is where our faith ultimately rests. We can have confidence that God has told us the truth because of the historical fact that God raised Jesus from the dead. The Resurrection cannot be explained away. We will explore this truth as we move deeper into Romans.

Loved by God

In the next section of his introduction to Romans, Paul makes a profound statement about the Christians in Rome—a statement that also applies to you and me as Christians today:

> And you also are among those who are called to belong to Jesus Christ.
> To all in Rome who are loved by God and called to be saints:
> Grace and peace to you from God our Father and from the Lord Jesus Christ. (Romans 1:6–7)

First, Paul says that Christians have a calling. We are not self-made or man-made saints; we are called by God to be His saints. The word *saint* comes from *sanctify*, which means to set something or someone apart for a specific purpose. So when Paul tells us we are "loved by God and called to be saints," he wants us to know that God cares deeply about us. He has called us and has set us apart for His eternal purpose.

God calls each of us in a unique way. But one common thread runs through every story of conversion to Christ: *God sought us out.* We may have thought we were seeking God, but the truth is that He sought us.

That is why Jesus said to His disciples, "All that the Father gives me will come to me, and whoever comes to me I will never drive away" (John 6:37). God sought us, God called us, God placed us in the care and keeping of His Son, Jesus.

Look again at Paul's remarkable statement that we are "loved by God." Later in Romans, Paul will have to scold these saints and correct them, so he begins by reminding them they are loved by God. He wants them to know that any correction that must take place will take place in a context of God's perfect love for them.

This is the basis of our relationship with God: *He loves us.* "Grace and peace to you from God our Father and from the Lord Jesus Christ," Paul writes. Grace and peace should characterize our lives. The grace and peace God gives us are proof of His love for us. We cannot earn grace; it is a gift of God's love.

Faith that Startles the World

Next, Paul highlights the faith of the Christians in Rome:

> First, I thank my God through Jesus Christ for all of you, because your faith is being reported all over the world. (Romans 1:8)

The whole world was talking about the faith of the Roman Christians! As Christians today, we tend to think the world will be impressed by the splendor of our church buildings, our growing congregations, or our glitzy, Broadway-class music programs. But these things do not impact the world for Jesus Christ. When God impacts the world through His saints, He does so through their *faith.*

The vibrant, vital faith of the Christians in Rome startled the entire world. Where did this vitality come from? Paul gives us this clue:

God, whom I serve with my whole heart in preaching the
gospel of his Son, is my witness how constantly I remember
you in my prayers at all times; and I pray that now at last by
God's will the way may be opened for me to come to you.
(Romans 1:9–10)

The faith of the Christians in Rome startled the world because
Paul and other Christians were praying for them. At this point in
his ministry, Paul had never been to Rome. Even so, he prayed
continually for the believers in Rome: "How constantly I remember you in my prayers at all times." That is why the church in
Rome was flourishing.

We need to recover this urgent sense of concern and prayer for
one another. I am convinced that it would make all the difference
in the world if we would continually uphold each other in prayer.

Set Apart from birth

Next, Paul points out that the Christians in Rome have been
strengthened by gifts of the Holy Spirit:

I long to see you so that I may impart to you some
spiritual gift to make you strong—that is, that you and I
may be mutually encouraged by each other's faith. (Romans
1:11–12)

Here we see what makes a church strong: the exercise of spiritual gifts. When Paul says he wants to impart a spiritual gift to the
Christians in Rome, he doesn't mean that he has all the gifts in
a bag and he doles them out wherever he goes. The word *impart*
means "to share." Paul can't give anyone a spiritual gift; only the
Holy Spirit can do that. Paul wants to share with the Roman Christians the gifts God has given. He wants to use his gifts among
them, and he wants to experience their gifts in his own life. Spiritual gifts are given so that Christians can be mutually strengthened in the faith. That is how a church should function. The saints

minister to each other, building up one another by their faith and by sharing and exercising their spiritual gifts.

Next, Paul defines himself as the great apostle to the Gentiles. As he writes, the good news of salvation by grace through faith in Jesus the Messiah is going out beyond Israel and into the world. Paul himself is helping build the bridge between Israel and the Gentiles.

In Romans 1:1, Paul identifies himself with these words: "Paul, a servant of Christ Jesus, called to be an apostle and set apart for the gospel of God." He is a *called* apostle, and it was God who called him. When did God call him? You might think Paul's calling took place when he had his blinding encounter with the Lord Jesus on the Damascus road (Acts 9:1–16). But no, Paul tells us in Galatians 1:15 that God "set me apart *from birth* and called me by his grace" (italics added).

God, who sees the end from the beginning, knows us and calls from a time before we even exist. That is the wonder of the God we serve. He sets us apart even before our lives and our awareness are formed. God used all the events of Paul's early life—his training under Gamaliel, his zeal as a young Pharisee, and even his early hatred of the gospel. This was all part of setting Paul apart as an apostle. When the time came for Paul to be converted, God opened the trap door on the Damascus Road and Paul fell through. That trap had been set for Paul long before he was born, and every experience of his pre-Christian life was designed to make him a more effective minister of the gospel.

So don't ever think that your life before you met Jesus was wasted. God can take all the sin, rebellion, sorrow, pain, and regret of your old life, and He can use it to make you a more effective minister of His grace in your new life in Christ. God doesn't merely redeem our souls. He redeems all the experiences of our lives, and He refashions them for His good, for our good, and for the good of the people around us.

What does Paul mean when he calls himself an apostle? What is an apostle? The word Paul uses that we translate *apostle* is *kletos* in the original Greek, which comes from *klesis*, "a divine calling or an invitation from God." Paul tells us in verse 5, "Through [Jesus] and for his name's sake, we received grace and apostleship to call people from among all the Gentiles to the obedience that comes from faith." So an apostle is someone called by God and set apart so that he might call others to faith and obedience. Paul continues:

> I do not want you to be unaware, brothers, that I planned many times to come to you (but have been prevented from doing so until now) in order that I might have a harvest among you, just as I have had among the other Gentiles.
>
> I am obligated both to Greeks and non-Greeks, both to the wise and foolish. That is why I am so eager to preach the gospel also to you who are at Rome. (Romans 1:13–15)

Note that phrase: "I am *obligated.* . . ." Here Paul tells us his mission in life. He is driven by a sense of purpose so clear and overwhelming that he considers it an obligation upon his life. He is obligated to preach the gospel to the Jews, to the Greeks, and to everyone else. He senses an urgent imperative to preach the gospel wherever he goes, to whoever he meets. Why? Because the gospel is the cure for sin!

If you were the sole possessor of a cure for cancer, would you be quiet about it? Or would you share the secret with everyone around you? Paul was intensely aware that he possessed the secret that everyone needs. He had the cure for the sin disease, and he was determined to share that cure with everyone he met.

Proud of the Gospel

What is this cure for sin that Paul feels driven to preach to the nations? He describes his message in the next two verses:

> I am not ashamed of the gospel, because it is the power
> of God for the salvation of everyone who believes; first for

the Jew, then for the Gentile. For in the gospel a righteousness from God is revealed, a righteousness that is by faith
from first to last, just as it is written: "The righteous will live
by faith." (Romans 1:16–17)

Paul closes with a quotation from the Old Testament: "The
righteous will live by his faith" (Habakkuk 2:4). This is the phrase
that gripped the heart of Martin Luther. This great truth, Paul says,
is the life-transforming message of the Christian gospel: If you
want to live a righteous life, then you must stop trying to achieve
it by your own efforts. The righteous life can only be achieved
by faith—that is, by a trust-relationship with God through Jesus
Christ.

This is a transforming truth, and Paul says he is not ashamed
of it. In fact, he is proud of it. He proclaims it boldly everywhere
he goes. He can't wait to get to Rome so he can preach this message there.

Paul is especially eager to proclaim this gospel in Rome
because the Romans appreciated power, just as Americans do
today. Roman military power had conquered the entire known
world. Roman knowledge was power—their road-building technology, their war-making technology, their legal knowledge, their
literary and artistic skill. Roman economic power had brought the
wealth of the world to Rome through both trade and conquest.

But Paul knew the Romans were powerless when it came to
changing hearts. Even with all its wealth and military might, the
Roman Empire was riddled with violence, corruption, despair,
and suicide. The "noble Romans" lived meaningless lives; their
wealth and power gave them no inner peace.

That is why Paul is proud of the gospel. That is why he is
eager to preach the gospel in the capital city of the Roman Empire.
The gospel of Jesus Christ is the power of God—power to do the
very things that Roman power could not do. We never need to
apologize for the gospel. It is power without rival, power to transform human lives, power to live a righteous life.

The righteousness of God, Paul says, is received by faith. We cannot earn God's righteousness, but we can receive it anytime we need it—and that is good news! Whenever we feel depressed, discouraged, or defeated, we can recall that God loves us, restores us, and gives us His righteousness to cover our own sin and inadequacy.

In the first seventeen verses of Romans 1, Paul has introduced the great themes of this letter. As we continue through this book together, I trust that these themes will transform our hearts as they have transformed the hearts of the first-century church, and of believers down through the ages. May you and I add our names to that list—Augustine, Luther, Bunyan, and Wesley—and may our hearts be strangely, wonderfully warmed by the life-changing truths of Romans.

CHAPTER 2

THE DIVINE DIAGNOSIS

Romans 1:18–32

The most famous mutiny in history was the rebellion aboard the HMS *Bounty* in April 1789. That incident inspired five motion pictures and numerous books. Three weeks after the *Bounty* left Tahiti with a cargo of breadfruit trees (a cheap food source for Caribbean slaves), the crew mutinied. First Mate Fletcher Christian, the leader of the mutineers, forced Captain William Bligh and eighteen loyal sailors into a small open boat and set them adrift.

The mutineers took the *Bounty* back to Tahiti. Sixteen crewmen chose to stay there. But Fletcher Christian and eight other men took some Tahitian islanders with them and set out for a safe hiding place. They chose a lonely, uninhabited island called Pitcairn.

One of the sailors made whiskey from the native plants, and the resulting drunken orgies quickly turned to violent brawls. Though the island looked like a paradise, the mutineers began to view it as a prison. One by one, the mutinous crewmen were either killed in fights or murdered in their sleep. Even Fletcher Christian died violently.

Finally, only one of the mutineers was left alive, a sailor named Alexander Smith. As the last man living, he felt responsible to look after the women and fatherless children who remained. Smith regretted the sinfulness of his past, and he knew he lacked wisdom to care for the women and children. He needed guidance from beyond himself.

Looking through a sea-chest, Smith found a Bible. Over the next few weeks, he read it from cover to cover. Then he asked God to take control of his life. He also taught the women and children to read the Bible. Fathered by various mutineers, those children grew up, married, and had children of their own.

In 1808, the American whaling ship *Topaz* stopped at Pitcairn. The Americans were the first visitors to the island since the mutiny on the *Bounty*, eighteen years earlier. The sailors from the *Topaz* were astounded to find an orderly Christian society in which there was no crime, no disease, no alcoholism, and no illiteracy.

Pitcairn had been hell on earth under the reign of Fletcher Christian and his fellow mutineers. The people had suffered under something called "the wrath of God"—the inevitable result of human hearts filled with murder, envy, lust, rage, rebellion, and drunkenness.

But when the last man on Pitcairn turned his heart over to God, the wrath of God was replaced by the love of God, and Pitcairn became a paradise on earth. The transformation of that tiny island is just a glimpse of what could happen in our own society. If we would choose to receive the love and mercy of God, we would escape the wrath of God now being revealed against the godlessness and wickedness of our age.

The Wrath of God

Following his introduction to Romans, Paul sounds a new and somber note. Beginning with verse 18, he introduces the troubling phrase "the wrath of God." Here, Paul begins a careful, logical analysis of the human dilemma:

> The wrath of God is being revealed from heaven against all the godlessness and wickedness of men who suppress the truth by their wickedness, since what may be known about God is plain to them, because God has made it plain to them. For since the creation of the world God's invisible qualities—his eternal power and divine nature—have been clearly seen, being understood from what has been made, so that men are without excuse. (Romans 1:18–20)

The wrath of God is a frightening subject, but it is necessary that Paul address this subject early in his letter. In these verses Paul tells us why we need the gospel. Human beings everywhere suffer under the wrath of God, and only the gospel can free us from that wrath.

What do you think of when you hear that phrase, "the wrath of God"? Most people think of something that follows death—the final judgment of God. It is true that hell is an expression of the wrath of God. But that is not what Paul means at this point. He refers to something present and active right now. As the text says, it is "being revealed from heaven" in the here and now. The wrath of God is inescapable, it is all around us. God's wrath is His invisible resistance to human evil.

This conception of the wrath of God did not originate with Paul. It is consistent with what the Old Testament tells us:

> All our days pass away under your wrath;
>   we finish our years with a moan.
> The length of our days is seventy years—
>   or eighty, if we have the strength;
> yet their span is but trouble and sorrow,
>   for they quickly pass, and we fly away.
> Who knows the power of your anger?
>   For your wrath is as great as the fear that is due you.
>   (Psalm 90:9–11)

The brevity of life, the sorrow and tragedy of the human condition—this is all part of what Paul captures in the phrase "the wrath of God." What provokes the wrath of God? Paul says it is caused by "the godlessness and wickedness of men who suppress the truth by their wickedness."

Notice the progression Paul describes: first godlessness, then wickedness. The order is never reversed. It is a godless attitude that produces wicked actions.

What is godlessness? It isn't necessarily atheism, the belief that God doesn't exist. Godlessness is thinking and acting *as if* God doesn't exist. A godless person doesn't have to deny the existence of God; he or she can merely disregard Him.

The inevitable result of godlessness is wickedness—those selfish and hurtful acts that people commit against each other. Why do we act selfishly? Why do we hurt each other? Because we disregard God.

And what follows as a natural consequence of our wicked actions? The truth of God is suppressed. In the next two verses, Paul sets before us the truth that human beings have wickedly denied:

> . . . what may be known about God is plain to them, because God has made it plain to them. For since the creation of the world God's invisible qualities—his eternal power and divine nature—have been clearly seen, being understood from what has been made, so that men are without excuse. (Romans 1:19–20)

The truth that people try to ignore and suppress is the existence of a God of eternal power and majesty. They try to suppress the greatness of God. Puny human beings strut about as if there were no God—indeed, as if *they* are gods! But there are times when human beings cannot avoid the reality of God. When those times come, they don't like to speak of God. They resort to saying that "nature" created us or that "fate" or "karma" controls their destinies.

But the reality of God can be avoided for only so long. The truth of God surrounds us and must eventually be faced—either willingly or unwillingly. God has revealed Himself, says Paul. He has made the truth about Himself plain. The reality of God is not a vague, incomprehensible enigma. The truth about God is obvious to all, even those who deny and avoid it. God has made the truth plain by displaying His eternal power and divine nature. So there is no excuse—the reality of God is on display throughout the universe. All human beings can read this revelation of God if they choose to do so.

One night my daughter, Laurie, and I were walking in the mountains of Southern California. We were away from the city smog, and the sky was filled with millions of stars. I pointed out the Milky Way and explained to her that it was part of the galaxy that our sun belongs to. I told her there are millions of galaxies just like it in distant parts of the universe that have never been explored by human beings. I pointed out the Big Dipper, the North Star, the Pleiades cluster, and we talked about the vastness and beauty of the universe.

"But remember," I added, joking, "that all of this happened purely by chance."

Laurie immediately began to laugh! How ridiculous that this vast array of beauty and complexity could have arisen by sheer chance! How can we say that a wristwatch can come about only as the result of intelligence and skill, yet a universe can arise, a baby can be born, a rose can bloom by sheer random chance? The idea is ridiculous on the face of it.

Yet many people make that godless claim. They willfully suppress the truth that stares them in the face. So the apostle Paul tells us that human beings are without excuse. If we want to find God, we do not have to search hard. In fact, we can't miss Him. Even God's invisible qualities—His eternal power and divine nature—are evident all around us.

Hebrews 11:6 tells us, "Without faith it is impossible to please God, because anyone who comes to him must believe that he exists and that he rewards those who earnestly seek him." First, we must believe that God exists, that He is there—and Paul says that everyone knows, deep down, that God is there. The evidence is beyond question. You must work hard to convince yourself otherwise, and only the very intelligent are able to accomplish this feat. The rest of us, who simply see the truth of the universe and believe it, accept the fact that God is there. And all of us are without excuse.

Next, as Hebrews 11:6 tells us, we must diligently seek this God whose existence is revealed in the universe around us. If we fail to find God, it is because we don't seek Him. If we seek Him, we will find Him.

In the next three verses, Paul tells us how human beings suppress the truth about God:

> For although they knew God, they neither glorified him as God nor gave thanks to him, but their thinking became futile and their foolish hearts were darkened. Although they clamed to be wise, they became fools and exchanged the glory of the immortal God for images made to look like mortal man and birds and animals and reptiles. (Romans 1:21–23)

Here, Paul traces a three-step process:

Step 1: People fail to glorify God and give thanks to Him. We see evidence of this throughout American society, where prayer has been banned from public schools, where Christmas is now called "winter break" and Easter is "spring break," where the words "under God" are edited out of our Pledge of Allegiance, where the Ten Commandments can no longer be displayed in our courthouses and other public buildings. God is no longer welcome in the public square. The powers that rule our society no longer wish to admit that God exists. They do not glorify Him as God, nor do they give Him thanks.

Paul says that, as a result, their thinking has become futile. What is futile thinking? This refers to human ideas, schemes, plans, institutions, and programs that seem so brilliant, but ultimately come to nothing. I have lived through the New Deal, the Fair Deal, the Great Society, Peace with Honor, the Great Recovery, and the New World Order—and all of them have failed dismally! These human programs begin with good intentions, brilliant planning, and shining promises, but always end in dismal failure.

Paul also says that "their foolish hearts were darkened." Human hearts are darkened by cynicism and selfishness. When a darkened heart sees human need, it does not feel compassion; it just shrugs and turns away. "It's too bad," the darkened heart says, "but it's really not my problem." That is the inevitable result of ignoring God.

Step 2: People claim to be wise. In other words, they place their own wisdom above the wisdom of God. They claim to know everything that can be known—and in so doing, they become fools!

You may recall the tale of the Sorcerer's Apprentice—the student magician who takes up the wand of his master and unleashes frightening powers he cannot control. Our "wise men" claim to have a godlike understanding of biology, chemistry, and physics, yet their "wisdom" has brought us to the brink of runaway biological, ecological, and nuclear catastrophes. These apprentice sorcerers have unleashed destructive forces upon our world—forces that are not only beyond our control but beyond our imagining. Claiming to be wise, they have become dangerous, destructive fools.

Step 3: People exchange the glory of the immortal God for images made like mortal man. They exchange the glory of the undying God for images made like dying creatures: men, birds, animals, and reptiles. Notice the descending order. Idolatry begins with statues of men. The world is filled with statues reflecting the images of heroes of the ancient Greek and Roman world. These images symbolize the ideas the people worship, and we still have such images today. But these images debase and dethrone God, replacing Him with something lesser, something human.

Idolatry begins first with men; then idolatry extends to birds, which are seen as heavenly creatures. Then idolatry descends to animals, the shaggy beasts of the earth. Finally, men even begin to idolize reptiles. When human beings cease to worship God, they begin to worship their own humanity—but they inevitably end up worshiping snakes.

You may think, "But people don't worship idols anymore!" If that is so, then why are movie stars, pop stars, and sports heroes called "icons" and "idols"? Famous people, with their glittering images (and their feet of clay) are worshiped today; they are given the honor and glory that should be given to God.

There are other things we worship today: Some of us worship power, such as military power or corporate power or economic power. Some of us worship money. Some of us worship sex. Some of us bow before idols of success, beauty, youth, and extreme adventure. We've exchanged the glory of the undying God for the worship of lesser things.

The consequences of idolatry are terrible to contemplate, and they descend upon both individual idolaters and upon an idolatrous society. These consequences are what Paul refers to when he speaks of "the wrath of God."

God Gave Them Over

In his book *The Great Divorce*, C. S. Lewis says that hell is made up of people who live at an infinite distance from each other. That is what happens when we lose the presence of God in our lives. Our relationships break down. We feel a loss of fellowship with the people around us. Even in a crowd, we experience loneliness and alienation.

In Romans 1:24–32, we will see that as human beings divorce themselves from God, they also divorce themselves from one another. We will also see that God, who has given all human beings the gift of free will, always allows us to make our choices freely. If we choose to reject God, He will step out of our way and let us reap the consequences of our choices.

We see this principle in this passage, where Paul repeats one somber phrase three times: "God gave them over." That phrase occurs in verses 24, 26, and 28, and it perfectly describes what is taking place in our culture today. Paul writes:

> Therefore God gave them over in the sinful desires of their hearts to sexual impurity for the degrading of their bodies with one another. (Romans 1:24)

The first mark of wickedness in a godless society is widespread sexual immorality—practices that degrade and dishonor the body. This sentence begins with the word *therefore*, which suggests a cause-and-effect relationship. The rise of sexual immorality is a direct result of the idolatry that Paul talks about in verses 21 through 23. Idolatry—the worship of people, objects, and ideas—leads inevitably to the spread and toleration of sexual immorality.

Immediately after the word *therefore*, we come upon Paul's first use of the phrase "God gave them over." Many people think Paul is saying that God gives up on people who do these things—that He turns His back on them forever. But that is not what Paul means.

The apostle is saying that when people reject the evidence of God in nature, when they commit idolatry and do not glorify God or obey His moral rules for a satisfying life, *God removes His restraints from society.* He allows what is done in secret to be uncovered. He lets sinful people operate as they wish, so that they reap the consequences of their choices.

We see this principle in our own society. Sexual immorality has always been present in human life, though immorality has largely been considered shameful and scandalous and was kept secret. Today, however, we see the most vile and ugly perversions breaking out into the open, flooding our news and entertainment media, clamoring for acceptance, demanding to be tolerated as "normal." Even pedophiles—those who sexually abuse children—are operating openly under a shield of "free speech," lobbying for a legal right to sexually exploit our children.

When sexual perversion is allowed to break out into the open and demand acceptance, it is a sign that God's wrath is at work. God allows us to experience the full effects of our own riotous self-will. He removes the lid and allows the bubbling pot of sin and evil to boil over.

When God removes His restraints from society, people tend to respond in one of two ways. Some witness the social destruction that sin causes, and they come to their senses. Like Alexander

Smith, the last mutineer on Pitcairn island, such people see the error of their ways, and they repent and turn to God for salvation.

But others refuse to learn the lessons of God's wrath. Instead of turning to God in repentance, they rage and rebel against Him. They blame Him for the consequences of their own sin. They plunge even deeper into immorality—and God gives them over to their own choices and the consequences they have heaped upon themselves.

The Worst Sins

You may ask, "Why is sexual immorality singled out as the sign of God's wrath? Why does sexual immorality signal the disintegration of a society?" There is a good reason for this—but not what you might think. It is not because sexual sins are the worst of sins. In his book *Mere Christianity*, C. S. Lewis observed:

> If anyone thinks that Christians regard unchastity as the supreme vice, he is quite wrong. The sins of the flesh are bad, but they are the least bad of all sins. All the worst pleasures are purely spiritual: the pleasure of putting other people in the wrong, of bossing and patronising and spoiling sport, and back-biting, the pleasures of power, of hatred. For there are two things inside me competing with the human self which I must try to become. They are the Animal self, and the Diabolical self. The Diabolical self is the worst of the two. That is why a cold, self-righteous prig, who goes regularly to church may be far nearer to hell than a prostitute. But, of course, it's better to be neither.[1]

The book of Romans confirms the words of C. S. Lewis. Human godlessness and wickedness begin with sexual impurity and proceed to sexual perversion. However, the ultimate degradation is not sexual sin but the sins of the spirit. Pride, hatred, bullying and bossing, wielding power over others, destroying lives and reputations with gossip—these are truly the worst sins.

The reason God uses sexual sins as a visible sign of spiritual disintegration is found elsewhere. Now, brace yourself, because you may find this shocking: the reason is that *sex is linked with worship*. Our sexual longings are intimately connected with our longing for genuine worship, for an intimate connection to God.

Our sex drive is nothing more or less than the desire to possess another person, body and soul, and to be possessed in the same way. That is why the sex drive has rightly been described as "the urge to merge." God intended that the human sexual urge should find its culmination in sexual relations in marriage, just as He intended that the soul find its delight in the "urge to merge" with God in worship. Whether we realize it or not, the deepest desire of the human soul is to possess and be possessed by God.

Jesus talked about this perfect union of souls when He prayed for His disciples, "that all of them may be one, Father, just as you are in me and I am in you. May they also be in us . . . I in them and you in me" (John 17:21, 23). Clearly, this is a spiritual prayer about a spiritual union, yet (as the Song of Solomon and other Scripture texts clearly show) the sexual union of marriage symbolizes the spiritual union in the worship relationship between God and His people.

The reason this idea seems shocking to us today is twofold. First, Victorian prudishness regards sex as something dirty, not to be mentioned in polite company. This is not a biblical or godly view of sex. Second, the Sexual Revolution that began in the 1960s has produced an anything-goes approach to sex that puts sexual behavior and even sexual deviancy on public display as if God's gift of sex was just so much meat in a butcher's window.

Both extremes demean God's beautiful gift of sex, turning it into something ugly and shameful. As God created it, there is nothing shameful about sex. It is a symbolic picture of the rapturous relationship we were made to experience with our loving Creator.

Many people mistakenly think that the sex urge is merely an animal drive for pleasure and procreation. But the sex urge is actually intertwined with our spiritual drive for communion and worship, an urge for oneness and fulfillment. That is why illicit sex leaves people empty and unfulfilled. Only union with God can satisfy that deep longing for complete unity—an experience of unity that is central to what we call worship. When we worship, we experience that sense of possessing and being possessed by God.

So when human beings seek a God-substitute in the form of illicit sex, God says, in effect, "You won't find fulfillment there. You can only find fulfillment in Me. If you deny Me and ignore Me, seeking to gratify your senses instead of satisfying your soul, you will remain empty. Still, if that is what you choose, I will not stop you."

So God removes the restraints and allows immoral sexual practices to become widely accepted. He knows that people who engage in such practices will end up as empty as when they started. But He also knows that many people will never turn to God until they reach the depths of hopelessness and despair. So He allows people to make their own choices in the hope that the consequences of those choices may ultimately drive them to Him.

God's View of Homosexuality

In the next few verses, Paul shows us another sign of a godless and wicked society:

> They exchanged the truth of God for a lie, and worshiped and served created things rather than the Creator—who is forever praised. Amen.
> Because of this, God gave them over to shameful lusts. Even their women exchanged natural relations for unnatural ones. In the same way the men also abandoned natural relations with women and were inflamed with lust for one another. Men committed indecent acts with other men, and received in themselves the due penalty for their perversion. (Romans 1:25–27)

Here, Paul speaks frankly about an issue that remains controversial in our society today: homosexuality. In fact, he tells us that open homosexual practice is another sign of a godless and wicked society. Because godless people have exchanged the truth for a lie, God has allowed them to exchange natural sexual functions for unnatural functions. He has removed the normal restraints so that homosexuality has become widely accepted in a godless society.

In the first-century world in which Paul lived, homosexuality was commonplace and accepted, much as it is in our society today. Many of the great philosophers practiced it. Socrates was a homosexual, as were fourteen of the first fifteen Roman emperors.

Tragically, many homosexual people have accepted the myth that homosexual tendencies are genetically predetermined, and that some people are "born homosexual." For example, in the early '90s, a study by Dean Hamer, published in the respected research journal *Science*, claimed that scientists were "on the verge of proving that homosexuality is innate, genetic and therefore unchangeable—a normal variant of human nature." The mainstream news media latched onto the story, proclaiming that scientists had discovered a "gay gene" that causes homosexuality.

Repeated attempts to confirm Hamer's findings have been unsuccessful. Though the public has largely bought the myth of the "gay gene," the best evidence shows that people are not "born gay," and that homosexual tendencies are probably the result of influences in childhood and adolescence. The fact that several organizations (such as the National Association for Research and Therapy of Homosexuality) report success in treating homosexuality would suggest that homosexual tendencies are treatable—not genetic.

Having met and talked to people who have been delivered from homosexuality, I know that there is help for homosexual people. It is not a sin to have homosexual tendencies; it is only a sin to indulge those tendencies—just as it is a sin to indulge heterosexual tendencies outside of marriage. No matter what sexual sin a person commits, he or she can be delivered and forgiven by the grace and power of the Lord Jesus Christ.

Paul speaks of a "due penalty" for homosexual sin. That penalty involves a loss of one's sense of identity and place in life. Engaging in homosexual sin creates an almost unbearable tension in any human being. Sexual confusion is an attack upon the delineation God made at creation when he made us male and female.

A Depraved Mind

Paul gives us another sign of a godless and wicked society in the concluding verses of Romans 1:

> Furthermore, since they did not think it worthwhile to retain the knowledge of God, he gave them over to a depraved mind, to do what ought not to be done. They have become filled with every kind of wickedness, evil, greed and depravity. They are full of envy, murder, strife, deceit and malice. They are gossips, slanderers, God-haters, insolent, arrogant and boastful; they invent ways of doing evil; they disobey their parents; they are senseless, faithless, heartless, ruthless. (Romans 1:28–31)

These sins mark a society that is approaching total collapse. These wicked acts are so rampant and hateful that they constitute a sociopathic contempt for all other human beings. They distill down to a simple willingness to use and exploit other people as if they are not human, as if they have no feelings. Godlessness eventually reduces all human beings to things.

When society reaches this point, Paul says, God gives those rebellious people over to "a depraved mind." Literally, Paul calls it an "unacceptable mind," a mind that cannot be lived with, a mind that is simply at odds with any rational concept of civilization. A depraved mind hates everything it sees and destroys everything it touches. A depraved mind is cruel and violent.

If we think that our own society has not yet reached the depths that Paul describes in Romans 1, we have only to look at the epidemic rates of child abuse, pornography, gang violence, and other senseless crimes in our land.

A depraved mind culminates in an attitude of callous disregard for God and an eagerness to drag everyone else into a pit of depravity. Paul writes:

> Although they know God's righteous decree that those who do such things deserve death, they not only continue to do these very things, but also approve of those who practice them. (Romans 1:32)

Fully aware that their actions are evil, they seek nevertheless to spread their wickedness, to seduce others into the same way of thinking and acting, to infect everyone around them with their godlessness and sin. They invade the fields of education, law, and government; they dominate the news and entertainment media; they attempt to control the institutions of society so that they can impose their will on society.

Clearly, the words of the apostle Paul are as relevant to our times as anything you will see in *USA Today* or on CNN or Fox News. Paul has given us God's diagnosis of the world we live in.

Yet, even as this moral and spiritual darkness spreads over the world, God does not turn His back on the human race. He has not merely given us His divine diagnosis, then left us to die in our disease. Instead, God has lovingly and graciously provided the cure. He is continually at work in our lives, trying to bring us to our senses, offering the gift of deliverance and forgiveness.

As the prophet Isaiah wrote, "The people walking in darkness have seen a great light; on those living in the land of the shadow of death a light has dawned" (Isaiah 9:2). When the world was shrouded in gloom and despair, when idolatry, wickedness, immorality, and oppression covered the land, a great light suddenly shone over the skies of Bethlehem. The night air reverberated with the music of angel voices, announcing the birth of a Savior.

Ever since humanity fell in the Garden of Eden, there has been only one hope for a world mired in sin: Jesus Christ. The wrath of God has been completely and fully met by the righteousness of God. God's righteousness cancels out His wrath—but only in the lives of those who receive His righteousness through faith in His Son Jesus.

Logically, you would think that people would be eager to receive the marvelous gift of God's righteousness—the gift that heals our hurts, corrects our errors, covers our sin, and brings peace, joy, and forgiveness to the heart. Incredibly, people stubbornly choose pain, darkness, death, and despair over eternal life through Jesus Christ.

Why? Why would anyone choose death over life, wrath over righteousness? In Romans 1, Paul correctly diagnoses the spiritual cancer that has infected the entire human race: Human beings have refused to glorify God and give thanks to Him. As a result, their hearts have become darkened. Claiming to be wise, they have become fools. They have depraved minds, and are full of envy, murder, strife, deceit, and more. That is the divine diagnosis of the human race. That is why the human race has incurred the wrath of a holy and righteous God.

But you and I do not need to fear the wrath of God. We can escape the wrath if we heed the message of Romans and receive the cure God offers us. As we shall see in the rest of this study, the message of Romans is the good news of Jesus Christ.

CHAPTER 3

SINFUL MORALITY

Romans 2

John Wesley, the founder of the Methodist movement, told of a man in his congregation who seemed to be greedy and stingy. The man had a good job and a nice home, yet he contributed only a paltry sum every year to the charities of the church. From the pulpit, Wesley once criticized the man for his stinginess.

Afterward, the man went to Wesley in private. "I know you think I've been holding back from the church," the man said, "but the truth is that I've been living on nothing but parsnips and water for weeks. You see, before I came to know Jesus Christ as my Lord and Savior, I lived irresponsibly and I ran up a great number of debts.

"Now, however, I'm trying to live within my means. I'm skimping on expenses for myself, and I'm paying off my debts, one by one. Within a year, I hope to be debt-free. In the meantime, with all of these bills to pay, I can only give a little more than a tithe to the church. But once I've settled up with the people I owe, I intend to give much more to the Lord's work."

With a heavy heart, Wesley apologized for misjudging the man. That day, Wesley learned a lesson that we all need to understand—the same lesson Paul wants to teach us in the second chapter of Romans: we often misjudge others because we cannot know another person's heart. Only God, who knows all things, has the wisdom and the authority to judge people righteously.

Stuck in denial

It is important to grasp the flow of Paul's argument as we come to Romans 2. In Romans 1, Paul has given us his penetrating analysis of the human condition. He has talked about humanity's rejection of the one true God who reveals Himself in nature and the human conscience. He has talked about how men and women have turned to false gods, sexual immorality, violence, and cruelty.

Romans 1 creates an instant division between "them" and "us," between people who are grossly wicked and those who are not. Most of us in the church would read Romans 1 and say, "I'm thankful I'm not like that! I'm a law-abiding, home-loving, clean-living, decent person. If only the world were filled with people like me instead of all of those criminals, rebels, prostitutes, and perverts!"

I call this attitude "sinful morality"—adopting a morally superior attitude toward others while denying our own sinfulness. It is a smug and false morality, rooted in a desire to build ourselves up by putting others down.

Here, in chapter 2, Paul turns and confronts all of us who are stuck in self-righteous denial. He attacks our "sinful morality" and cuts off our escape, forcing us to confront the truth about ourselves: We are not as decent and innocent as we suppose! We, too, are subject to God's judgment.

In Romans 2, Paul turns the white-hot glare of his spotlight upon us with a devastating three-step argument. Let's examine his argument, step by step.

Step 1: You Are Guilty Because Your Own Judgment Condemns You

The first step of Paul's argument is found in the first verse of Romans 2:

> You, therefore, have no excuse, you who pass judgment on someone else, for at whatever point you judge the other, you are condemning yourself, because you who pass judgment do the same things. (Romans 2:1)

If you have never passed judgment on another human being, then feel free to skip this chapter and move on to the next. In my own case, however, I must honestly confess that I am guilty. I have passed judgment on others. To all of those, myself included, who come under the condemnation of this passage, Paul has two important points to make.

First, he points out that people who judge others clearly know the difference between right and wrong; otherwise they would not presume to judge. They understand moral standards. So they know which actions merit the judgment and wrath of God. This wrath, as Paul explained in Romans 1, primarily involves God's removal of all restraints upon human wickedness. As God allows evil to reign in society, that society degenerates and human misery compounds.

Second, Paul points out that people who judge others are guilty because they do the same evil things themselves. They are hypocrites.

This point reminds me of our Lord's account of His promised return, when all of the nations will come before Him to be judged (see Matthew 25:31–46). Jesus said He would separate the people of the world into two groups, the sheep and the goats. What determines whether you are a sheep or a goat? Jesus says the test is simple: You will be judged based on how you have treated others.

When He renders judgment, Jesus will say to the sheep, "I was hungry and you gave me something to eat, I was thirsty and you gave me something to drink, I was a stranger and you invited me in, I needed clothes and you clothed me, I was sick and you looked after me, I was in prison and you came to visit me." And to the goats, He will point out that they did none of these things. Both the sheep and the goats will be surprised. The sheep will say, "We don't remember doing those things for you!" And the goats will say, "We never saw you in such need!" But Jesus replies that whatever we have done—or have failed to do—for other people will be counted as our treatment of Jesus Himself.

I have to confess that I remember times when I have been more goat-like than sheep-like. I confess that I have often been blind toward my own faults. Oh, I can pick out these same faults in the people around me, but I just can't find them in myself. There are things that I have casually, thoughtlessly done to others, thinking nothing of it—yet if those same acts were done to me, I would be outraged and offended.

How blind I am to my own faults! I simply do not see them— yet I am so quick to judge others for the same offenses. In so doing, I come under the condemnation of Romans 2.

At other times, I may be aware of my own sins and faults, yet I simply assume that God will let it slide, that He is easygoing and indulgent. I am so quick to forgive myself and forget my faults. As my own sin fades from my memory, I assume it will fade from God's memory as well.

One area in which most of us are prone to do this is in our thought-life. Jesus, in the Sermon on the Mount, told us that God looks at the heart and judges our attitudes and intentions. He doesn't judge as people judge, by merely looking at the outward reality. God knows that if we are full of hate and resentment toward another person, then we have committed murder in our hearts. He knows that if we have lustful thoughts, then we have committed fornication or adultery in our hearts. If our thoughts are full of self-righteous arrogance and pride, He sees that we are guilty of the worst of sins.

We think these hidden sins will go unnoticed, forgetting that nothing is hidden from God. He sees all that we ignore. He remembers all that we forget. He knows when we speak spitefully toward others, when we cheat others, when we destroy reputations with malicious gossip, when we behave stubbornly or arrogantly or vindictively toward others. He sees when we are quick to judge others but slow to judge ourselves.

Another way we come under the judgment of Romans 2 is the way we label our behavior and the behavior of others. We accuse other people of lying—but we ourselves merely "stretch the truth." Others steal; we merely borrow. Others are biased and stubborn; we have convictions. Our euphemistic labels may keep us in denial, but they do not fool God. He sees the reality of our hearts.

Step 2: You Are Guilty Because God Judges Truthfully

Paul goes on to develop Step 2 of his argument by asking two powerful, confrontational questions. Here is the first:

Now we know that God's judgment against those who do such things is based on truth. So when you, a mere man, pass judgment on them and yet do the same things, do you think you will escape God's judgment? (Romans 2:2–3)

We foolishly think that God will harshly judge other people, but He will not judge us! We know that He sees the innermost thoughts and intentions of all people, yet we expect Him to overlook our sins while punishing the sins of others.

People often ask, "How can a good and loving God permit so much evil and suffering in the world? Why doesn't God immediately judge the sins of evil people who kill, steal, rape, and oppress the innocent?" But if we were honest with ourselves, the question we truly ought to ask is, "Why didn't God judge me yesterday when I said that harsh, hurtful word to my spouse? Why didn't God shrivel my hand when I cheated on my income tax? Why didn't God strike me silent when I gossiped on the phone this morning?"

We blame God for not judging the evil of others, yet think it perfectly natural that He indulge our sins and hurtful behavior. So Paul asks us, in effect, "Don't you know that God judges truthfully? And if so, then how can you pass judgment on others when you are guilty as well? How will you escape God's judgment, which is based on absolute truth?"

Paul then poses his second question:

Or do you show contempt for the riches of his kindness, tolerance and patience, not realizing that God's kindness leads you toward repentance? (Romans 2:4)

Paul's second question is, "Why do you act the way you do? You judge others, but you don't judge yourself! If God judges on the basis of truth, then you must be included in that judgment as well! God's kindness toward you is not intended to give you more opportunities to sin, but to lead you toward repentance and righteousness."

Our tendency is to take God's kindness for granted. But God wants us to respond to His kindness in gratitude. He knows that we are blind and filled with denial. He urges us to open our eyes and take His grace and kindness toward us as an opportunity for repentance and change.

Step 3: You Are Guilty Because God Does Not Show Favoritism

In the third and final step of his argument, Paul describes what lies ahead for those who refuse to face the actual condition of their lives:

> But because of your stubbornness and your unrepentant heart, you are storing up wrath against yourself for the day of God's wrath, when his righteous judgment will be revealed. God "will give to each person according to what he has done." To those who by persistence in doing good seek glory, honor and immortality, he will give eternal life. But for those who are self-seeking and who reject the truth and follow evil, there will be wrath and anger. There will be trouble and distress for every human being who does evil: first for the Jew, then for the Gentile; but glory, honor and peace for everyone who does good: first for the Jew, then for the Gentile. For God does not show favoritism. (Romans 2:5–11)

I am amazed at how many times I have expected God to show favoritism toward me. Even as a Christian, I expect God to ignore my sins and flaws, and I feel ill-treated when God points them out to me! Yet the Scriptures tell us that God is constantly bringing these issues to our attention for our own benefit. When God holds a mirror up to us, forcing us to face our sinful and flawed condition, we should thank Him for His love, learn from the experience, repent and grow—not retreat into denial.

Paul says that when we refuse to judge these areas of our lives, we store up wrath for ourselves. The original Greek word translated "storing up" literally means "to heap up a great treasure." Here, Paul draws an ironic parallel between "the riches of [God's] kindness" (verse 4) and heaping up a great "treasure" of God's wrath. If we do not judge our own hearts, then we are laying up a horrible "treasure" of judgment and condemnation.

We are constantly making deposits in a bank account. That bank account is continually accruing a terrible interest as God allows us to deteriorate as human beings. We are steadily becoming less and less of what God intended us to be. C. S. Lewis put it this way in *Mere Christianity*:

> People often think of Christian morality as a kind of bargain in which God says, "If you keep a lot of rules, I'll reward you; and if you don't, I'll do the other thing." I do not think that's the best way of looking at it. I would much rather say that every time you make a choice, you are turning the central part of you, the part that chooses, into something a little different than what it was before. And, taking your life as a whole, with all your innumerable choices, all your life long you are slowly turning this central thing either into a heavenly creature or into a hellish creature; either into a creature that is in harmony with God and with other creatures and with itself, or else into one that is in a state of war and hatred with God and with its fellow creatures and with itself. To be the one kind of creature is heavenly, i.e., it is joy and peace and knowledge and power; to be the other means madness, horror, idiocy, rage, impotence, and eternal loneliness. Each of us, at each moment, is progressing to the one state or the other.[1]

Lewis is telling us the same thing that Paul brings out in Romans 2: God is a righteous God. He judges human beings and assesses wrath against those who do wrong. The wrath of God operates as a principle throughout human life—but a day of judgment is also coming when God's righteousness and wrath will be revealed.

So Paul's question to us is this: What are you seeking in life? If you persistently do good, seeking glory and honor and immortality, then you will find it. God will give you eternal life. You will find Jesus as your Redeemer and Lord and Savior. You will grow increasingly like Jesus as you judge those evil areas of life and honestly repent of them before God.

But if what you really want is *not* God, truth, life, glory, and immortality—if you merely seek pleasure, fame, wealth, and power—then you are storing up a treasury of wrath for yourself. As Paul puts it, "There will be trouble and distress for every human being who does evil: first for the Jew, then for the Gentile." God plays no favorites. Your skin color, your ethnicity, your national origin, your church membership will make no difference before God.

If you think that this description of God and His judgment makes Him seem harsh and unloving, then you have not understood the passage in its context. The judgment of God and the wrath of God are in no way inconsistent with the love of God. The Bible clearly shows us that God loves human beings and wants to restore humanity, not destroy it. God loves us so much that He tells us the truth about ourselves and about Himself; that is true love. He is not willing to leave us in a muddle of self-deception and denial. Only the truth can set us free.

God lovingly seeks to move us toward a recognition of our sinfulness. Once we recognize our hopeless condition, we can accept the fact that God has dealt with our sinfulness in Christ. On that basis, God offers us full and free forgiveness. There is no other way.

Anyone who thinks there is any other way of escape from sin needs a soul-shaking blast of truth! Such a person needs to know that he or she is storing up a treasure-house of wrath. That realization should drive any rational person to God. If we surrender ourselves to God, if we give up seeking our own will and our own way, then we can begin to live for the God who made us and who loves us. We can get off the road to hell and set our feet toward heaven. If you lose your life—surrender it completely to God—then you will save it. If you submit your desires and ambitions to Him, you will gain eternal life. But if you look out for yourself, defend yourself, excuse yourself, and rationalize your sins, your life will become a ruin, and your soul will end up in darkness.

That is the gospel. We are all without excuse. We all need God's forgiveness. You and I are as much in need of His forgiveness as any cold-blooded murderer. We have no right to see ourselves as superior to anyone else. Our condemnation of others only blocks the flow of God's life and power in our lives. If we want to enjoy the peace and power of God on a daily basis, then we must stop judging others and we must begin judging ourselves.

Four Kinds of People

God has promised us an ultimate destiny that is beyond all our wildest dreams—and infinitely beyond our deserving. Yet I am continually amazed that people so often resist and refuse the good news of eternal life through Jesus Christ.

One reason people struggle against the gospel is that it cannot be received until we admit our need. Many people resist to the death—to an eternal death!—having to admit their hopelessness and helplessness. We do not like to confess that we need help. We cling to our illusion of self-sufficiency because admitting helplessness is humiliating. We want to believe that salvation is something we can earn for ourselves.

In Romans, Paul describes four types of people who refuse the gospel. At the conclusion of Romans 1 he describes *Type 1: The Flagrantly Wicked*. Such people are filled with every kind of wickedness, evil, greed, depravity, envy, murder, deceit, and malice. Flagrantly wicked people flout morality and defy God. They are not content to destroy their own souls, but encourage others to destroy themselves as well.

Then, in Romans 2, Paul introduces the second group of people who refuse the gospel—*Type 2: The Self-Righteous Moralists*. These people are outwardly concerned with a form of morality, but are inwardly filled with resentment, jealousy, murder, hatred, and envy. These people are as sinful as the flagrantly wicked people of Romans 1. Because they maintain a facade of morality and respectability, they think God will overlook their hidden sin. They think they will be excused from God's judgment because of their self-righteousness and their harsh judgment and condemnation of flagrantly wicked sinners.

Next, Paul will introduce two more types of people who refuse the gospel, beginning with *Type 3: The Unenlightened Pagans*. Here Paul deals with a troubling question: What will God do with those who have not heard the gospel? What about those who live where the Bible is unknown and who have never had a chance to hear about the life, death, and resurrection of Jesus Christ? In this passage Paul says that their problem is that they defile their consciences.

In the same passage, Paul also introduces us to *Type 4: The Religious Devotees*. These people believe that God is pleased by religious rites and rituals. They ignore the fact that God's Word repeatedly states that God judges on the basis of the reality of a person's thoughts and behavior. Religion and rituals cannot save us from God's judgment. Only a sincere and authentic faith relationship with Jesus Christ can save.

The last two types of people are introduced by this statement of the universal lostness of humanity:

> All who sin apart from the law will also perish apart from the law, and all who sin under the law will be judged by the law. For it is not those who hear the law who are righteous in God's sight, but it is those who obey the law who will be declared righteous. (Romans 2:12–13)

This is probably the strongest statement from the hand of Paul. It answers the most common question that non-Christians ask Christians: "What about the people who have never heard of Jesus Christ?" Usually, the people who ask this question are thinking of people in remote parts of the world, such as the Amazon jungle.

What these people fail to realize when they ask this question is that people in the Amazon jungles are in exactly the same spiritual condition as people in the concrete jungles of any American city. Paul's answer to this question is that all people will be judged by their own standards. God judges people according to what they know, not according to what they don't know.

So far in Romans, Paul has made three great statements about the basis of the judgment.

First, in Romans 2:2, Paul says that God's judgment is according to the truth; it is based in reality. God judges only according to what is actually in our hearts and our behavior. God cannot falsely convict anyone but He judges according to truth.

Second, in Romans 2:6, Paul says that God judges according to our works. This gives us some insight into the patience of God. Though He sees what is going on in our hearts and minds, He waits patiently for our inner attitude to work itself out in words or actions that we manifest openly. So God allows us to be our own judge, to see for ourselves that our words and deeds manifest what is inside us.

Third, in Romans 2:9–10, Paul says that the judgment of God is according to light. In other words, God will not judge humanity on the basis of the Ten Commandments. We will be judged on the basis of our own inner standards of morality. He will say to each individual, "What did you think was right and wrong?" When the individual answers, God will then ask, "According to your own standard, did you do the right—or the wrong?"

By that standard, of course, everyone fails. I fail, and so do you. Paul tells us, "All who sin apart from the law will also perish apart from the law." The fact that a person has never heard the Ten Commandments is no excuse. That person will perish in the judgment not because he or she didn't know what God expected, but for failing to do right according to his or her own moral expectations.

Next, Paul goes on to take up the case of the group of people we identified as Type 3: The Unenlightened Pagans.

(Indeed, when Gentiles, who do not have the law, do by nature things required by the law, they are a law for themselves, even though they do not have the law, since they show that the requirements of the law are written on their hearts, their consciences also bearing witness, and their thoughts now accusing, now even defending them.) This will take place on the day when God will judge men's secrets through Jesus Christ, as my gospel declares. (Romans 2:14–16)

The New International Version places verses 14 and 15 in parentheses because this comes within the context of Paul's argument regarding the coming day of judgment when God will judge the secrets of human beings everywhere, and all that is hidden will be revealed. Jesus spoke of this same day of judgment in Luke 12:3: "What you have said in the dark will be heard in the daylight, and what you have whispered in the ear in the inner rooms will be proclaimed from the roofs" (Luke 12:3).

There were some in Paul's day who said that, because the Jews possessed the Law of Moses and knew God's truth, they would not be condemned in that judgment. But Paul is saying, "If your knowledge of God's Law saves you, then everyone will be saved, even the pagans, because they have a law, too. It is written on their hearts. Their consciences act as judges within them."

Of course, God does not judge according to what we know. He judges according to what we do with what we know. All people have an inner standard of right and wrong. They show it by the way they talk and the way they live their lives.

Some years ago, missionary Don Richardson wrote a book called *Peace Child*, the story of his encounter with the Sawis, a society of cannibals in New Guinea. When Richardson and other missionaries arrived there in 1962, they discovered a tribe that had become so degraded and immoral that they actually idolized treachery. They admired the man who could win someone's trust, then betray and murder that person. Richardson was shocked to find that when he told the gospel story to the Sawi people, they thought that the hero of the story was Judas, not Jesus!

Because of this lack of a common understanding of morality, the Christian missionaries despaired of ever reaching the Sawi tribes for Christ. It seemed impossible to appeal to a society whose moral standards were completely inverted.

But as the missionaries lived among the Sawi people, they discovered one area of life in which these tribal people were bound to a recognizable moral standard: the *peace child*. If one Sawi tribe gave a gift of a baby to another Sawi tribe, then that other tribe was bound to keep its agreements and honor its treaties. If the tribe did not honor the gift of the peace child and keep its agreements, that tribe would lose face and be utterly disgraced.

This gave Richardson and the other missionaries an idea for a way to introduce the Christian gospel. They told the Sawi people that God had given them a peace child, the baby Jesus. As a result, the Sawis were bound to honor God.

"The key God gave us to the heart of the Sawi people," Richardson said, "was the principle of redemptive analogy—the application to local customs of spiritual truth. . . . God had already provided for the evangelization of these people by means of redemptive analogies in their own culture."[2] By using the analogy of the peace child as a stepping stone to biblical truth, the missionaries were able to bring the gospel to the Sawis. Many of the Sawi people became Christians, and Sawi society was transformed.

It seems that God always prepares humanity for the gospel by building into every culture a concept that is ready and waiting when the gospel comes. All people have an inner sense of right and wrong, though that moral standard may be hard to find. The Sawi people were living according to the rule of conscience—a conscience that was so twisted that right seemed wrong and good seemed bad to these people.

The human conscience cannot produce inner peace, nor can it produce peace with God. But the innate moral sense of the human conscience can sometimes provide a pathway for the gospel to enter the human heart.

The Religious Devotee

Next, Paul deals with the religious devotee of his day: the committed, religious Jew. At first glance, you might think, *This passage does not speak to me—I'm not a religious Jew.* But we need only to substitute "church member" for "Jew," and this passage becomes a pointed indictment of many Christians in the twenty-first century. There are many parallels between first-century Jews and twenty-first-century Christians. As evangelical Christians, we are proud of our knowledge, understanding, and defense of Christian truth. Some of us go so far as to smugly assume that our biblical knowledge and doctrinal purity will deliver us from God's judgment. Paul wants us to know that this is a tragically mistaken assumption. He writes:

> Now you, if you call yourself a Jew; if you rely on the law and brag about your relationship to God; if you know his will and approve of what is superior because you are instructed by the law; if you are convinced that you are a guide for the blind, a light for those who are in the dark, an instructor of the foolish, a teacher of infants, because you have in the law the embodiment of knowledge and truth—you, then, who teach others, do you not teach yourself? You who preach against stealing, do you steal? You who say that people should not commit adultery, do you commit adultery? You who abhor idols, do you rob temples? You who brag about the law, do you dishonor God by breaking the law? As it is written: "God's name is blasphemed among the Gentiles because of you." (Romans 2:17–24)

Paul lists five great advantages that the Jews of his day prided themselves in.

First, they prided themselves on possessing the Law of Moses. Many evangelicals today take similar pride in possessing the Bible. We have the Bible in a hundred different versions, and we claim to have correct, orthodox, evangelical doctrine. In the church today, we often hear people bragging about their understanding of God's truth, while putting down anyone who takes a different view of this or that doctrinal fine point. That is precisely the attitude of the deeply religious Jew of Paul's day.

Second, the Jews of Paul's day prided themselves on having a special, unique relationship with God. They were God's chosen people. Today we often hear evangelicals talk about their special relationship with God that people of other traditions or denominations don't have.

Third, the Jews of Paul's day claimed to know the will of God. They had the Scriptures, the Law of Moses, and the Prophets. Many Christians today claim to have a similar knowledge of God's will. They claim to know the only God-approved mode of baptism, the only God-approved view of worship, the only God-approved view of Bible prophecy. They boast of their knowledge of God's Word and God's will, and they are smugly secure in that knowledge.

Fourth, the Jews of Paul's day prided themselves on their moral superiority. There were certain things that no self-respecting Jew would ever do, just as many Christians today pride themselves in the long list of "Thou shalt nots" that they observe: Thou shalt not dance, thou shalt not drink, thou shalt not go to movies, and so forth. Some Christians today practice a negative religion of restrictions and prohibitions, and they think their rigid observance of these restrictions makes them morally superior to everyone else.

In the same verses, Paul goes on to list four privileges that the Jews claimed because of the advantages that were theirs.

First, these religious Jews felt that they were guides to the spiritually blind. Today, many Christians seem to feel entitled to correct anyone around them. They make it their mission in life to impart the truth of God to their poor, ignorant brethren.

Second, these religious Jews felt that they were a light to those in darkness. Their Christian counterparts are with us today, trying to dazzle us with their Bible knowledge. They have it all figured out: the year of the Lord's return, the identity of the Antichrist, the election-predestination debate, the elective decrees of God, the various views of the fall of man, and on and on. Such people take great pride in their knowledge.

Third, these religious Jews felt that they were instructors of the foolish. Many Christians today take the same position. Without any consideration for the feelings of others, these sharp-tongued saints never miss an opportunity to set others straight.

Fourth, these religious Jews felt privileged to be teachers of children. I've seen many Christians today who are of the same mind. It is wonderful, of course, when people volunteer to teach Sunday school or to be youth advisors. Unfortunately, I have seen many volunteer for such positions *not* because they have been called and gifted by God to teach the young, but because they derive ego gratification from being in charge and helping to "straighten out" the next generation.

Paul pronounces a judgment against all such people, telling them, in effect, "You are outwardly righteous and correct, but inwardly you are doing the wrong thing. You religious zealots are dangerous people. You are envious, proud, covetous, lustful, and bitter. You preach against stealing, but do you steal? You condemn adultery, but do you commit adultery?" Paul brings them sharply to task for their hypocrisy.

Then Paul delivers the most devastating judgment of all. He says, in effect, "You brag about God's Law, yet your own behavior brings dishonor upon God's name. The Gentiles blaspheme God because of you." That was the ultimate judgment upon the Jews. To them, blasphemy was the worst of sins. Yet Paul tells them that people have turned away from God and dishonored His name because of the actions of these oh-so-religious Jews.

Blatant examples from American Christianity instantly leap to mind. We see pastors of prominent churches caught in sex scandals; televangelists caught abusing their prominence to gain sex, money, and power; so-called "faith healers" who get rich by exploiting the pain and desperation of the faithful; and church members who seem holy and pious on Sunday, but Monday through Friday they cheat their customers, abuse their employees, and otherwise disgrace the name of God. They consider themselves guides to the blind, lights to those in darkness, instructors of the foolish, and teachers of the young—yet they are actively hurting the cause of Christ.

When we as Christians try to share the gospel or invite a non-Christian friend to church, we are told, "Are you kidding me? I don't need your gospel and I wouldn't go near a church! Churches are full of hypocrites!" Some Christians keep records of how many people they win to Christ, yet they have no idea of how many people they have driven away from Christ by their spiritual arrogance, their unkind words, and their unrighteous example. The name of God is blasphemed because of such people.

What Is a Real Christian?

Next, Paul singles out the supreme symbol of Jewish separatism, the Jewish rite of circumcision:

> Circumcision has value if you observe the law, but if you break the law, you have become as though you had not been circumcised. If those who are not circumcised keep the law's requirements, will they not be regarded as though they were circumcised? The one who is not circumcised physically and yet obeys the law will condemn you who, even though you have the written code and circumcision, are a lawbreaker. (Romans 2:25–27)

First-century Jews prided themselves on the rite of circumcision, the symbol that they were God's people. Many Christians today derive a similar pride from baptism or church membership. Paul goes on to say that such outward signs are meaningless if there has been no "circumcision of the heart" (that is, inner transformation):

> A man is not a Jew if he is only one outwardly, nor is circumcision merely outward and physical. No, a man is a Jew if he is one inwardly; and circumcision is circumcision of the heart, by the Spirit, not by the written code. Such a man's praise is not from men, but from God. (Romans 2:28–29)

There is a significant play on words in that last phrase. The Greek word for "praise" comes from the word for "Judah," from which we get the word "Jew." Paul says that when a person is truly a Jew, when there is not merely an outward symbol of circumcision but a genuine circumcision (transformation) of the heart, then that Jew receives praise not from people but from God.

To this day, one of the most hotly debated questions in the state of Israel is this: What constitutes a true Jew? Is it religion? Is it observing the Old Testament Law? Keeping a kosher kitchen? Many Jews are atheists; they do not believe in God or in the Jewish Scriptures, yet they claim to be Jews on the basis of their ancestry. Is that a valid basis for claiming to be Jewish?

Paul tell us that there is nothing outward that makes you a true Jew. One becomes a Jew through the transformation of the heart. You become a true Jew when you believe in (to use His Hebrew name) Yeshua Hamashiach, Jesus the Messiah. Authentic Jewishness, Paul tells us, is not your culture, your ancestry, or the rites and rituals you observe. It is the fact that you have come to know the Lord Jesus Christ. That is what makes you a true Jew—and a true Christian.

Paul put it this way in another of his letters:

If you belong to Christ, then you are Abraham's seed, and heirs according to the promise. (Galatians 3:29)

Paul's conclusion of Romans 2 is that a human being without Christ is hopelessly lost. Outward rites and rituals have no value if there is not an inward transformation on the basis of a relationship with the Lord Jesus. That, and that alone, makes a Christian.

CHAPTER 4

THE HEART OF THE GOSPEL

Romans 3

Imagine an island that lies in eternal darkness. The sun never shines. Thousands and thousands of people live on that island, wandering in the darkness. There is never any joy, any peace, any happiness.

The people on the island yearn to escape—and, indeed, there is a pathway of escape that they can take if they can find it. The problem is that the only path of escape is a narrow bridge. That bridge stretches from a high cliff at the edge of the island, and it leads over a deep chasm. If your feet stray to the right or the left, you'll fall to your death—and there is no light by which to find your way across the narrow bridge.

Everyone on the island has a little penlight that dimly illuminates no more than a foot or so in all directions. But there is one group of people who have been given a powerful searchlight. That searchlight casts a brilliant beam that provides light for up to half a mile. This searchlight was given for two reasons: (1) These people are to use the light to find their own way across the bridge, and (2) they are to share that light with others.

So what do these specially chosen people do with the powerful searchlight they've been given? Tragically, they do not point it at the bridge. Instead, they point their searchlight at the nearest haystack and proceed to search for needles in that haystack.

That is a fitting analogy for what Paul says the Jews of his day were doing. The Jewish nation had been given the light of God's truth. Yet, instead of using that truth to point the way of escape from spiritual darkness, the Jewish religious leaders pointed that light at meaningless theological debates over tiny differences in interpretation. Jesus, in Matthew 23:24, described such behavior this way: "You strain at a gnat, but swallow a camel."

The Jewish religious leaders engaged in lengthy debates over how many footsteps constituted a violation of the Sabbath, or whether it is right to spit during the Sabbath day (they decided that spitting on a rock is permissible while spitting in the dust is not). This is how they used the searchlight of God's Law. Meanwhile, the people continued to wander in darkness. Though the Jews had a tremendous advantage in having the Law, Paul indicts them for failing to use it as God intended.

A Squandered Advantage

Romans 3 carries Paul's argument forward with a clear and carefully thought-out construction. In verses 1–8, Paul creates an imaginary dialogue between himself and a typical religious Jew of his day—a dialogue that grows from the issues he raised in Romans 2. In Romans 3:9–20, Paul describes the condition of fallen humanity before a holy, righteous God. At the end of that section, the condition of the human race seems hopeless.

Then, in Romans 3:21–31, we encounter a dramatic turning point in Paul's argument. A light suddenly shines into the darkness of the human condition. The righteousness of God suddenly appears, coming to the rescue of the fallen human race.

Let's begin by looking at the first eight verses of Romans 3. Here, Paul imagines that he is facing a Jewish objector. It is as if one of the Jews that Paul described in Romans 2 suddenly jumps up to argue with him. No doubt, Paul had experienced many *real* dialogues with angry Jewish objectors during his travels. Paul often taught and preached in the Jewish synagogues, and there were undoubtedly times when a Jewish rabbi would rise to debate him. That is what Paul suggests to us in this dialogue.

Is there a twenty-first-century counterpart to this imaginary Jewish objector in our own culture? Of course, there is. You can easily substitute any religionist for the Jewish objector in this dialogue—Mormon, Muslim, Hindu, Christian Scientist, Buddhist, Catholic, Baptist, or Presbyterian. Anyone who relies on religion for his salvation will offer the sort of argument Paul poses here.

Paul imagines a Jewish objector saying, "Hold on, Paul! These things that you say don't count are the very things God has given to us—rituals, rites, doctrines, the Law of Moses, circumcision! Paul, you're setting aside things that God Himself established. If these things don't count, then what advantage is there in being a Jew? What is the advantage in being religious?"

In these two verses, Paul succinctly phrases those questions and begins to give us his answer:

> What advantage, then, is there in being a Jew, or what value is there in circumcision? Much in every way! First of all, they have been entrusted with the very words of God. (Romans 3:1-2)

Here Paul says that, "First of all," that is, chiefly and supremely, the Jews have the advantage of the Law of Moses, "the very words of God." This is a tremendous advantage. Through Moses, the Jews were given the written Word of God, permanently engraved on tablets of stone. In this way, the Jews were entrusted with a knowledge of the mind, will, and character of God that other human tribes did not possess. The Jews had a greater opportunity to know and obey God than anyone else in that day—a tremendous advantage.

Yet, for those Jews who failed to make use of this advantage, it did them no good at all. In fact, a Jew who did not use this advantage to obey God was no better off than if he had never known the Law at all!

Now, here is the parallel to our own situation today: Most of us, as Christians, have been raised in church and Sunday school. We have been taught the Word of God, and we may have even read it from cover to cover. We have memorized passages of Scripture. Bibles are available to us in dozens of translations. The mind of God is available to us.

But are we any better off for having this advantage? Have we put our biblical knowledge to good use, studying God's Word so that we can obey Him and serve Him better? If not, then we are no better off than those who have never seen a Bible or heard the name of Jesus. We have squandered our God-given advantage!

Let God Be True

The dialogue continues as the imaginary rabbi comes back at Paul with a second objection:

> What if some did not have faith? Will their lack of faith nullify God's faithfulness? Not at all! Let God be true, and every man a liar. As it is written:
>
> "So that you may be proved right when you speak and prevail when you judge." (Romans 3:3–4)

The imaginary rabbi says, "Paul, are you suggesting that if *some* of the Jews did not believe, then God might forget His promises to *all* of the Jews? Are you saying that just because some of us didn't measure up to what God required in the Law, everyone in Israel has lost the promise that God gave them? You seem to suggest that God is not interested in the very rituals that He Himself instituted. Are you saying that circumcision and all of the other rites and rituals of the Old Testament mean nothing to God?"

Paul's answer uses the strongest words of denial possible in the Greek language: "Not at all!" Or, as other translations put it, "By no means! May it never be! God forbid!" To suggest God would go back on His promises is tantamount to saying that God is dishonest and unfaithful. Paul says that such a suggestion is totally unthinkable: "Not at all! Never let that be! Let God be true, and every man a liar." No matter how many human beings may fail, God always keeps His word.

Paul then quotes from Psalm 51, the beautiful psalm of confession David wrote after his sin of murder and adultery. For a year and a half, David hid his sins and refused to admit them to God or anyone else. Finally, God sent Nathan the prophet, who exposed David's sins (see 2 Samuel 12). At that moment, David broke down and confessed to God.

In his psalm of confession, David told God, "Against you, you only, have I sinned and done what is evil in your sight, so that you are proved right when you speak and justified when you judge." In other words, "You are not to blame, God; I did this sin, and you are right and justified in judging me for it." Or, as Paul puts it, "Let God be true and every man a liar."

Next, the imaginary rabbi raises a third objection, and Paul responds:

> But if our unrighteousness brings out God's righteousness more clearly, what shall we say? That God is unjust in bringing his wrath on us? (I am using a human argument.) Certainly not! If that were so, how could God judge the world? (Romans 3:5–6)

As Paul notes, this is a common human argument. We often hear this same argument today. People say, "If my sin makes God look good because it gives Him a chance to show His love and forgiveness, then how can He condemn me? I've given God a chance to reveal Himself, and that's what He wants. In fact, I should sin even more and make Him look all the better!"

To this argument, Paul replies, "Let's carry this to its logical conclusion. If everyone lived on that basis, then nobody could be judged and God would be removed as judge of all the world." In short, such reasoning would demean God. He would have no right to judge our sin if He had arranged the universe so that sin would glorify Him. If God does not judge the world, then sin cannot be arrested.

Sin never glorifies God. Sin always has evil results. As the Scriptures tell us, those who plant seeds of sin reap only corruption (see Galatians 6:8). This is a law of nature, ordained by God, which no one can break.

Next, Paul reinforces his argument with a personal illustration:

> Someone might argue, "If my falsehood enhances God's
> truthfulness and so increases his glory, why am I still
> condemned as a sinner?" Why not say—as we are being
> slanderously reported as saying and as some claim that we
> say—"Let us do evil that good may result"? Their condem-
> nation is deserved. (Romans 3:7–8)

Translators of the New International Version erred by adding
a phrase that is not in the original Greek text: "Someone might
argue. . . ." The New King James Version renders this passage
more accurately:

> For if the truth of God has increased through my lie to
> His glory, why am I also still judged as a sinner? And why
> not say, "Let us do evil that good may come"?—as we are
> slanderously reported and as some affirm that we say. Their
> condemnation is just. (Romans 3:7–8 NKJV)

There is an interesting progression here, as if Paul is drawing
a noose around himself. In Romans 1 he talks about "they," as in
"They are without excuse." In Romans 2, he talks about "you," as in
"You are without excuse." In Romans 3, he talks about "our unrighteousness." Finally, in verses 7 and 8, he tightens that noose around
his own neck, saying, "my lie." He has included himself in the circle
of sin, judgment, and condemnation. I love to see this, because it tells
me that Paul does not hold himself up as better than anyone else.

Paul says, in effect, "Wouldn't it be logical to simply say, 'Let's
do evil that good may come'? What a ridiculous argument! That
kind of false 'logic' removes all differences between good and evil!"

Here, we see the timeliness of Paul's message in Romans,
because this, in fact, is what many people are saying today: "There's
no such thing as good or evil. Whatever you like is good; whatever
you don't like is evil. Morality is all in your mind!" Paul says that

such false "logic" is an absurdity, producing moral anarchy. Such thinking is precisely why our society is in moral chaos today.

No One Is Righteous

The dialogue continues. In the next section, Paul introduces another question, along with his answer:

> What then? Are we better than they? Not at all. For we have previously charged both Jews and Greeks that they are all under sin. (Romans 3:9 NKJV)

The phrase "Are we better than they?" would be better translated "Do we have any standing at all?" Paul is looking at the entire human race and asking, "Is there any way that a human being can please God apart from faith in Christ?" His answer: None at all. Whether Jew or Gentile, our situation is hopeless.

Paul has already shown that blatantly wicked people have no hope because they defy God. The self-righteous have no hope because they delude themselves, thinking themselves to be morally superior to everyone else. The unenlightened pagans, whether in the Amazon jungles or the concrete jungles, have no hope because they do not even live up to their own standards. The religious zealots have no hope, because they cannot live up to their own teachings.

Finally, Paul seals his argument with the iron-clad authority of Scripture. He gathers up a compilation of passages from the Psalms, Proverbs, and Isaiah to show that he is not introducing a new doctrine. He is simply stating what God has already said throughout His Word. The Scripture passages Paul cites deal with three themes: (1) God's view of human character; (2) God's view of human conduct in speech and action; and (3) the root cause of human character and conduct. He writes:

> As it is written:
> "There is no one righteous, not even one."
> (Romans 3:10)

Isn't that an amazing statement? Here, Paul quotes God's all-inclusive indictment of humanity in Psalm 14:1. Think of all the nice, kind, gracious people you know. You may think of them as "good" people, "good" neighbors, "good" friends. You may think of yourself as a "good" person. But God's verdict on the human race is universal and all-inclusive: "There is no one righteous, not even one." Paul continues:

> ". . . there is no one who understands, no one who seeks God." (Romans 3:11)

Here, Paul quotes Psalm 14:2. All over the world, in secular universities and religious temples, human beings are searching for the answer to the mystery of life—and God says that there is not one who understands, not one. Moreover, God says that there is no one who truly seeks Him! The world is filled with millions of religious people, streaming into houses of worship, observing rites and rituals—but are they looking for God? No, says God. They may be looking for peace or answers to their prayers or feelings of religious ecstasy, but God says that there is no one who truly seeks God Himself.

> "All have turned away, they have together become worthless; there is no one who does good, not even one." (Romans 3:12)

Paul quotes Psalm 14:3. This statement could not be any clearer: There is no one who does good, not even one. We read this and think, "But I'm not such a bad person! Everybody knows I'm moral and decent!" Does God, who knows your innermost thoughts, agree? If all your thoughts throughout the day were recorded and broadcast to the world, would everybody still regard you as moral and decent?

It is easy to fool the world and hide our innermost selves from others. It is impossible to hide our souls from God. He looks on the heart, He knows our thoughts, and His verdict is clear: There is no one who does good, not even one.

Next, Paul cites Psalm 5:9, 140:3, and 10:7 to give us God's perspective on why there is no one who does good. The first area he deals with is our speech:

> "Their throats are open graves;
>   their tongues practice deceit."
> "The poison of vipers is on their lips."
> "Their mouths are full of cursing and bitterness."
>
> (Romans 3:13–14)

Quoting three passages from the Psalms, Paul covers the whole realm of the sins we commit with our speech. It begins deep within us, in the grave-like darkness of the throat; it proceeds to the tongue, then the lips, and finally the whole mouth. The sins we do with our words come from our innermost selves and proceed outward. When God looks upon our sinful speech, He sees an open grave with a rotting corpse, with a horrible stench billowing forth.

What are the sins of speech? There are sins of offensiveness and vulgarity, of spewing filthy words that cause people to feel repulsed and violated. There are sins of scorn and insult, of treating people with disrespect and abuse.

"Their tongues practice deceit," says God, highlighting our sins of hypocrisy and lying. Some of our deceptions are stark and openly destructive. Others are "little white lies," those tissue-thin facades we put up so that no one will know what we are *really* like.

"The poison of vipers is on their lips," says God. This is a picture of the tongue being used to destroy reputations, to gossip and slander, to cruelly wound another person.

"Their mouths are full of cursing and bitterness." Cursing is profanity and blasphemy, taking God's name in vain, or blaming God, or placing oneself in God's place, verbally condemning another human being to eternal punishment. Bitterness is reproaching God for one's own circumstances. We hear cursing and bitterness all the time, from the people around us, from our TV and movie screens, and even (I'm sad to say) from Christians.

Next, Paul cites Isaiah 59:7–8 to describe the acts that follow the sins of human speech:

> "Their feet are swift to shed blood;
>   ruin and misery mark their ways,
>   and the way of peace they do not know."
>
> (Romans 3:15–17)

Wherever humanity goes, ruin follows. Every great city has its crime- and poverty-ridden slums. All of our beautiful wilderness regions and rivers are endangered by litter and pollution. Crime, violence, and war are an inescapable part of the human condition. Ruin is in the heart of humanity. I have often thought this statement would be an appropriate slogan for the United Nations: "The way of peace they do not know."

Next, Paul quotes Psalm 36:1:

> "There is no fear of God before their eyes." (Romans 3:18)

This statement recalls Paul's words in Romans 1:18: "The wrath of God is being revealed from heaven against all the godlessness and wickedness of men who suppress the truth by their wickedness." The wrath of God is revealed against humanity because "there is no fear of God before their eyes."

The Purpose of the Law

In Romans 3:19–20, Paul connects the sinfulness and wretchedness of humanity to the Law of Moses. His goal is to show us clearly why God gave the Law. The Jews of Paul's day were convinced that God had given them the Law as a special privilege. In these verses, Paul punctures their self-righteous pride—and ours:

Now we know that whatever the law says, it says to those who are under the law, so that every mouth may be silenced and the whole world held accountable to God. Therefore no one will be declared righteous in his sight by observing the law; rather, through the law we become conscious of sin. (Romans 3:19–20)

Reading this description of God's view of humanity, we are tempted to respond, "Enough! Wipe them all out!" In view of our wretchedness, deceit, hypocrisy, vulgarity, and blasphemy, wouldn't the universe be better off without us? Wouldn't God prefer a universe free of our moral and spiritual pollution?

Amazingly, the same God who rendered this terrible verdict on humanity has also found a way to suspend the sentence of death that we so richly deserve. As John 3:16 tells us, God loved the world so much that He gave us His only begotten Son to take our penalty upon Himself.

The Law of God condemns us, proving that we deserve eternal death. But God did not send the Law to destroy us. He sent the Law to us to keep us from false hope and false pride in our own "good" works. He sent the Law to keep us from taking a false path of do-it-yourself righteousness. The Law condemns us—yet it is the very condemnation of the Law that makes us willing to listen to God, so that we will find the right path.

Paul says the Law does three things to us: First, it silences us. You can always tell that someone is close to becoming a Christian when they stop making excuses. Self-righteous people say, "Yes, I've done bad things, but I've also done many good things." But when the true meaning of the Law becomes clear to people, they realize good deeds can never outweigh the immense burden of sin we all carry. That realization silences all excuses.

A friend of mine once received a traffic ticket. She felt that, even though she had committed the offense, her actions were justified because of extenuating circumstances. So she went to court to plead her case. She imagined that the judge would ask her if she was guilty or not guilty, and she would answer, "Guilty—but I have an explanation." Then she would make her case and the judge would agree with her and the case would be dismissed. After the hearing, she told me what happened. "I had my argument all prepared," she said, "but when I stood there all alone before the judge in his robe, and he looked over his glasses and said, 'Guilty or not guilty?' all my arguments evaporated. I said, 'Guilty.'" Her arguments and excuses were silenced.

Next, Paul says that the whole world will be held accountable to God. Time and death do not erase our sins. As the book of Hebrews tells us, "It is appointed unto men once to die, but after this the judgment" (Hebrews 9:27 KJV).

What does the Law want of us? Jesus said that the two greatest commandments are, "Love the Lord your God with all your heart and with all your soul and with all your mind," and, "Love your neighbor as yourself." The entire Law, He added, is summed up in these two commandments to love (see Matthew 22:37–40).

All the Law asks us to do is to love God and love one another. When we face ourselves before the Law, we have to confess that the greatest sins of our lives have been the many times we have failed to love. So, Paul says, we cannot be declared righteous by observing the Law. The purpose of the Law is not to make us free from sin, but to make us conscious of how sinful we are. Only when we are conscious of our sin are we willing to receive God's solution for our sin.

"But Now . . ."

A major transition occurs at verse 21, signaled by the first two words, "But now. . . ." The first twenty verses of Romans 3 have been a depressing assessment of the human condition. At verse 21, we feel a sudden spiritual lift, as if a brilliant ray of heavenly sunlight has broken through the overcast of our sin, bringing light and warmth to our souls. God has not left us under a sentence of eternal death. Though we were incapable of fulfilling the Law, God now shows us what perfect love looks like by sending us His Son. Here is Paul's joyful transition:

> But now a righteousness from God, apart from law, has
> been made known, to which the Law and the Prophets tes-
> tify. (Romans 3:21)

In the face of human failure comes God's "But now"! Humanity can never supply its own righteousness—but now a righteousness from God has appeared to solve the human crisis!

In this concluding section of Romans 3, Paul explores
what this "righteousness from God" means. In verse 21, Paul
announces that God's answer to the human crisis has arrived.
In verses 22–24, he explains how this gift of righteousness can
be obtained. In verses 25–26, he tells us how this gift works. In
verses 27–31, he explains the results that follow in our lives when
we receive this gift.

What is this "righteousness from God" that Paul announces in
verse 21? Elsewhere in the New Testament, Paul refers to it as "the
glorious gospel of the blessed God" (1 Timothy 1:11), the good
news that Jesus Christ has become our righteousness.

This word *righteousness* is widely misunderstood these days.
People tend to associate "righteousness" with "good works."
But in the book of Romans, Paul uses the word *righteousness* in a
way that has nothing to do with works. In fact, he makes it clear
that we cannot achieve righteousness by observing the Law. The
phrase "righteousness from God" does not refer to anything we
do; it refers to *what we are* in God's sight. The gift Paul talks about
is the gift of a *righteous standing* before God.

But the real meaning underlying this word *righteousness* is
found in the word *worth*. People everywhere are looking for a
sense of worth. Psychologists tell us that a sense of worth is essential to human well-being. We cannot function if we see ourselves
as worthless and unworthy, so we are all on a quest for a sense of
worth.

The good news of the gospel is that God has given us the gift
of true worth, a righteousness that comes directly from Him. Some
people will labor in vain all their lives to find that which God gives

us as a free gift. We cannot earn a sense of worth. We can only reach out and accept it.

Now, perhaps, we begin to see that the gospel is significant not merely for its promise of an afterlife, but for what it means in the here and now. The good news of the gospel is that we are people of worth, thanks to the free gift of God.

Unfortunately, many people—including many in the church!—do not realize that this is what the gospel is truly about. Young people and old people, rich people and poor people, and people of every race and color are looking for a sense of worth, a sense that they are loved and accepted. The place where they should hear the good news of their own worth to God should be the church; tragically, many churches do not preach that wonderful news. That is one reason why many people have turned their backs on the church.

God offers us the gift of His own perfect righteousness, His own true and satisfying sense of worth. By faith in Jesus Christ, we receive that amazing, healing sense of worth and acceptance. There could be no better news to any searching, aching heart.

Paul goes on to add two important clauses to his argument about this "righteousness from God." Let's look at this statement again:

> But now a righteousness from God, apart from law, has been made known, to which the Law and the Prophets testify. (Romans 3:21)

Notice, first, that this righteousness is *apart from the Law*. In other words, it is not something we can earn by obedience to the Law. It is a gift. Anyone who tries to achieve righteousness (a sense of worth and right standing before God) by keeping the Law has already failed. No one can measure up to God's standards of perfection. Nevertheless, God has found a way to give us the gift of righteousness.

Second, Paul says that this righteousness is witnessed by the Law and the Prophets. It is not something that popped into existence, unannounced, when Jesus Christ was born. This righteousness has been foretold down through the centuries, in the books of the Law (the first five books of the Bible: Genesis, Exodus, Leviticus, Numbers, and Deuteronomy) and in the writings of the Old Testament prophets. The saints who lived before the birth of Jesus knew and experienced the wonder of this gift just as we do today, although they came to it by a different process.

The Law bore testimony to this righteous gift of God by providing a series of sacrifices. The Jews knew that they did not measure up to God's standards, so the Law itself provided a system of sacrifices that could be offered on the altar. The entire sacrificial system of Old Testament worship symbolized the coming One who would be "the Lamb of God, who takes away the sins of the world" (see John 1:29).

The Prophets—such as Abraham, Moses, David, Isaiah, Jeremiah, and many others—not only talked about this gift but experienced it in their own lives. David, for example, wrote, "Blessed is the man whose transgression is forgiven, to whom the Lord will not impute iniquity, whose sins are covered" (Psalm 32:1). David wrote those words hundreds of years before Jesus died upon the cross of Calvary, yet David understood that God had found a way to cover those sins and give the unearned gift of righteousness to a sinner like himself.

The righteousness from God is not a new concept. It was thousands of years old by the time Paul wrote the book of Romans. Yet the source of that righteousness from God was difficult to understand until we could see it flowing to us from the cross of Jesus.

The Gift Must Be Accepted

In the next section, Paul tells us how to obtain this gift. Perhaps you are looking for this sense of being loved and accepted by God. How do you receive it? Here is Paul's answer:

This righteousness from God comes through faith in Jesus
Christ to all who believe. There is no difference, for all have
sinned and fall short of the glory of God, and are justified
freely by his grace through the redemption that came by
Christ Jesus. (Romans 3:22–24)

There is only one way to receive the righteousness and worth
that comes from God. It is expressed here in four different aspects,
but there is only one way: faith in Jesus Christ.

First, notice how Paul's answer centers on the person of the
Savior—not merely on His work or His teaching, but on His person. It is not by giving mental agreement to His teachings that we
are saved. Rather, we are saved by believing and trusting in Jesus
Himself. The gift of the righteousness from God requires that we
have a relationship with a living person, Jesus Christ.

That is why the Bible never tells us, "Believe in what Jesus
did." Rather, it tells us, "to all who received him, to those who
believed in his name, he gave the right to become children of God"
(see John 1:12). That means there must come a time when you
open your life to Christ, when you ask Him to be what He offers
to be—your Lord and Savior.

Later in Romans, Paul writes, "That if you confess with your
mouth, 'Jesus is Lord,' and believe in your heart that God raised
him from the dead, you will be saved [being "saved," of course,
is another term for this gift of righteousness]. For it is with your
heart that you believe and are justified, and it is with your mouth
that you confess and are saved" (Romans 10:9–10).

There is no other way to receive the righteousness from God,
the gift of salvation. No way can be found in all the religions of
earth that can bring people to a place of righteousness and right
standing in God's sight except the way of faith in Jesus Christ.

Second, notice that Paul stresses the fact that all who believe
are saved; those who do not believe are not saved. The righteousness from God is not automatically and universally applied to

the entire human race. It is a free gift, but it is a gift that must be accepted in order to be received.

There are many religious groups today that teach a false doctrine called universalism, the belief that all people will be saved or made happy in the afterlife, regardless of their sins. Some claim that the death of Christ was so effective that all are saved, whether they trust in Him or not. Others claim that a loving God would simply not allow anyone to suffer eternal death.

But Paul clearly states that there is no such thing as universalism in God's plan. Salvation, says Paul, is a result of God's grace through the redemption that comes by faith in Jesus alone. Grace is the gift God offers. Faith is the hand that accepts and receives that gift. A gift is of no use unless it is accepted and received.

Third, Paul describes how we obtain the gift of the righteousness from God through the phrase, "justified freely by his grace." The gift of salvation is all God's doing, and none of ours. We are justified and declared righteous by God's grace. That word *grace* is defined as "God's unmerited favor toward sinners." We do not deserve grace, nor can we earn grace. There is nothing we can add to grace.

Many people mistakenly think that baptism is a substitute for grace, or that church membership is an add-on that completes grace. We cannot contribute a thing to the grace of God. As in the words of the old hymn, "Nothing in my hand I bring; Simply to Thy cross I cling."

The Heart of the Gospel

Next, Paul offers a brief explanation of how and why this redemption works. "How" is found in the opening words of verse 25; "why" is found in the rest of this passage:

> God presented him as a sacrifice of atonement, through faith in his blood. He did this to demonstrate his justice, because in his forbearance he had left the sins committed

beforehand unpunished—he did it to demonstrate his justice at the present time, so as to be just and the one who
justifies those who have faith in Jesus. (Romans 3:25–26)

This is the heart of the gospel and the ground of our assurance
as Christians. Many Christians struggle with assurance. They have
a sneaking suspicion that perhaps God is not quite satisfied with
them. They worry that, even after receiving Jesus as their Lord and
Savior, they might still somehow be lost. Pay careful attention to
Paul's argument, because this is the answer to that struggle.

First, Paul says that God has accomplished a sacrifice of atonement through faith in His blood. This phrase, "sacrifice of atonement," is actually a single word, *hilasterion*, in the original Greek.
This Greek word is also sometimes translated "expiation" or "propitiation"—theological terms that may not make much sense to
you. But the meaning of "sacrifice of atonement" or "expiation"
or "propitiation" is actually quite simple—and it is the heart of
the gospel.

Expiation is that which satisfies justice; *propitiation* is that
which awakens love. Both of these terms are involved in the death
of Jesus, but expiation does not go quite as far as propitiation. Propitiation carries us clear through to the awakening of God's love
toward us. So I think "propitiatory sacrifice" is a better translation
than the word "expiation."

Let me illustrate the difference: Suppose someone is injured
at work in an industrial accident. He is left partially paralyzed,
and the company is at fault for neglecting to provide a safe work
environment. As a result, the company is held accountable for the
man's injury and paralysis. The court awards this man a tremendous sum of money, to be paid by the company. When the money
is paid, the company has expiated its wrongdoing and has satisfied
the demands of justice. It no longer has any legal responsibility
toward this man. That is expiation.

But expiation does nothing about how the man feels toward
the company. Though he has collected a great sum of money, the

man may spend the rest of his life hating the name of that company. The debt has been expiated, but it has not been propitiated.

Paul tells us that human sin has injured God, just as that man was injured by the negligence of the company. Justice demands that we be punished for our sin. That punishment was accomplished by the death of Jesus on the cross; with His death, God's justice was satisfied. That is expiation.

But the reality of the cross goes much deeper than mere expiation. Paul is telling us that the death of Jesus on the cross also awakened God's love toward us. Because of the sacrifice of Jesus, God grants us a sense of worth, acceptance, and value in His sight. That is what propitiation means. That is what the death of Jesus does. It not only satisfies God's justice, but it awakens His love. As a result, He pours out His love upon us.

Paul shows us why this had to happen, beginning in the middle of verse 25: "He did this to demonstrate his justice, because in his forbearance he had left the sins committed beforehand unpunished." Here Paul refers to all the centuries when God apparently had done nothing about human sin. We often hear people questioning God on this very point. "Where is the God of justice?" they ask. "How can a just God allow tyranny, oppression, poverty, slavery, and genocide? Where is the justice of God?"

These questions are even found throughout the Bible: "Why does the way of the wicked prosper?" (Jeremiah 12:1). "Why do the wicked live on, growing old and increasing in power?" (Job 21:7).

The last time in history the human race saw God's holy justice on display was during the Flood of Noah. In response to human wickedness, God wiped out the whole human race except for eight people. The Flood was a testimony to God's sense of justice; there has never been a manifestation of God's justice to that degree since that time. So people ask, "Doesn't God care about evil and injustice?"

The truth is that God has patiently held back His hand of justice so that the human race may continue to exist. Humanity does not see that, and shows no gratitude for God's restraining grace. To most people, it seems that God doesn't care about sin.

But God cares deeply about sin. The cross is proof of that. And He cares deeply about human beings. The cross is proof of that, too. The cross is where the justice of God meets the love of God. All the stored-up punishment that we deserve was poured out upon Jesus at the cross. God did not spare His Son one iota of the wrath that the human race deserves.

That outpouring of God's wrath explains the awful cry of abandonment that comes from the cross, "My God, my God, why have you forsaken me?" (Mark 15:34). There Jesus entered into the eternal emptiness of God's judgment.

Paul's argument is that God presented Jesus as a sacrifice of atonement in order to demonstrate His justice, so that He would maintain His own justice while still being free to extend love and mercy to undeserving human beings. That is the amazing good news of the gospel. God's love has been freed to act toward us, yet at the same time His justice has been satisfied. At the cross, His justice was satisfied—yet His mercy and love were also satisfied. That is the heart of the gospel.

Three Final Questions

In the closing paragraph of Romans 3, Paul shows us the results of this forgiveness:

> Where, then, is boasting? It is excluded. On what principle? On that of observing the law? No, but on that of faith. For we maintain that a man is justified through faith apart from observing the law. Is God the God of Jews only? Is he not the God of Gentiles too? Yes, of Gentiles too, since there is only one God, who will justify the circumcised by faith and the uncircumcised through that same faith. Do we, then, nullify the law by this faith? Not at all! Rather, we uphold the law. (Romans 3:27–31)

Paul raises—then answers—three basic questions to show us the natural result of God's merciful acceptance of us through faith in Jesus Christ. First question: Who can boast? Paul's answer: No one. How can you boast when you have received the gift of grace without any merit on your part? If we can't boast, then we can't look down on others for their sins. All boasting is excluded. All religious and moral snobbery is excluded. We are accepted by God on the basis of the free gift of grace.

Second question: "Is God the God of Jews only?" In other words, are Jews the only recipients of God's grace? Are the non-Jewish Gentiles excluded by God? Does God grant special favors to this group or that group because of their ethnicity, ancestry, or national origin? Is there one God for the Jews and another for the Gentiles? Paul's answer: Of course not. There is only one God, and He is the God of both Jews and Gentiles, because both must come to God on exactly the same basis: by grace through faith in Jesus alone. The ground is level at the foot of the cross. No one can stand on any other basis but the work of Jesus Christ.

Third question: "Do we, then, nullify the law by this faith?" In other words, does faith cancel out the Law? Does faith mean that we no longer need the Law? Paul's answer: No, faith in Jesus fulfills the Law. The righteousness which the Law demands is the same righteousness that is given to us in Christ. So if we have the righteousness from God as a gift, then we no longer need to fear the Law, because its demands—demands that are nothing less than absolute perfection!—have been met.

Having received the righteousness from God, we are forgiven. But receiving God's forgiveness is not something we do only once; it is something we must experience again and again. It is the cleansing basis on which we are to live from day to day. The apostle John puts it this way:

If we confess our sins, he is faithful and just and will forgive us our sins and purify us from all unrighteousness. (1 John 1:9)

Forgiveness is God's gift, and we need to receive it daily, even hourly, from the hand of God. When we slip into self-righteousness and pride, when we treat others with criticism or sarcasm, when we indulge in evil speech, talk, or thoughts, then we need to acknowledge our sin before God. When we return to Him in confession and repentance, we will find His love is still there. He accepts us, values us, and restores us. He is our Father, we are His dearly loved children, and He will never change.

That is what God's gift of righteousness means to us. It is good news indeed, so that we never need to fear God or His judgment. The God of ultimate holiness is also the Father of infinite mercy. He has covered our worst sins with His own gleaming righteousness.

CHAPTER 5

THE FATHER OF FAITH

Romans 4

One of the most honored people in human history is Abraham, the forefather of the Hebrew people. There are few names that are as honored throughout the world as the name of Abraham. He is revered by three faiths: Judaism, Islam, and Christianity. The apostle Paul spends the entire fourth chapter of Romans exploring the meaning of Abraham's life, lifting him up as an example of what it means to live by faith.

In Romans 3, Paul told us how to receive the free gift of a righteousness from God to cover our own sinfulness and guilt. That righteousness from God gives us a sense of worth, value, and acceptance by God, and He offers it to us through the sacrifice of atonement that Jesus made upon the cross. That righteousness lies at the heart of the Christian gospel.

Now, in Romans 4, Paul points us to one of the clearest Old Testament examples of how human beings can receive the gift of the righteousness from God. That Old Testament example is Abraham—a man who lived thousands of years before Jesus was born, yet he received the gift of righteousness, acceptance, and right standing before God.

Faith in God's Promise

In Romans 4, Paul raises two important questions about Abraham: (1) When was Abraham made righteous? (2) Why was Abraham made righteous? Paul introduces the first question in the first three verses:

What then shall we say that Abraham, our forefather, discovered in this matter? If, in fact, Abraham was justified by works, he had something to boast about—but not before God. What does the Scripture say? "Abraham believed God, and it was credited to him as righteousness." (Romans 4:1–3)

Paul says that Abraham could have chosen two ways to gain a sense of worth and right standing before God. The first choice Abraham could have made: good works. There is no question that Abraham was a man of good works. We first meet Abraham in Genesis 11. His name at that time was Abram, and he was living in the city of Ur of the Chaldeans in the Mesopotamian Valley. Abram was a religious man, but his religion was idolatry; he worshiped the Chaldean moon goddess—though he did so in ignorance.

While Abram was in that condition of ignorance, God appeared and spoke to him, commanding him to go to a new and strange land. Abram believed God and obeyed. Stepping out in simple trust, Abram gathered his family and possessions, and he launched out into the unknown. He trusted God to lead him to a land he had never seen before. So Abram/Abraham appears in Scripture as a man of good works.

But was Abraham justified, saved, and made righteous by his good works? Paul answers the question this way: "If, in fact, Abraham was justified by works, he had something to boast about—but not before God." Another word for "good works" is *performance*. We all know that if you give a good performance in any endeavor, you will be highly thought of by people. You will receive praise, awards, commendations, and testimonials.

But God is not impressed by the things that people find impressive. God knows the heart. He knows that grand performances are usually motivated by selfishness, ego, and greed. When we give a grand performance and receive our applause and accolades, we may experience a temporary sense of worth. But that is not the true, lasting worth that comes from possessing the righteousness from God. It is fleeting. It evaporates as soon as the applause no longer echoes in our ears, leaving us feeling empty and unfulfilled. Only the righteousness that comes from God lasts throughout our lives, and beyond, for all eternity.

That is the righteousness Abraham discovered—a righteousness that comes not from good works or grand performances, but from a secure and eternal Source. What is the Source of this righteousness Abraham found? To answer that question, Paul points us directly to God's Word. "What does the Scripture say?" he asks—then he quotes Genesis 15:6: "Abraham believed God, and it was credited to him as righteousness."

That statement comes from the story in which God took Abraham out one night and showed him the stars in the heavens. "Abraham," He said, "look up at the heavens and count the stars if you can!" Abraham looked at the stars blazing in their glory—and there was no way he could number them all. Then God said, "So shall your offspring be." And at that point we find the statement Paul quotes: "Abraham believed God, and it was credited to him as righteousness." That was when Abraham received a sense of worth, acceptance, love, value, and right standing in the sight of God.

There is a common misunderstanding concerning God's promise, "So shall your offspring be." People assume that God is promising to give Abraham a vast multitude of descendants, but that is not the true meaning of this promise. In Galatians 3:16, Paul explains what this promise actually meant: "The promises were spoken to Abraham and to his seed. The Scripture does not say 'and to seeds,' meaning many people, but 'and to your seed,' meaning one person, who is Christ."

So when God said, "So shall your offspring be," He was not talking about a multitude of offspring (plural), but of one Offspring (singular), who was Jesus Christ. In other words, God told Abraham that there was One coming who would give Abraham a heavenly seed or offspring as well as a physical seed or offspring. Through Jesus, God would give Abraham a multitude of *spiritual* descendants—people descended from Abraham not merely by physical ancestry but by having the same *faith* that Abraham had.

This explanation of the promise was affirmed by Jesus Himself. He was talking to the Pharisees and they said to Him, "Abraham is our father." Jesus replied, in effect, "If Abraham were your father, you would believe in me, because Abraham saw my day and was glad" (see John 8:56).

So we can only conclude that God revealed to Abraham (and Abraham understood by faith) that the Seed of righteousness, Jesus the Lord, was coming and He would remove the penalty of sin from all who believe in Him. We don't know how detailed God's explanation of this promise was or how clearly Abraham understood it. But we know that Abraham believed God, and that his faith was credited to him as righteousness.

It is interesting that the apostle James also quotes Genesis 15:6: "And the scripture was fulfilled that says, 'Abraham believed God, and it was credited to him as righteousness,' and he was called God's friend." Note that last phrase: "and he was called God's friend"! That is genuine acceptance and worth, to be called a friend of God. Abraham became God's friend because he believed God's promise. And if you and I have faith like Abraham, we also become friends of God.

Every year, I sit down and fill out my income tax. I have to confess that there is one tantalizing regulation in the tax code that tempts me every year. That regulation says that money that is given to you as a gift is not taxable. This rule tempts me to look for ways to make it appear that the money I receive from my various functions as a pastor is really a gift, not wages. But I know that the Internal Revenue Service will never accept such reasoning. I am a pastor, and the money I receive is payment for the work I do, so it must be reported as taxable income. Paul uses an almost identical illustration in the next two verses of Romans 4:

Now when a man works, his wages are not credited to
him as a gift, but as an obligation. However, to the man who

does not work but trusts God who justifies the wicked, his faith is credited as righteousness. (Romans 4:4–5)

Paul's argument is clear: If you work, then you have *earned* your wages. Wages are not a gift but an obligation that must be paid. A worker is entitled to take credit for what he has earned, but he cannot take credit for what he receives as a free gift.

It is the same way in the spiritual realm. If we could earn our salvation by our own good works, then we could take credit for our own salvation. But if we receive salvation as a free gift from God, then all credit goes to God alone. When we place our faith in God through Jesus Christ, our faith is credited as righteousness—not because we have earned that righteousness, but because we have received it as a gift.

Who is Paul talking about in these verses? From the context, it is clear that Paul is talking about Abraham. He is saying that Abraham, despite his good works, was not saved by his own works. Abraham was saved by his faith, which was credited to Abraham as righteousness.

Next, Paul points us to another Old Testament figure to confirm his argument: David the Psalmist. Paul says that David expressed the same idea—that faith is credited by God as righteousness—when he wrote these words (quoted by Paul from Psalm 32:1–2):

David says the same thing when he speaks of the blessedness of the man to whom God credits righteousness apart from works:

"Blessed are they
　　whose transgressions are forgiven,
　　whose sins are covered.
Blessed is the man
　　whose sin the Lord will never count
　　　　against him."

(Romans 4:6–8)

It is truly remarkable that David found this gift of the righteousness from God after his soul was stained by the murder of Uriah the Hittite and by his adultery with Uriah's wife. David sinned grievously—yet he came to God in faith and repentance, and his sins were forgiven, his right standing before God was restored.

Paul makes it clear that Abraham never found the righteousness of God by being devout and moral. He found it when he believed God's promise of the Seed that was to come—Jesus. In the same way, King David did not find forgiveness for his sins by being a mighty king of Israel or by any other good works. David found forgiveness because he believed (as he wrote in Psalm 51:16–17) that God did not delight in the sacrifice of animals, but in the sacrifice of a broken and repentant heart. Because of his faith, David was called a man after God's own heart (see 1 Samuel 13:13–14 and Acts 13:21–22).

Wouldn't you like to be called a friend of God? Wouldn't you like to be called a man or woman after God's own heart? Paul's message to us is that we can become God's friends—not by our performance, but by placing our faith in Jesus Christ.

A Sign and a Seal

So Paul has answered the first of the two questions he raised: When was Abraham made righteous? Paul's answer: When he believed God and His promise of the One who was to come, the One who would die for the sins of the world. Now Paul moves to the second question: Why was Abraham made righteous? He writes:

Is this blessedness only for the circumcised, or also for the uncircumcised? We have been saying that Abraham's faith was credited to him as righteousness. Under what circumstances was it credited? Was it after he was circumcised, or before? It was not after, but before! And he received the sign of circumcision, a seal of the righteousness that he had by faith while he was still uncircumcised. (Romans 4:9–11)

Many people today are embarrassed by God's emphasis upon circumcision. This is not hard to understand, because circumcision is performed on the male sex organ, and many people have been raised with a taboo on even discussing such matters. But the truth is that our bodies do not end at the waist. Pretending that they do is an unhealthy view of our bodies.

God chose circumcision as a symbol of the marvelous truth we are discussing in this chapter. He gave the rite of circumcision to the Jewish people for a specific purpose. Because God is not embarrassed to discuss circumcision, we shouldn't be either.

Paul makes two important points about circumcision. The first is that rituals such as circumcision are powerless to save. He points out that Abraham was circumcised years after he was pronounced righteous by faith. Clearly, then, the ritual of circumcision has no saving value whatsoever. Abraham was a friend of God long before he was circumcised. Paul underscores this point to silence the arguments of those who trusted in this ritual to make them acceptable to God.

Paul's argument also cancels out any modern analogies to circumcision, such as baptism. People are justified—made righteous and accepted in God's sight—not by being baptized, but by having faith in the Lord Jesus Christ, in His sacrificial death and His resurrection.

The second point Paul makes about circumcision is that the real purpose of this ritual is twofold: It is a sign and a seal. I don't wish to offend the reader, but it is important to set aside our prudery and discuss this matter candidly. There is a reason God chose this particular place on a man's body to place His sign—and the reason is obvious. God wants us to remember what the rite of circumcision stands for, so he placed this sign on an organ that a man must see several times a day. God made sure that His sign in human flesh was impossible to overlook.

Paul calls this rite "the sign of circumcision, a seal of the righteousness." Circumcision is not only a sign, but a seal. What is a seal? It is a guarantee of permanency. Circumcision, the removal of the foreskin of the male organ, is an unchangeable act. Once done, it cannot be undone. It is God's way of saying, in visible and indelible terms, "You have been accepted by Me, and that acceptance will never change."

Next, Paul explains why Abraham was made righteous. Beyond Abraham's own need of personal salvation, God had another reason:

> So then, he is the father of all who believe but have not been circumcised, in order that righteousness might be credited to them. And he is also the father of the circumcised who not only are circumcised but who also walk in the footsteps of the faith that our father Abraham had before he was circumcised. (Romans 4:11–12)

The gift of being made acceptable before God, of receiving the righteousness from God, was given to Abraham, not only to save him, but to make him a father of many more yet to come. God promised Abraham that he would become the father of many spiritual descendants, more numerous than the stars in the heavens, and that promise is still in the process of being fulfilled. When we receive the righteousness from God by faith in His Son, Jesus Christ, then we become spiritual descendants of Abraham. This is true, Paul says, whether we are circumcised or uncircumcised, whether we are Jewish or Gentile.

This is the great secret of life. We do not have to earn God's love and forgiveness. It is already ours every day. There is no more liberating truth than that. We do not have to live for a fleeting sense of worth that comes from the applause and praise of others. We have an eternal sense of worth that comes from our right standing before God.

The Law Brings Wrath

In the concluding half of Romans 4, Paul explores the nature of Abraham's faith. In the process, he explains what authentic faith is—and is not. Sometimes the best way to learn what a thing is, is by learning what it is not. Paul writes:

> It was not through law that Abraham and his offspring received the promise that he would be heir of the world, but through the righteousness that comes by faith. For if those who live by law are heirs, faith has no value and the promise is worthless, because law brings wrath. And where there is no law there is no transgression. (Romans 4:13–15)

Faith, Paul says, is *not* trying to obey and fulfill a law. Faith is *not* doing your best to live up to a moral standard. Those who do so are not living by faith, but by works. If you live on those terms, you will find that you cannot receive what God wants to give you. If you think that God is going to accept you because you tried hard to live a moral life, you are on the wrong track. Paul explains why.

First, notice that Abraham received the gift, the promise of righteousness, long before the Law was ever given. "It was not through law," Paul says, "that Abraham and his offspring received the promise." Galatians 3:23–29 tells us that Abraham received the gift of righteousness centuries before the Law was given. So righteousness clearly could not come by law.

Second, the Law renders the promise worthless. "For if those who live by law are heirs [of the promise to Abraham], faith has no value and the promise is worthless." Let me put this another way. Suppose I promised you a million dollars if you could broad-jump the Grand Canyon. Would that promise actually be worth a million dollars? No. It wouldn't be worth one cent, even if I made that promise in all sincerity and had the bank account to back it up. Why? Because such a promise depends on a human being doing what is humanly impossible.

In the same way, if God promises that you will have right standing with Him if you keep the Law of Moses perfectly, then His promise would also be worthless. Such a promise is based on a human being doing what is humanly impossible. With the exception of Jesus alone, no human being can live a sinless life.

But Paul does not stop there. He says there is another reason why we cannot gain righteousness by trying to keep the Law: the Law brings wrath. If you fail to keep it, the Law makes you subject to punishment.

As we have seen, wrath is defined in Romans 1. The wrath involves God's removal of all divine protection and restraint—we can do anything we want. As C. S. Lewis once observed, there are two kinds of people in the world. There are those who say to God, "Thy will be done," and there are those to whom God says, "Thy will be done." When God gives us over to do what we want to do, that is wrath.

The Law brings wrath. Paul amplifies this by saying, "Where there is no law, there is no transgression." In other words, where there is no law, people disobey in ignorance, not as deliberate law-breakers. For example, many young people today live together without marriage. Some were raised to know that this is wrong, so they are deliberate law-breakers. But others were never raised to know that living together without marriage is wrong, so they do so in all innocence of any transgression.

Don't misunderstand: What they are doing is still wrong. But the people who do so in ignorance do not realize how damaging and destructive it is to live together without marriage. They lack the light of understanding. They fail to see that their lifestyle is destroying them in subtle ways, bringing harm to themselves, to their children, and to society.

When Paul says, "Where there is no law, there is no transgression," he means that death and hell are taking their toll on human beings whether they know it or not. He will expand this idea in Romans 5, but for now his point is that when the Law comes, it makes you aware of what is wrong in your life. In a sense, the

Law just makes us more miserable and more responsible for our sins, because when we sin with an awareness of the Law, we are deliberately disobeying God.

The Object, the Obstacles, and the Objective

Next, Paul tells us two things that faith does:

> Therefore, the promise comes by faith, so that it may be by grace and may be guaranteed to all Abraham's offspring—not only to those who are of the law but also to those who are of the faith of Abraham. He is the father of us all. As it is written: "I have made you a father of many nations." (Romans 4:16–17)

First, the promise comes by faith. You actually obtain what you desire by faith—a sense of being approved, loved, and accepted by God. You are a part of God's family and you are forgiven of all your sins. What works could not do, faith does.

Second, faith introduces the principle of *grace*. Law and grace do not cancel each other out, but they accomplish two very different things. We need both law and grace. We should never say, "I am under grace, so I don't need the Law." The Bible never takes that position. It is the Law of God that draws you to the grace of God.

What, then, is grace? There are many ways to define it. One excellent definition is an acronym: G.R.A.C.E. stands for God's Riches At Christ's Expense. Grace is all the richness of life—love, joy, peace, and fulfillment—that we receive but do not deserve. It is a gift of God's unmerited, undeserved favor toward us.

The Law put us down. Grace lifts us up. If salvation depended upon our effort to keep the Law, we would have no hope. But if salvation comes to us by grace, then we receive it as a free gift from God. That is why Paul says, "Therefore, the promise comes by faith, so that it may be by grace and may be guaranteed to all Abraham's offspring—not only to those who are of the law but also to those who are of the faith of Abraham."

Next we come to the heart of Romans 4, where Paul explains to us what faith truly is:

> He is our father in the sight of God, in whom he believed—the God who gives life to the dead and calls things that are not as though they were.
>
> Against all hope, Abraham in hope believed and so became the father of many nations, just as it had been said to him, "So shall your offspring be." Without weakening in his faith, he faced the fact that his body was as good as dead—since he was about a hundred years old—and that Sarah's womb was also dead. Yet he did not waver through unbelief regarding the promise of God, but was strengthened in his faith and gave glory to God. (Romans 4:17–20)

Paul explains the nature of faith in three dimensions: (1) the object of faith, (2) the obstacles to faith, and (3) the objective of faith.

First, Abraham believed God. God is the object of faith. The power of your faith depends upon the object in which your faith is placed. The amount of faith has nothing to do with it. That is why Jesus told us that even a tiny faith, like a grain of mustard seed, is powerful. It is not a question of how big your faith is, but how big your God is!

Abraham believed in the God who gives life to the dead. If your God has power over life and death, then you will never despair. And Abraham believed in the God who calls into existence things that do not exist. If you have a God of such vast creative power, you will never lose hope.

Second, Abraham faced obstacles to faith. Whenever you are called to exercise faith, there will be obstacles. What obstacle did Abraham face? The obstacle of *hopeless circumstances*. He and his wife were old and barren, yet God had promised him a child through whom would come the promised Seed, Jesus Christ. Paul makes a tremendous statement: "Without weakening in his faith, he faced the fact that his body was as good as dead." Abraham was realistic about the fact that there was no imaginable way that God's promise could be fulfilled, yet his faith in God's ability to do the impossible never wavered.

Though there was no hope, Abraham believed and hoped. Why? Because he remembered that God has the power to raise the dead; he remembered that God has power to create something out of nothing. Despite the obstacles to his faith, Abraham kept his faith focused on the Object of all faith, the infinite, omnipotent God.

Third, Abraham attained the objective of faith. Paul says that Abraham "did not waver through unbelief regarding the promise of God, but was strengthened in his faith and gave glory to God." As we remain focused on the Object and overcome the obstacles, we attain the objective. The objective of faith is growth and maturity in faith. As Abraham obeyed in faith, he was strengthened in his faith and he gave glory to God. Faith never glorifies man; it glorifies God.

Faith Grasps the Promise

Many people mistakenly think of faith as "belief without evidence." In reality, faith is trust in what we have every reason to believe is true. Faith is not an unsupported, irrational hope, but the grounding of our lives in the truth about God. That is how Paul describes Abraham in the next two verses:

> being fully persuaded that God had power to do what he had promised. This is why "it was credited to him as righteousness." (Romans 4:21–22)

Abraham was grounded in the truth. He was fully persuaded. His was no irrational hope of "pie in the sky when I die, by and by." Abraham knew God and walked with God. When God spoke, Abraham obeyed. God overcame unbelievable obstacles in Abraham's life, so Abraham was fully persuaded. This proven, persuaded faith was credited to him as righteousness.

Faith grasps the promise. Faith lays hold of what God offers. As Abraham's faith grew, he grasped the promise and found himself loved and accepted by God. And that is why Abraham was a friend of God.

In the centuries since Abraham, many children of Abraham—children of the faith—have grasped the same promise that was offered to the patriarch. Many have believed in the God of Abraham, and in the Son of God, and they have crossed over from death to life. These are the ones to whom Paul turns his attention as Romans 4 comes to a close:

> The words "it was credited to him" were written not for him alone, but also for us, to whom God will credit righteousness—for us who believe in him who raised Jesus our Lord from the dead. He was delivered over to death for our sins and was raised to life for our justification. (Romans 4:23–25)

Astounding! Those words "it was credited to him as righteousness" were not written for Abraham alone. They were written for you and me, today! We look at the faith of Abraham and say, "What an extraordinary faith!" But Paul says that Abraham's faith was not extraordinary at all—it was an ordinary faith. Anyone can exercise the faith of Abraham. I can. So can you.

You can have the righteousness from God. You can be a friend of God, accepted by Him, with worth and value in His sight. You not only receive the righteousness from God at the beginning of your Christian experience. You actually receive His righteousness *every day*—a renewed sense of worth fresh from His hand each morning.

If you believe in a God who is the Lord of Life and the Great Creator, raising life from the dead and calling everything into existence out of nothing, then you are going to experience an exciting, adventure-filled life! You are going to live the adventure of faith!

CHAPTER 6

REJOICING IN GOD

Romans 5

I was in Honolulu, Hawaii, during World War II. The whole city had celebrated when the war ended in Europe, though the celebration was muted by the fact that war still raged in our part of the world. The citizens of Honolulu were glad that the fighting in Europe had concluded, but we knew that many bloody battles lay ahead in the South Pacific.

Suddenly, in August 1945, came the shocking news of the atomic destruction of two Japanese cities, Hiroshima and Nagasaki. On September 2, 1945, Japan signed a formal declaration of surrender on the deck of the battleship *Missouri* in Tokyo Bay. World War II was officially over.

I vividly remember the throngs of people pouring into the streets and onto the beaches of Honolulu. There was music and dancing, whooping and shouting. Streetlights and neon signs, darkened for years due to wartime blackouts, now burned brightly in the night. It was a wild and joyful celebration of the peace the world had waited for.

To me, that memory has long been a symbol of the joy and celebration that takes place in our hearts when we realize that we have been justified through faith. The long, agonizing war is finally over. All conflict has ceased. We are at peace with God.

Justified Through Faith

In Romans 5, the apostle Paul traces the results of receiving the righteousness from God. The opening word of this chapter marks a major transition: "Therefore. . . ." With that word, Paul sends a signal that everything he has said in Romans 1 through 4 is bringing us to a specific conclusion. He writes:

> Therefore, since we have been justified through faith, we have peace with God through our Lord Jesus Christ, through whom we have gained access by faith into this grace in which we now stand. And we rejoice in the hope of the glory of God. (Romans 5:1–2)

That little word *rejoice* is the key to Romans 5. Paul develops this theme of rejoicing in three stages: Stage 1—We rejoice in the hope of the glory of God (Romans 5:1–2). Stage 2—We rejoice in sufferings (Romans 5:3–10). Stage 3—We rejoice in God our Friend (Romans 5:11–21). Each of these stages represents a level of Christian growth. The overall theme of Romans 5, then, is learning to rejoice at these various stages.

If you understand what it means to be a Christian, you will be rejoicing—even in the midst of suffering. Some Christians seem strangely unable to grasp this idea. They trudge through life, dour and grim-faced, looking as if they are marinated in embalming fluid.

We are not talking here about people who suffer from clinical depression or bipolar disorder or some other medical condition that causes a state of depression. It is not sinful or unspiritual to be afflicted with a mental disorder. Paul directs his concern at those Christians who are capable of rejoicing if they would simply focus on their Christian hope instead of on thoughts of bitterness and self-pity.

The Christian gospel was designed by God to produce a spirit that can't help but rejoice. Christian joy is not an artificial happiness. It does not mean putting on a plastic smile and pretending everything is wonderful when it's not. It does not mean saying, "Happy day! I'm going bankrupt!" or "Hallelujah! I've got cancer!" Rejoicing is a deep sense of security in God, even when the circumstances of our lives are crumbling.

Our first and most immediate cause for rejoicing is that we have been justified through faith, which brings us peace with God. That is why we rejoice in the hope of the glory of God. As we saw in the previous chapter, the term "justified through faith" was exemplified for us in the person of Abraham. Abraham, of course, did not earn God's acceptance. He received justification as a free gift through faith at the moment he believed that God would do what He had promised.

The same is true for us. We receive justification as a free gift by faith alone, with no merit or worthiness on our part. When we believe the promise of God, that He will save us according to the atoning work of His Son on the cross, then we are justified through faith.

Three results flow from being justified through faith. First: We have peace with God. All the conflict between ourselves and God is ended. We lose our fear of God.

Something in all of us instinctively fears God. When I was a boy, I thought of God as a heavenly policeman, watching and waiting to catch me in some sin. I will never forget the joy that came into my heart when I realized that God was no longer my judge but my Father. Having been justified through faith, I lost my fear of God.

Second: If we are justified through faith, we are no longer afraid to die.

As a boy, I lived for a while in the Red River Valley of North Dakota. As a Scottish Presbyterian settlement, the town had an old custom of ringing the church bell when someone died. I remember lying in my bed, listening to that slow, solemn death-knell, and feeling the cold clutch of fear as I thought about facing my own death. I knew I would die someday, and that death could come even for a boy, as it had come for a young friend of mine. I was terribly afraid of death.

When I came to know Jesus as my Lord and Savior, I experienced the joy that comes from being set free of that terrible fear. As Hebrews 2:15 tells us, Jesus has liberated "those who all their lives were held in slavery by their fear of death."

Third: We have an answer for our guilt. When we sin, our conscience accuses us and we feel guilty. Sometimes our guilt shouts at us, "How can you call yourself a Christian? No real Christian could do what you've done!" But when we know that we are justified through faith, we can remind ourselves, "My standing before God does not depend upon me. My sin is covered by the saving, atoning work of God's own Son."

So we have three wonderful results of being justified through faith: We have peace with God, freedom from the fear of death, and an answer to guilt. Whenever we are tempted to feel afraid of God, afraid of death, or afraid that our sin has canceled out our salvation, we can answer those fears with this firm statement of assurance: "I have been justified through faith."

A Hope of Coming Glory

Next, Paul talks about our standing before God. Through our Lord Jesus Christ, Paul says, "we have gained access by faith into this grace in which we now stand." In other words, we have access to continued grace to enable us to stand in the midst of pressures, problems, and trials. This is a *constant supply* of grace because we have instant access to the God of all grace.

An account in the book of Esther beautifully illustrates this principle: Esther was a lovely Jewish woman held captive in the land of Persia. The king of Persia was smitten by her and made her his queen. After Esther became queen, a plot was hatched to destroy all the Jews in the land. The king was manipulated into signing a death decree against the Jews.

Queen Esther's godly uncle, Mordecai, urged her to go to the king and tell him that this decree was wrong and would destroy her people. Esther knew that Mordecai's plan could easily get her killed. It was the law that no one could come before the king without being summoned by him—not even the queen herself. Esther had only one chance of surviving: If the king extended his golden scepter toward her when she entered the throne room, she would live. If he didn't, she would be executed.

But if she didn't try, her people would be destroyed.

So Queen Esther fasted for three days and nights to prepare herself spiritually. Then she dressed herself in robes of beauty and glory. When she was ready, she went to the throne room of the king and appeared alone before him. The king was shocked at the queen's bold, death-defying entrance.

But as he looked upon his beautiful queen, his heart went out to her. He stretched forth his scepter. Queen Esther was granted access to the king.

This is a picture of what Paul tells us in Romans 5:2. Who would dare stand before the God of all the earth, the all-powerful and glorious King of the universe, without being granted access and standing? God's amazing promise to us is that, now that we are justified through faith, we have access to His presence. Dressed in robes of beauty and glory that do not belong to us—the garments of the righteousness of Jesus—we can step boldly into the presence of our King. We do not have to be afraid of Him. He extends toward us the golden scepter of His love.

As we read in Hebrews 10:19 and 22, "Therefore, brothers, since we have confidence to enter the Most Holy Place by the blood of Jesus . . . let us draw near to God with a sincere heart in full assurance of faith, having our hearts sprinkled to cleanse us from a guilty conscience and having our bodies washed with pure water."

Next, Paul tells us, "And we rejoice in the hope of the glory of God." We think of the word *hope* as referring to a wishful possibility, a chance of things working out in our favor: "Oh, I hope this is the winning lottery ticket!" But the word *hope*, as it is used in the Bible, has a very different meaning. It speaks of a well-founded *certainty* of something that is not yet visible.

Our Christian hope is based on the promises of God. Jesus promised us the hope of a future resurrection: "Because I live, you also will live" (see John 14:19). That is the certain hope of everyone who has been justified through faith. You cannot see the resurrection, but you have a sure and certain hope of the resurrection because you have God's word on it.

A friend who lives in the Midwest told me of an experience he had in the dead of winter. He looked out the window of his farmhouse, across the snowdrifts that buried his front yard, and saw the mailman placing something in his mailbox. Eager for a letter to lift his wintry spirits, my friend hurried out to the mailbox. There he found only one piece of mail: a seed catalog.

How disappointing! No personal letter from family or friends, just a seed catalog. He went back inside and was about to toss the catalog on the kitchen table—then on a whim, he started thumbing through it. On page after page, he saw the brilliant colors of flowers and vegetables. He could almost taste the cool crunch of a cucumber. He imagined the perfume of sweet alyssum, lemon mint, and zinnias. He could practically taste the sweet-tangy juice of a red, ripe tomato on his tongue. For a few moments in the dead of winter, the colors and fragrances of springtime came alive in his heart. My friend experienced a few moments of the coming glory of springtime.

That is what the Christian hope is like. In this world, life is like a cold, snowy winter. But we know that a brilliant and wonderful glory waits beyond this life. When we rejoice in the hope of the glory of God, we experience a glimpse of His springtime amid the winter of our discontent. That is the hope of all who have been justified through faith. It is cause for rejoicing.

Rejoicing in Suffering

Next, we come to Stage 2 in our experience of Christian rejoicing: We rejoice in our sufferings. During my years as a pastor, I have been impressed by the number of wonderful Christians who have gone through severe trials and sufferings. I recall one couple who awoke one morning to find their troubled teenage son standing in the doorway with a gun in his hand. The boy shot the father one time and the mother twice. Both survived and their son was captured by police and confined in a mental hospital.

God has since used the father in a powerful way. Before this harrowing experience, he was reluctant to talk to other people about his faith in Christ. But after he and his wife survived their brush with death, he rejoiced to be alive. He felt that the experience had drawn himself and his wife closer to God. Suddenly, he was eager to share his faith with others. He traveled around the state, telling large groups that Jesus Christ is a reliable friend in times of trial and suffering.

I have met many other Christians who suffer with the loss of a child, with cancer, with multiple sclerosis, with AIDS, with ALS, with Alzheimer's disease, with the aftermath of a rape or other assault. Again and again, I am impressed with the fact that suffering is something that all Christians experience in one way or another. To me, there is no question more difficult to answer than this one: "Why do Christians suffer?"

We rejoice that our sins are covered, that we are justified through faith, and that we have a sure and certain hope of future glory with the Lord. But as we probe deeper into Romans 5, Paul introduces us to a different kind of rejoicing—a Christian joy that is much more mysterious than the initial rejoicing that we experience as a result of our conversion experience. This rejoicing is the result of a deeper and more mature stage of the Christian faith. Paul calls it "rejoicing in suffering." He writes:

> Not only so, but we also rejoice in our sufferings, because we know that suffering produces perseverance; perseverance, character; and character, hope. And hope does not disappoint us, because God has poured out his love into our hearts by the Holy Spirit, whom he has given us. (Romans 5:3–5)

These words tell us clearly that Christians should expect suffering. Elsewhere, Paul puts it bluntly: "For it has been granted to you on behalf of Christ not only to believe on him, but also to suffer for him" (Philippians 1:29). So if you became a Christian in the belief that Christians are spared from suffering, then you have been seriously misled!

The next question that naturally arises is, "How can anyone 'rejoice in sufferings'? When I suffer, I moan, I groan, I cry out in pain—but I don't rejoice! Does God expect Christians to take some sort of masochistic pleasure in being tormented?" Clearly, the concept of "rejoicing in our sufferings" does not seem natural or rational.

I am reminded of the woman who was complaining about her troubles to her pastor. She went on and on about all of her sufferings, and finally the pastor stopped her. "Sister," he said, "you really should not complain so. The Bible says that Christians are to rejoice in tribulations."

"Well, I know that, pastor," the woman said, "but I think that when God sends us tribulations, He expects us to tribulate a bit!"

We all have times when we feel like "tribulating" over our sufferings, and some of us do so freely and with gusto. But in those times when we feel like tribulating, we should remember that it is not only Paul but *all* of the New Testament writers who urge us to rejoice in our sufferings.

The apostle Peter puts it this way: "Dear friends, do not be surprised at the painful trial you are suffering, as though something strange were happening to you. But rejoice that you participate in the sufferings of Christ, so that you may be overjoyed when his glory is revealed" (1 Peter 4:12–13). Suffering is normal, so rejoice that you can share the sufferings of your Lord.

The apostle James puts it this way: "Consider it pure joy, my brothers, whenever you face trials of many kinds." There it is again: have joy when you face trials.

Even the Lord Jesus told us: "Blessed are you when people insult you, persecute you and falsely say all kinds of evil against you because of me. Rejoice and be glad, because great is your reward in heaven" (Matthew 5:11–12). Paul's call to rejoice in suffering is echoed throughout Scripture. Let's take a closer look at what rejoicing in suffering truly means.

First, rejoicing in suffering is not stoicism. It is not a "grin and bear it" or "tough it out" attitude. It is not a spiritual contest to see who can take the worst punishment.

Second, rejoicing in suffering is not masochism. God does not expect us to enjoy our pain. Paul is not telling us that we should be glad when tragedy strikes. There is something twisted and unnatural about a person who actually *enjoys* being hurt, and that is not the position Paul urges us to take toward our sufferings.

Third, rejoicing in suffering is not an act. God does not expect us to pretend we are happy in times of suffering. Christianity is not phoniness or dishonesty. When we suffer, it's okay to say, "This is hard. This hurts. I wish it would stop."

Paul reveals a deep truth when he tells us to rejoice in our sufferings. He is saying that even though we are not stoics or masochists, even though we are honest about the pain we are going through, we can still experience a genuine sense of rejoicing. We can authentically say to people around us, "I am suffering, and I hate to suffer—but even through this pain, I am experiencing the joyful presence of our loving God. I have peace and joy even through this time of trial and testing."

Don't feel bad if you don't immediately feel like rejoicing in your suffering. When suffering strikes, it's normal to cry out in pain, bewilderment, and even anger. Give yourself time to adjust to the experience you are going through. As you gain the ability to reflect on your trial, listen carefully for the truths and lessons that God wants to teach you through this painful experience.

I once knew a man who had to have a leg amputated due to an advancing disease. Unfortunately, even the amputation failed to arrest the disease, and it soon became clear that he was going to die. I visited him in the hospital just a few days before his death and he told me, "I never would have chosen any of the trials I have gone through, but I wouldn't have missed any of them for the world! God has taught me so much about Himself through my trials that I never could have learned from a life of ease."

That is what it means to rejoice in suffering. This man didn't choose his trials, and he didn't enjoy his pain. He freely admitted that these trials had inflicted enormous misery on him—yet he rejoiced in the spiritual growth and Christian maturity he had gained through those trials.

Reason for Rejoicing

How do you reach a place where you can rejoice in suffering? That is what Paul wants us to understand. He says, "We also rejoice in our sufferings, *because. . . .*" There is a reason to rejoice. What is that reason?

Paul explains: ". . . because we know that suffering produces perseverance; perseverance, character; and character, hope." Suffering produces something in our lives. It is the product of suffering that causes us to rejoice. What, then, does suffering produce?

Paul lists four products of suffering. First, suffering produces *perseverance*. The Greek word literally means "to remain firm under pressure." Pressure is something we want to get out from under, but suffering teaches us to stand firm under pressure. Another word for perseverance is *steadiness*. God uses our trials to make us more mature, stable, and steady under pressure.

Once, when Jesus and the disciples were crossing the Sea of Galilee in a fishing boat, a storm arose. While Jesus slept in the back of the boat, the disciples panicked. They shook Jesus and said, "Wake up! Don't you know we're about to perish?" And Jesus stood up and told the disciples, "Don't panic!" Then He commanded the wind and waves to be still, and the storm immediately ended. Jesus had a purpose for that storm in the lives of His disciples. He wanted them to learn steadiness under pressure.

And our Lord wants you and me to learn the same lessons. That's what suffering does: it steadies us and teaches us not to panic. The process often works like this: We go through a time of trial and we panic. Then the Lord calms the stormy trial and we think, "I'm glad that's over! I've learned my lesson!" A few weeks or months pass—and suddenly there is another storm! But this time, you don't panic, at least not as badly as the first time. You respond with greater steadiness, greater faith. You discover you're not as strong as you thought, but at least you are stronger than you used to be. You've grown.

With each new trial, you learn and grow a little more. Your faith becomes a little more resilient. In time, you find that you are handling challenges that you never imagined you could withstand. That's how suffering produces perseverance.

The second product of suffering is *character*. Paul says that perseverance produces character. The Greek word for character connotes being put to the test and approved. Perseverance under pressure produces proven, reliable character qualities. When you show yourself to be steady under pressure, people know they can rely on you in challenging situations.

On D-Day, June 6, 1944, Allied forces landed on the beaches of Normandy, France. That day was the beginning of the end of World War II, but it was a costly day for the Allies. Over 2,500 fine young soldiers from the free nations of Europe and North America died on that day alone. They scaled cliffs under a hail of machine-gun fire. They crawled across sandy beaches and grassy fields that had been sown by the Nazis with over 6 million landmines. They cut through coils of barbed wire and attacked steel bunkers bristling with machine gun muzzles.

The story is told of one particular sandy ridge where scores of Allied soldiers tried to punch their way up from the beach. That ridge was strewn with landmines. Soldiers went up that ridge only to have their legs blown to pieces out from under them. As those men lay dying, they spent their last breaths warning the men who came behind them—"The mines are right here! The safe path is over there!"

Some of the men of D-Day suffered, sacrificed, and died. Others suffered but lived to see the liberation of Europe. They remained steady under pressure and demonstrated perseverance under fire. They were the veterans of World War II.

God is in the business of making veterans. A veteran is a person who has been through trial and pressure, a person who has been tested and proven. When the apostle Paul wrote about rejoicing in sufferings, he was speaking as a tested veteran. Here are his credentials:

> We do not want you to be uninformed, brothers, about the hardships we suffered in the province of Asia. We were under great pressure, far beyond our ability to endure, so that we despaired even of life. Indeed, in our hearts we felt the sentence of death. But this happened that we might not rely on ourselves but on God, who raises the dead. He has delivered us from such a deadly peril, and he will deliver us. On him we have set our hope that he will continue to deliver us. (2 Corinthians 1:8–10)

Those are the words of a veteran. Paul had been through unbelievably difficult experiences, to the point where he had given up hope of survival. God brought him safely through it—yet Paul knew that there were even more perils ahead. Still, he trusted that God, who raises the dead, would deliver him. Perseverance had produced character and faith in the life of this seasoned veteran, the apostle Paul.

The third product of suffering is *hope*. In verse 2, Paul said, "And we rejoice in the hope of the glory of God." He spoke of hope for a future beyond this life, beyond death. Now, in verses 4 and 5, he says that character produces hope—"and hope does not disappoint us." Here, Paul speaks of the hope that we will share the character of God and the glory of God right now. We have the hope that God is producing a Christlike character within us right now.

Remember, when Paul talks about hope, he is not talking about a wish or a possibility, but about a *certainty*. He is not saying that we *might* be changed and made more Christlike; he is saying we *are* being changed, we *are* becoming more like Jesus! We are growing in Christlike love, maturity, wisdom, and patience. Through our sufferings, God is doing the work He promised to do: He is transforming us into the image of His Son.

What does Paul mean when he says, "and hope does not disappoint us"? Perhaps it would be clearer to look at that phrase in the King James Version: "And hope maketh not ashamed." Here Paul uses a figure of speech called a *litotes*, a negative understatement to underscore a positive idea (another example of a litotes: "This is no small problem," meaning, "This is a *huge* problem"). Paul uses a similar figure of speech in Romans 1:16 where he says, "I am not ashamed of the gospel of Jesus Christ." Properly understood, Paul is not merely saying that he is unembarrassed; he is actually saying he is proud, confident, bold, excited, and exuberant about the gospel.

So when Paul says, "And hope maketh not ashamed," he is actually saying, "Our hope makes us bold, proud, excited! We have a hope that sends the spirit soaring!"

Suffering and the Love of God

Paul goes on to explain why our hope does not disappoint us. He says it is "because God has poured out his love into our hearts by the Holy Spirit, whom he has given us." I am convinced that this is one of the most important verses in the book of Romans. It is significant because it adds a statement to Paul's argument that we have not yet heard in this book. This statement is Paul's explanation of how to rejoice in suffering.

This statement is also significant because it is the first time the Holy Spirit is mentioned in the book of Romans—and it is the first mention in Romans of the love of God.

That brings us to the fourth product of suffering, which is *love*. Paul raises the issue of Christlike love here in verse 5, and he will develop it more fully in verses 6–11. It is important to see verse 5 in context with verses 6 through 11 so that we will understand Paul's true meaning. Here is the flow of his discussion of God's love:

> . . . God has poured out his love into our hearts by the Holy Spirit, whom he has given us.

You see, at just the right time, when we were still powerless, Christ died for the ungodly. Very rarely will anyone
die for a righteous man, though for a good man someone
might possibly dare to die. But God demonstrates his own
love for us in this: While we were still sinners, Christ died
for us.

Since we have now been justified by his blood, how
much more shall we be saved from God's wrath through
him! For if, when we were God's enemies, we were reconciled to him through the death of his Son, how much more,
having been reconciled, shall we be saved through his life!
(Romans 5:5–10)

It is important to grasp the flow of Paul's argument. If we
understand what Paul is truly telling us, then we will know how
to rejoice in suffering.

I know many Christians who suffer. Some are becoming
increasingly more steady, reliable, and confident in their sufferings; tragically, others are becoming steadily more bitter, resentful, and angry—even to the point of denying their faith. Suffering,
you see, does not automatically produce good qualities.

What makes the difference between a Christian whose faith
grows through suffering and a Christian whose faith withers
under suffering? The difference is here in this passage, and it has
to do with how we view God and His love. If we see our suffering as evidence of God's love, we will rejoice in our sufferings. If
we see our suffering as evidence of God's wrath, we will become
embittered and angry.

To rejoice in our sufferings, we must allow the Holy Spirit to
fill our hearts with an experience of the love of God—an experience so rich, radiant, and glorious that we can't help but rejoice.
We associate love with times of blessing, warmth, and ease—but
when we suffer, we naturally tend to feel broken and forgotten. At
such times, says Paul, we need to return to the place where we first
felt God's love for us. What place is that? The place of the cross.

At the foot of the cross, we realize that God loves us even though we are worthless and sin-ridden. At the cross, we clearly see ourselves and our sinfulness. At the cross, we see God's amazing love for us, in that while we were broken and sinful, Christ died for us.

Then comes the full force of Paul's argument: "For if, when we were God's enemies, we were reconciled to him through the death of his Son, how much more, having been reconciled, shall we be saved through his life!" In other words, if we clearly experienced God's love when we first gave our hearts to Christ—when we were nothing more than enemies of God, helpless and powerless—how much more can we count His love now that we are His children! Even though we are suffering, we can rely on the fact that God loves us.

When that is our perspective, then we realize that our suffering is not the result of God's anger toward us; it is the result of His love. God is using this time of suffering in our lives to produce character qualities that will enable us to become the people God wants us to be. He will lovingly carry us through whatever suffering we face.

An Avalanche of Love, Grace, and Forgiveness

Next, we come to Stage 3 in our experience of Christian rejoicing: We rejoice in God our Friend. Here, Paul introduces this concluding theme of Romans 5:

> Not only is this so, but we also rejoice in God through our Lord Jesus Christ, through whom we have now received reconciliation. (Romans 5:11)

We rejoice in God Himself! In my book *Authentic Christianity*,[1] I call this "an unquenchable optimism." Christians always have grounds for rejoicing. The three stages of rejoicing described in Romans 5 represent three levels of maturity. We don't necessarily experience these levels in chronological order, but they are levels of understanding and responding to God's truth with a deepening maturity.

Notice the rich phrase Paul uses: "we also rejoice in God through our Lord Jesus Christ, through whom we have now received reconciliation." As he so frequently does, Paul reminds us that everything good comes through our Lord Jesus Christ. The Lord Himself said, "I am the way and the truth and the life. No one comes to the Father except through me" (see John 14:6).

Jesus is the way to God. He has reconciled us to God, so that God the Father is now our Friend. When we see the greatness of Jesus, we see the greatness of God. When we know the love of Jesus, we know the heart of God. That is why we rejoice in God through our Lord Jesus Christ.

After introducing his theme of rejoicing in God, verse 11, Paul launches into an argument in four movements. *First Movement*, verses 12–14: Sin entered the world through Adam, the first man. *Second Movement*, verses 15–17: The first man, Adam, versus the God-man, Jesus. *Third Movement*, verses 18–19: The disobedience of Adam versus the obedience of Jesus. *Fourth Movement*, verses 20–21: The Law versus grace. Let's examine each of these movements of Paul's argument in turn, beginning with Paul's discussion of the fall of the human race:

> Therefore, just as sin entered the world through one man, and death through sin, and in this way death came to all men, because all sinned. (Romans 5:12)

Paul begins with the phrase, "Therefore, just as . . . ." Any grammarian will tell you that when you have the phrase "just as" in a sentence, it must eventually be followed by the phrase "even so." Paul is making a comparison here. The Greek text actually has the phrase "even so." The New International Version doesn't translate it that way, so permit me to offer a more accurate version of this verse:

> Therefore, *just as* sin entered the world through one man, and death through sin, *even so* death came to all men, because all sinned. (Romans 5:12, author's translation)

This is Paul's argument. He starts with two indisputable facts: (1) the universality of sin and (2) the universality of death. Everywhere we look we see evidence of the twin evils of sin and death. Paul says that sin entered the world by one man, Adam. And along with sin came death. From the moment we were born, we began to die. Later on in this passage, Paul says, "Death reigned." Near the end of Romans 5, he says, "Sin reigns." So in these two forces that have been introduced into humanity, we have a pair of oppressors who rule over the human race.

How did sin and death gain control of our race? Through one man, Adam. That is the key to this section. Paul is contrasting two men: Adam and Jesus. Death and sin came through Adam; life and forgiveness came through Jesus. In each case, our entire existence has been altered by a single man, either Adam or Jesus.

We sin and die because we are sons and daughters of Adam. The sins of Adam have injected us with the poison of death. Even before we are sufficiently aware to commit sins of our own, we are subject to death. Even babies, who have never sinned, sometimes die—and they die because the sin of Adam overshadows us all. This is Paul's argument as he writes:

> Before the law was given, sin was in the world. But sin is not taken into account when there is no law. Nevertheless, death reigned from the time of Adam to the time of Moses, even over those who did not sin by breaking a command, as did Adam, who was a pattern of the one to come. (Romans 5:13–14)

Paul's point is that death is the punishment for breaking God's command. In the Garden of Eden, God said to Adam, "You must not eat from the tree of the knowledge of good and evil, for when you eat of it you will surely die" (see Genesis 2:17). Adam violated that command and ate of the fruit. In so doing, he chose to be independent from the God who made him. It was an act of rebellion and even idolatry. Adam enthroned himself as a god in the place of the one true God. As a result, death and sin passed upon all his descendants.

Paul is saying that death is the result of breaking a command. There must be a law in order for a command to be broken. You may have had the experience of driving through an unposted intersection for years—then one day a stop sign is placed at that intersection. You never stopped at that intersection before, and you were never penalized. But now the law has come, and if you do what you have always done—if you roll through that intersection without stopping—you will be breaking the law and incurring a penalty.

In order for death to come, says Paul, a commandment had to be broken. Yet we know that there was death in the human race long before the Law was given to Moses. How could that be, if death is the result of breaking a command? Paul concludes that the whole race actually sinned when Adam sinned. When Adam broke the command of God in Eden, we all broke it.

You may respond, "But that isn't fair! God is punishing us all for Adam's sin!" That argument fails to take into account the nature of our humanity. As human beings, we are all connected to each other. As the poet John Donne observed, "No man is an island, entire of itself; every man is a piece of the continent." It is a mistake to think that we stand alone, as though no one else exists. Human choices have consequences that radiate out to others. When Adam chose to sin, he plunged his whole race into disaster.

The most important phrase in this section is the last one: "Adam . . . was a pattern of the one to come." In the rest of Romans 5, Paul will present Adam as a contrast to Christ. Paul writes:

> But the gift is not like the trespass. For if the many died by the trespass of the one man, how much more did God's grace and the gift that came by the grace of the one man, Jesus Christ, overflow to the many! (Romans 5:15)

The gift of righteousness from God through Jesus Christ is not like the trespass of Adam. The trespass came through Adam's disobedience in the Garden of Eden; the gift came through the Lord's obedience in the Garden of Gethsemane.

Death came to all through the disobedience of Adam—but we die only once, don't we? So Adam brought to us the experience of the first death. But Jesus brought to us the experience of new life, a life that is renewed and re-experienced day after day. We can receive life from Jesus a *thousand* times a day! We can accept the gift of righteousness and worth over and over again. So Jesus is greater than Adam because the trespass of Adam brought death once, but the obedient sacrifice of Jesus brings life many times over.

Next, Paul writes:

> Again, the gift of God is not like the result of the one man's sin: The judgment followed one sin and brought condemnation, but the gift followed many trespasses and brought justification. (Romans 5:16)

Adam's single trespass brought judgment—death—upon the entire human race. The Lord's single gift of obedient sacrifice brought justification—life—to those who committed a multitude of trespasses. Adam sinned once and brought death to many; Jesus died once and brought life to many. There is a powerful principle here for your life and mine: No matter how many times we sin, God's forgiveness is greater than our deepest sin.

Next, Paul writes:

> For if, by the trespass of the one man, death reigned through that one man, how much more will those who receive God's abundant provision of grace and of the gift of righteousness reign in life through the one man, Jesus Christ. (Romans 5:17)

Paul's argument is that Adam's transgression permitted death to reign over the entire human race. When Paul speaks of death, he means more than just the funeral at the end of your life. He is saying that, because of Adam, death reigns throughout our lives. Paul is talking about forms of death besides the mere cessation of life.

What is life? It is love, joy, vitality, and fulfillment. Death is the absence of all of those things; it is emptiness, loneliness, depression, and restlessness. How much of your life is made up of death? Probably a great deal of it. In fact, some people never seem to have anything but death in their lives. Death reigns because of Adam's transgression.

Paul says that Christ's death provides an abundance of life, even amid the pressures, troubles, and suffering of this life. You can be alive and joyful, experiencing joy, peace, and fulfillment. You can have all of this through the sacrificial death of the Lord Jesus Christ. What you lost in Adam, you regain in Jesus—plus so much more!

Just as a mountain climber can dislodge a pebble that rolls downhill and becomes an avalanche, so Adam's sin dislodged a pebble that has grown into an avalanche of sin and death that sweeps across our entire race. But Jesus has unleashed an avalanche of love, grace, and forgiveness that covers all the sin and death that Adam has caused.

The "Gift" of Adam and the Gift of Jesus

Paul continues his argument:

> Consequently, just as the result of one trespass was condemnation for all men, so also the result of one act of righteousness was justification that brings life for all men. For just as through the disobedience of the one man the many were made sinners, so also through the obedience of the one man the many will be made righteous. (Romans 5:18–19)

Judgment or condemnation, says Paul, is a "gift" from Adam—the most terrible "gift" of all. Since we are born in Adam, sin and guilt are not an option with us. We *will* sin because sin is part of our nature. Paul then contrasts the "gift" of Adam with the wonderful gift of Jesus, which is the righteousness from God—the love, acceptance, and worth we all need in order to truly live.

Paul concludes Romans 5 with a discussion of the role the Law plays in the scheme of sin and grace—and he begins with a startling statement:

> The law was added so that the trespass might increase. But where sin increased, grace increased all the more, so that, just as sin reigned in death, so also grace might reign through righteousness to bring eternal life through Jesus Christ our Lord. (Romans 5:20–21)

Paul says that the Ten Commandments were never given to make people do right. This is a shocking notion. In our everyday experience, the function of laws—whether criminal laws or civil laws or traffic laws—is to govern human behavior. But Paul says that is not true of the Law of Moses, the Ten Commandments.

The Law, he says, was added to show human beings how wrong they already are. The commandments were actually given to make human beings sin more and to increase their trespass! Why would God do such a thing? Paul's answer: "Where sin increased, grace increased all the more." In other words, the more we fling ourselves into rebellion and sin, the closer we are to being broken, to coming to the end of ourselves so that we can receive the cleansing, forgiving grace of Jesus Christ.

As special counsel to the president, Charles Colson was known as Richard Nixon's "hatchet man." He pleaded guilty to crimes connected with the Watergate scandal and served seven months in a federal prison in 1974. Shortly before he entered the penitentiary, Colson made a decision to receive Jesus Christ as his Lord and

Savior. Many people were skeptical of his conversion experience, but time has proven that his relationship with Christ is genuine.

While in prison, Colson found another Christian brother and they began praying together for their fellow inmates. Soon, they saw God begin to work. One by one, they saw hardened, violent, brutal men—men who had spent their lives in rebellion against God—begin to break down and seek God's grace. If there is one place where it can truly be said that sin abounds, it is in a prison! Yet, as Charles Colson saw, where sin increased, grace increased even more.

The One who breaks through sin with the power of grace is Jesus. Adam ruined our lives, making us slaves to sin and death. Only Jesus Christ can set us free. He is the head of a new race, the forerunner of a new humanity. He comes to live within us, to infuse us with His strength and purity, His wisdom and power. So we rejoice through our Lord Jesus Christ, who has reached down to us, lifted us up, and reconciled us to God the Father, God our Friend.

CHAPTER 7

WHOSE SLAVE ARE YOU?

Romans 6

Over the years, I have encountered a number of people who call themselves Christians, yet who claim that they have the right to live in blatant sin because their sins are forgiven through Christ. Are they right? Now that you are a Christian—now that the sacrifice of Jesus Christ has settled the debt of your sins—do you have the right to continue in sin?

In the first five chapters of Romans, Paul has been building an argument concerning the enormous breakthrough in history that resulted from the death and resurrection of Jesus Christ. In chapters 6 and 7, Paul interrupts his argument to address two practical questions. The question he deals with in Romans 6 is, "What about the sins of believers?" The question he deals with in Romans 7 is "What about the Ten Commandments and the demands they place on us?" Then, in Romans 8, Paul returns to his argument and continues to explore the tremendous impact of Jesus Christ on human history and the human condition.

So let's examine with Paul this crucial question that is as relevant today as ever: "Can Christians continue to sin?" Paul writes:

> What shall we say, then? Shall we go on sinning so that grace may increase? By no means! We died to sin; how can we live in it any longer? (Romans 6:1–2)

That is Paul's argument in a nutshell. He will expand on the logic of this argument in the verses that follow, but for now he puts his entire case into one concise rhetorical question: "We died to sin; how can we live in it any longer?"

A Ghastly Thought

Three aspects of these verses are worthy of our careful attention:

First, notice that Paul's approach is *logical*. "Shall we go on sinning so that grace may increase?" That is a reasonable question. If our preaching of the gospel does not arouse this question in people's minds, our message is likely flawed. The grace of God logically gives rise to this issue. If the sin problem has been so completely solved by the forgiveness of Christ, then we don't need to worry about sin, do we? We are free to sin because the consequences of sin have been removed by the cross of Christ—haven't they?

Second, Paul's approach is *natural*. He understands that it is only human nature to ask such a question. We think of sin as fun, and that's why we like to do it! It is great fun to gossip about others, to elevate ourselves by putting others down; it is great fun to engage in sexual sins; it is fun to covet and take what is not ours. Sin is fun. So any suggestion that we can sin and get away with it—that we can have our sin and heaven too—is immensely appealing to our fallen nature.

Understand, when Paul talks about sin here, he is not talking about one or two isolated failures, but a *lifestyle* of sin. He is talking about Christians who live as they did before they were Christians. When he says, "Shall we go on sinning . . . ?" he is using the present continuous tense, which refers to an action that occurs on a continual basis. Later, in Romans 6:15, Paul will discuss the effect of a single act of sin on a believer's life; but here, in Romans 6:1–2, Paul talks about a lifestyle of habitual sin.

Third, Paul puts the question in a way that sounds *pious*. He is anticipating the question of someone who would rationalize sinning on the grounds that increased sinning would be a "good" thing, since it would lead to increased grace. Some people are so eager to rationalize their sin that they pretend they are *doing God a favor* by sinning! After all, God loves to show His grace, so if we sin more, God will have more opportunities to be gracious. Paul wants to put an end to such self-deceiving rationalizations. His answer is emphatic:

> What shall we say, then? Shall we go on sinning so that grace may increase? By no means! (Romans 6:1–2)

Paul's answer is as blunt, forceful, and absolute as it can possibly be: "By no means!" The original Greek form states literally, "May it never be!" The King James Version expresses offense at the suggestion: "God forbid!" The Phillips version conveys a note of horror: "What a ghastly thought!" Clearly, Paul wants us to understand that the idea of deliberately sinning in order to increase grace is an unthinkable abomination. Why? He explains:

> We died to sin; how can we live in it any longer? (Romans 6:2)

With four one-syllable words, Paul makes an airtight case. He will spend the rest of the chapter expounding and expositing that statement, but the logic of those four words is inescapable: *We died to sin.* That is all the argument anyone should require. But just to make sure that no one could misunderstand, Paul adds, "How can we live in [sin] any longer?"

Understand, when Paul said, "We died to sin," he didn't mean that sin is dead in us, that we have reached a point where we cannot be tempted to sin. Even though we are covered by the righteousness from God, the principle of sin is still at work in us, like an addiction that we can never break free of in this life.

Once, when I was working in the city of Pasadena, I went to a barbershop for a haircut. I sat in the chair, and as I chatted with the barber, I learned that he was a Christian. He told me that seventeen years earlier he had been "sanctified." According to the doctrinal traditions of his denomination, this meant that he was no longer able to sin. For seventeen years, he had lived without sinning—not even once!

I began to discuss this doctrine with him, and I raised certain Bible passages that seemed to contradict his views. The discussion turned into an argument. The more we talked, the hotter he got—all while he was cutting my hair. When I saw how upset he had become, I said to him, "Look, if you can become so angry when you have no sin in you, what would you be like if you were a sinner like the rest of us?"

It was two weeks before I dared to appear in public after that haircut!

When Paul says, "We died to sin," he is not saying that we are incapable of sin. Entire religious movements have been based on the idea that we are commanded to "die to sin." You can attend conferences and camp meetings where you are exhorted to "die to sin," to be "sanctified" so that you can reach a state of continual sinlessness.

But I submit to you that Paul never tells us that we should "die to sin." He is telling us that *we have already died to sin.* He is speaking of an accomplished fact.

Some people say that Paul means *we are dying to sin.* In other words, the Christian is gradually changing and growing, and the more mature he becomes, the more he dies to sin. Eventually, says this view, a time will come in the life of the Christian when he or she outgrows sin.

But that is clearly not what Paul is saying. He puts his statement in the Greek aorist tense, which means that this statement is true, once and for all: *We died to sin.* It is done, it is accomplished, period.

In Romans 5, Paul makes it clear that sin is our heritage in Adam. We can't escape it because Adam passed the taint of sin and death to us all. As children of Adam, we will sin. Even though we are Christians, we will sin.

Paul is saying that when you became a Christian, you received the gift of God, which is Jesus Himself and His righteousness. At that moment, you were no longer in Adam but in Christ.

Some Bible scholars teach that the believer has two natures, a new nature in Christ and an old nature of Adam. I disagree with that view. Yes, there are two natures—but only one of them is yours! Yes, there are two forces at work within us, and we feel the conflict between them—but only one of those forces belongs to us. We were once in Adam; now, as Christians, we are no longer in Adam but in Christ.

Having said that, we have to face the fact that Christians (who are no longer in Adam but in Christ) do sin, and they do die. Romans 5 told us that sin and death are the results of Adam's transgression. How can we be free from Adam and still suffer the results of Adam's transgression?

The answer lies in the nature of our humanity. I believe this tension is easily resolved once we see what Scripture reveals about who we are as human beings.

The "Cup" of the Human Spirit

The Bible tells us we are *spirit*; we have bodies and souls, but the most essential part of ourselves is our spirit. That may sound "spooky," but that is because we can see our material bodies and we can't see our spirits. We have been brainwashed by the world to believe only in what we can see and feel—and who can see or feel a spirit? The Scriptures tells us that the most fundamental nature of our being is spirit. (God, too, is spirit, which is why He cannot be seen.)

The Scriptures often use a metaphor to describe the human spirit: a "vessel," like a cup or bowl. You can think of your spirit as a little cup inside of you, made to hold something. Of course, picturing the spirit as a cup is speaking in metaphors, but it is necessary to use symbols and metaphors when discussing things that cannot be seen.

The Scriptures tell us that, in the beginning, this cup was made to hold none other than God Himself. All the greatness and glory of God could be poured into that tiny human cup. That is what Adam was, as he came fresh from the hand of God. But when Adam sinned and fell, that cup was emptied, then filled again with a kind of poison. This satanic poison has sickened all our humanity.

When that poison fills the cup of the spirit, it overflows into the soul, which is the realm of the mind (reason and intelligence), the will (the power to choose), and emotion (the power to feel). The Bible tells us that all of these areas of our being have been poisoned by sin, so that we are unable to think, choose, and feel as we should. Ultimately, when the spirit and the soul have been poisoned, that harm is expressed in the functioning of the body. The poisoning power of sin always flows from the inside out. Jesus put it this way:

> "For from within, out of men's hearts, come evil thoughts, sexual immorality, theft, murder, adultery, greed, malice, deceit, lewdness, envy, slander, arrogance and folly. All these evils come from inside and make a man 'unclean.'" (Mark 7:21–23)

The evils that Jesus lists are the poisons that come to us from the original transgression of Adam. These are the poisons in the cup of the human spirit, and they will come out—nothing can stop them from spilling out.

What happens when a poisoned human spirit turns to Jesus and receives the gift of righteousness and worth that comes from God? According to Paul's argument in Romans 5, the tie with Adam is broken. The spirit is emptied of its satanic poison—sin— and it is filled again with the Holy Spirit, who releases the life of Jesus to operate within the human spirit. That is what the Holy Spirit has come to do. Our human spirit, our essential nature, is no longer in Adam but in Christ. We have died to sin.

The problem is that our souls and bodies, which have functioned for years under the control of sin, are still going on in the same old way, operating according to the habits and patterns of the life of Adam. That is where the evil and sin in a believer's life come from. So as we mature in the Christian life, we must reeducate the soul and the body. We will experience many failures until we allow the Holy Spirit to bring every aspect of our lives under the control of the new life in Jesus Christ. It is a process, but it will happen.

The new life of Jesus is more powerful and persistent than the power of death from Adam ever was. If Jesus Christ truly fills the cup of the human spirit, He will continually work to bring the soul and body into conformity with His image. Just as we could not avoid sin while we were in Adam, so we cannot avoid becoming increasingly more Christlike if we are in Christ.

That is why Paul tells us, in effect, "Since we have died to sin, how can we live any longer in it? Why, it's impossible! It's not a question of *should* we continue in sin; it's a question of *can* we! And the only possible answer is: 'What a ghastly thought! It cannot be!'"

Indwelt by Adam or Christ?

In our neighborhood is a home that has been occupied by a number of different families over the years. One of those families allowed the place to fall into unsightly disrepair. The lawn died for lack of watering and became littered with trash. The house was a shambles, inside and out.

Eventually, that family moved out and another family moved in. The new family shoveled all the trash and filth from the house, patched and repainted the walls, replanted the lawn, and repaired the fence. The most wretched house in the neighborhood suddenly became one of the most beautiful homes in the neighborhood. The reason for this change was obvious: The house was indwelt by someone new.

The same is true of a human "dwelling place," a human being. When we are indwelt by Adam, we are filthy and wretched, inside and out. When Someone new comes to dwell in us—Jesus Christ—the change is evident to everyone. The transformation takes place inside and out.

What does it mean, then, if a Christian goes on sinning? What if someone claims to be forgiven yet goes on living a sinful lifestyle without any sign of a spiritual change? The biblical answer to this question is simple: These "sinning Christians" show that they are not truly Christians. They are deceiving themselves and others. They may believe they are Christians, but they are not genuine Christians because Jesus is not their Lord.

A "lord" is a master—someone who must be obeyed. If we call Jesus "Lord" but do not obey Him and do His will, then He is not truly our Lord. This is the point Jesus made when He said, "Not everyone who says to me, 'Lord, Lord,' will enter the kingdom of heaven, but only he who does the will of my Father who is in heaven" (Matthew 7:21), and "Why do you call me, 'Lord, Lord,' and do not do what I say?" (Luke 6:46).

It is impossible for your lifestyle to continue unchanged if Jesus is truly your Lord. When Jesus comes to live in you, a change must take place, beginning in your spirit, and moving outward into your soul and your body. Those who say they can be Christians while continuing in a life of sin reveal that there has been change in their spirit, no break with Adam. They are still in the same poisoned condition. They are indwelt by Adam, not by the Lord Jesus Christ. As Paul writes elsewhere:

> Of this you can be sure: No immoral, impure or greedy person—such a man is an idolater—has any inheritance in the kingdom of Christ and of God. Let no one deceive you with empty words, for because of such things God's wrath comes on those who are disobedient. (Ephesians 5:5–6; see also 1 Corinthians 6:9–11)

The biblical position on a sinful lifestyle is clear. So we must ask ourselves, *Is Jesus truly the Lord of my life and my lifestyle? Do I truly hate sin as God hates it? Do I truly want to be free from sin, delivered from its power, healed of its poison?* The power of sin will never be broken in your life until the Lord Himself comes into your heart to fill the cup of your spirit with a new Spirit. It is time to stop flirting with the poison of sin. It's time to put sin out of your life.

Can we go on sinning? By no means! What a ghastly thought! May it never be!

The True Baptism

In verses 3–14, Paul expands on what he means when he says we have died to sin. In this next passage, he uses two visual aids to make his meaning clear: baptism and the grafting of a branch into a tree. He writes:

> Or don't you know that all of us who were baptized into Christ Jesus were baptized into his death? We were therefore buried with him through baptism into death in order that, just as Christ was raised from the dead through the glory of the Father, we too may live a new life. (Romans 6:3–4)

Most people, when they encounter the word *baptism*, immediately "smell water." When I was a boy in Montana, I had a horse that could smell water from a great distance. I'd be riding that horse across dry, parched plains when he would suddenly prick up his ears and quicken his pace. I knew that he smelled water and he invariably found it. If you "smell water" when you see that word *baptism*, I want to assure you that there is no water here. This is a "dry" Scripture passage. The baptism Paul speaks of in these verses does not involve water.

This passage deals with the issue of how we have died to sin. In other words, Paul is talking about how we became separated from our old nature in Adam, and how we became joined to Christ. No water can do that. Baptism with water is merely a visible symbol of the *true* baptism that Paul speaks of here—the baptism of the Holy Spirit.

This is the same distinction John the Baptist made when he told the people, "I baptize you with water. . . . But after me will come one who is more powerful than I. . . . He will baptize you with the Holy Spirit" (see Matthew 3:11). Paul makes the same point when he writes, "For we were all baptized by one Spirit into one body—whether Jews or Greeks, slave or free—and we were all given the one Spirit to drink" (1 Corinthians 12:13).

Notice that Paul emphasizes that all believers were baptized into one body. If you are a Christian, you are baptized into one body and given one Spirit to drink; if you are not a Christian, you are not baptized into the body of Christ. Some churches teach that a Christian needs to experience a baptism of the Holy Spirit *after* conversion, but that is not what the Scriptures teach. This passage (and others) make it clear that you are baptized with the Holy Spirit when you become a believer, and you can't be a believer without also being baptized with the Spirit.

Historically, the baptism of the Spirit occurred first on the day of Pentecost, when the Holy Spirit came upon 120 people who were gathered in the courts of the temple at Jerusalem. This event fused them into one body, joining them to the Head, which is Jesus. At that moment, the church, the body of Christ, was formed, and all believers became members of one another and of the Lord Jesus Himself.

The baptism of the Holy Spirit is not something that is felt or experienced through the physical senses. It is something that the Holy Spirit does within the human spirit. Though invisible to the human eye, this baptism is essential to becoming a Christian. It is part of the process by which we share the life of Jesus Christ.

The way Paul speaks of the baptism of the Spirit, it is clear that he expects all Christians to know about it. He asks, "Don't you know that all of us who were baptized into Christ Jesus were baptized into his death?" At this time, Paul had never been to Rome and had never preached to the Roman Christians. Why did he expect them to know of the baptism of the Holy Spirit?

Here is where water baptism comes in. Water baptism teaches us—by picture and symbol—the meaning of the baptism of the Holy Spirit. Water baptism is the shadow; the baptism of the Spirit is the reality. Paul expects that the water baptism the Roman Christians have undergone has helped them to understand the reality of the baptism of the Spirit in their lives.

Notice, too, that Paul relates the issue of baptism directly to the fact that we have died to sin. He writes: "We were therefore buried with him through baptism into death." When we were baptized by the Holy Spirit at the moment of conversion, we were buried with Jesus; we became partakers in His death.

Paul is still discussing the question, "Can a believer go on sinning?" Paul answers, "No, because we died to sin." How did we die to sin? Paul explains it this way: Upon our conversion and baptism of the Holy Spirit, the Spirit caused us to be intimately identified with all that Jesus did. Christ died, and we died; Christ was buried, and we were buried with Him; Christ rose again, and we rose with Him. That is how we died to sin.

What's more, this magnificent truth is one of the most important truths of the Christian life: We are dead, buried, and raised with Christ. Our union with Christ is the central truth from which everything else in Scripture flows. If we understand what this truly means, it changes everything about our lives. That is why Paul so urgently wants us to understand this truth.

Grafted into Christ

Next, Paul introduces the metaphor of being grafted into Christ as a branch is grafted into a living tree, although that metaphor may not be immediately apparent. He writes:

> If we have been united with him like this in his death, we will certainly also be united with him in his resurrection. For we know that our old self was crucified with him so that the body of sin might be done away with, that we should no longer be slaves to sin—because anyone who has died has been freed from sin. (Romans 6:5–7)

When Paul writes, "If we have been *united* with him," he is using a word from botany that refers to grafting a branch into a tree. Just as you can graft a branch from a nectarine tree into a peach tree, so that the life of the peach tree flows into the nectarine branch, so we are grafted into the life of Jesus. We are united with Him and His life becomes our life. We are no longer in Adam; we are in Christ. We are grafted into His death and we are grafted into His resurrection.

Paul goes on to say that because Jesus was crucified, we were crucified too. The Adam within us has been nailed to a cross and put to death. Jesus was crucified "so that the body of sin might be done away with." In other words, Jesus was crucified so that the sin which was in His body on the cross should come to an end, so that His body would be rendered powerless with respect to sin.

You may be thinking, *That's wrong! There was no sin in Jesus!* And that's true, Jesus was the only sinless being who ever lived. There was no sin in Him—until He was placed on that cross. Then, as Paul tells us elsewhere in the New Testament, something amazing happened: On the cross, "God made him who had no sin to be sin for us, so that in him we might become the righteousness of God" (2 Corinthians 5:21).

Sin, in the believer, is located in the body. That is why sin is described in Jesus in terms of the body. On the cross, His body became possessed by sin. That is why His body died; that is why He was buried.

Why do we bury a corpse? Because it is dead and useless. There is nothing more anyone can do with it, so we bury it. Jesus was buried to prove that the sin in His body was ended. The body was useless and dead. Paul says that the same thing happens to us when we receive Jesus as Lord and Savior: Our spirit, which is identified with Christ, dies in Christ, and the body of sin is rendered powerless.

Paul says that our old self was crucified with Jesus "so that the body of sin might be done away with." What does he mean by the term "body of sin"? He means the physical body that is dominated and controlled by sin. In Adam, sin filled the whole of our humanity—spirit, soul, and body. That is why we must sin when we are in Adam. Even though a person in Adam tries to be good, it is impossible.

A person in Adam, says Paul, is a slave to sin. No matter how much a person in Adam wants to be good, it is impossible. Sin is the lord and master of a person in Adam.

But a person in Christ, says Paul, is no longer a slave to sin. The bond has been broken. In Christ, the human spirit is free. It is united with Jesus, grafted into Him, dead and buried with Him, risen with Him, and free from sin. This explains the intriguing passage in 1 John 3:9: "No one who is born of God will continue to sin, because God's seed remains in him; he cannot go on sinning, because he has been born of God." John is talking about your spirit, the essential you. In that sense, it is proper to say of believers, "We cannot sin," because the regenerated spirit is born of God and cannot sin.

As Christians, we do not have to sin. If we do, it is because we allow it to happen. But we are no longer slaves to sin. The body is the means by which we are tempted to sin. There is nothing inherently sinful about our bodies, but the alien power of sin remains in them. Sin comes from the body, not the spirit. That is why, throughout our lives, even as Christians, we will struggle with the temptation to sin.

Dead to Sin, Alive to God

Even though we will be tempted, we are no longer slaves to sin. We have been set free, so that we can choose not to sin. Moreover, a new power to resist sin has been given to us, as Paul now explains:

> Now if we died with Christ, we believe that we will also live with him. For we know that since Christ was raised from the dead, he cannot die again; death no longer has mastery over him. The death he died, he died to sin once for all; but the life he lives, he lives to God. (Romans 6:8–10)

Once we consider ourselves dead to sin, nothing remains but for us to proceed onward and upward to life. Once Jesus died, He could not go back into sin and death again. Sin and death were ended, and no longer had any claim on Him. Once we have died to sin through our identification with Christ, the same is true of us: sin and death are ended and no longer have any claim over us. So we need to recognize that we have died to sin with Christ, and that His life is in us now. When we decide not to sin, we have the power to carry it out, because Christ is alive in us. It all comes down to two simple steps that Paul describes in the next verse:

> In the same way, count yourselves dead to sin but alive to God in Christ Jesus. Therefore do not let sin reign in your mortal body so that you obey its evil desires. Do not offer the parts of your body to sin, as instruments of wickedness, but rather offer yourselves to God, as those who have been brought from death to life; and offer the parts of your body to him as instruments of righteousness. (Romans 6:11–13)

This is the first time in the book of Romans that we are given a command or an exhortation. Prior to this point, Paul has been building an argument about what God has done for us. Now we are told to do something: "Count yourselves dead to sin but alive to God in Christ Jesus."

Two principles that flow from this command will help you in times of temptation. First principle: When tempted, remember that you don't have to obey sin. Don't allow sin to reign in your mortal body. Don't obey its evil desires. You are free to say, "Sin has no right to use my body for evil purposes."

Second principle: When tempted, remember that the power of Christ in you enables you to offer your body to God, to be used for His purposes. You have been brought from death to life by a power that is greater than sin, greater than temptation. Of course, when you are tempted, you will be in for a struggle. After all, the strength of sin is very powerful in the body. But we have an even greater power living in us, if we will rely upon it: the power of God Himself, living in us.

We will always struggle with temptation, but we have the strength and the right to resist sin. We have the freedom not to sin and the desire not to sin. That is what God has given to us through Jesus Christ. That is how to win over temptation.

Paul closes this section of Romans 6 with this powerful statement:

> Sin shall not be your master, because you are not under law, but under grace. (Romans 6:14)

Why does Paul talk about the Law at this point? Because he is dealing with one of the most basic problems of the Christian struggle—an issue that depresses Christians more than any other issue of the Christian life: the feeling of condemnation we experience when we sin.

The Law condemns. The Law tells us that we have failed, we are washed up, and God wants nothing to do with us. Countless times, I have counseled Christians who feel defeated and discouraged because they are convinced that God is angry with them. That sense of defeat and discouragement comes from the condemnation of the Law.

But Paul says that we are not under the Law. We are not accused before God. We are under grace and God understands our struggle. He knows that we battle temptation, and He is not angry with us. He is alongside us, eager to pick us up when we stumble.

Sin is not your master. The Law is not your master. Your Lord and Master is Jesus Christ, who brings you His righteousness and forgiveness. When you fail, you need only go back to God, confess your sin, and receive His forgiveness—then get on with the business of living for Him.

This verse, Romans 6:14, first came alive for me when I was a young man in the service during World War II. I was on a watch one night, reading the book of Romans from my pocket New Testament. I had been wrestling with guilt over some failures in my life, and I was in a depressed mood as I read.

Suddenly, this verse leaped off the page and into my heart. The Holy Spirit made it come alive! In a flash, I saw the great promise of this verse, and I knew that all the things I struggled with as a young man would ultimately be mastered. They would be mastered *not* because I was so smart, but because God was teaching me and leading me into victory. I remember pacing excitedly back and forth, my heart overflowing with praise to God as I rejoiced in the promise of that verse: "Sin shall not be my master, because I am not under law, but under grace!"

Looking back across the years since that night, I clearly see that God has broken the grip of many temptations and problems that held me down. Other problems have come, and in the power of my Lord and Savior, I am battling them and experiencing victory. The struggle remains, but the promise of God will outlast even the struggle: "Sin shall not be your master, because you are not under law, but under grace."

Whose Slave Are You?

Some years ago in Los Angeles, I saw a man walking down the street with a large sign. The front of it read: I'M A SLAVE FOR CHRIST. As he passed by, I saw that the back of the sign read: WHOSE SLAVE ARE YOU?

That is a good question. We are all slaves to someone. We are either slaves to sin or slaves to righteousness. We have no other choice. By the very nature of our humanity, we are made to serve forces beyond our power. So the question that confronts us in the closing section of Romans 6 is the same question that man wore on his back: Whose slave are you? Here is how Paul frames the question:

> What then? Shall we sin because we are not under law but under grace? By no means! Don't you know that when you offer yourselves to someone to obey him as slaves, you are slaves to the one whom you obey—whether you are slaves to sin, which leads to death, or to obedience, which leads to righteousness? But thanks be to God that,

though you used to be slaves to sin, you wholeheartedly obeyed the form of teaching to which you were entrusted. You have been set free from sin and have become slaves to righteousness.

I put this in human terms because you are weak in your natural selves. Just as you used to offer the parts of your body in slavery to impurity and to ever-increasing wickedness, so now offer them in slavery to righteousness leading to holiness. (Romans 6:15–19)

"I put this in human terms," Paul says, meaning that he is using the image of slavery, one of the common features of the first-century world, to give us a word-picture of the human spiritual condition. He pictures us as slaves, because he wants to make us aware of a profound psychological and spiritual fact: Human beings are made to be mastered.

The great question is: Who is our master? Who controls the choices we make? Paul shows us that our range of options is limited. In fact, there are only two: Righteousness and sin—or, to put it another way, God and Satan. The one you choose to obey is your master. If you choose God as your master, you choose life; if you choose Satan as your master, you choose death. If you yield yourself to sin, you become the slave of sin—and sin is a deadly master.

This principle didn't originate with Paul. Jesus taught the same principle in John 8:34: "I tell you the truth, everyone who sins is a slave to sin." What is a slave? A person who is under the complete control of another. A slave is someone whose will is not his own.

If you tell one lie to cover up a sin, you will find yourself telling more lies to cover up the first lie, and the second, third, and on and on. You may not want to lie. You may wish you had never told the first one, but soon you are in so deep that you can no longer see any way out of the thicket of lies you have created.

Anger, gossip, greed, coveting, sexual immorality, foul language, gambling, drinking, drug abuse—all of these sins are addictive. It is easy to yield to them a little bit at a time. The sin seems minor at first. But each time we yield to sin, it becomes a little easier to yield the next time, and the next, and the next—until we suddenly wake up and realize that we are enslaved by it. We are the slaves of that which we obey.

Paul continues to explore this theme:

> When you were slaves to sin, you were free from the control of righteousness. What benefit did you reap at that time from the things you are now ashamed of? Those things result in death! (Romans 6:20–21)

I'm sure you can think of past sins that make you blush with shame. There are moments we can vividly recall in flashback, moments we wish we could take back. Such moments are a stain on our memories. Sin—no matter how small it may seem at the moment—always leads to shame.

But sin also produces something worse than shame—death! "Those things," Paul says, "result in death!" The sin of Adam placed him and all of our race under a sentence of death. And the sins of our race—your sins and mine—nailed our Lord Jesus to the bloody cross of Calvary. Why would we want to do the things that result in shame and death?

The Wages of Sin

In the closing verses of Romans 6, Paul sets before us a choice between life and death:

> Now that you have been set free from sin and have become slaves to God, the benefit you reap leads to holiness, and the result is eternal life. For the wages of sin is death, but the gift of God is eternal life in Christ Jesus our Lord. (Romans 6:22–23)

The death he speaks of is both physical and moral. Physical death is a picture of moral death. Physical death involves darkness, the end of light and life. And physical death involves corruption—the corruption of a decaying corpse.

That is what happens when we sin as believers. We experience moral darkness and moral corruption that is every bit as real as the darkness and corruption of physical death—indeed, it is *more* real. I've met many Christians who do not seem to understand this principle of God's Word. They deliberately allow things in their lives that they know are wrong, things that are sinful, dark, and corrupt. They don't realize that they are allowing death into their lives, into their souls, into their families.

When we as Christians allow sin, darkness, and death to enter our lives, we inevitably reach a point where we are sickened by it. We may not know why we feel sick of living the way we do; we only know that something about our lives has become nauseating and unbearable. Have you ever felt that way? Then that just might be the stench of death, the stench of the sin that you have been yielding to for too long. You have allowed yourself to become a slave of sin.

If that is your condition right now, then I have good news for you. Throughout Romans 6, Paul has stressed again and again that we do not have to remain in bondage to sin. "You have been set free from sin," he says. Now that you have been set free, you no longer have to live in darkness, corruption, and death. You can choose life, light, and freedom.

The challenge of Romans 6 is this: Jesus Christ has made you free—free to be a whole person, free to experience an intimate relationship with the Lord and Creator of the universe. That is why Paul closes this chapter of Romans with these words: "The wages of sin is death, but the gift of God is eternal life in Christ Jesus our Lord." Jesus Himself described eternal life in these words: "Now this is eternal life: that they may know you, the only true God, and Jesus Christ, whom you have sent" (John 17:3). Eternal life is knowing God.

We have been called into an intimate relationship with the infinite God, called to life and light and joy—yet we foolishly toss it all away for a lifestyle that leads to slavery, shame, and death. "It is for freedom that Christ has set us free," Paul tells us. "Stand firm, then, and do not let yourselves be burdened again by a yoke of slavery" (Galatians 5:1).

Jesus has purchased you and led you out of the slave market and into the bright sunlight of God's love and freedom. Turn your back on the slave market of sin. Hold your head high and walk as a new, liberated person in Christ.

CHAPTER 8

THE NEVER-ENDING STRUGGLE

Romans 7

Comedian Red Skelton portrayed many characters in his comedy sketches, including Freddie the Freeloader, Sheriff Deadeye, San Fernando Red, and Clem Kadiddlehopper. One of his most famous characters was Junior, the Mean Widdle Kid. Junior continually got into conflict with himself as he pondered whether or not he should commit some act of mayhem. He would say to himself, "If I dood it, I'll get a whipping!" His inner conflict would last about half a second, ending in a mischievous leer and the words, "I dood it anyway!"

That is the struggle many of us know all too well: We are confronted with the temptation to sin, we know that there will be consequences if we sin, we ponder the temptation for about half a second, then we "dood it anyway." In Romans 7, Paul summarizes this struggle with these words: "I have the desire to do what is good, but I cannot carry it out. . . . When I want to do good, evil is right there with me."

Romans 7 is a commentary on Paul's great declaration of Romans 6:14: "Sin shall not be your master, because you are not under law, but under grace." The central question of Romans 7 is this: "Does the Law help us handle the problem of sin in our lives?" Paul's answer is, in effect, "Yes—and no. Yes, the Law does help us up to a point. It helps us define the problem. It helps to drive us to God. But no, the Law is no help at all in delivering us from sin. In fact, the Law actually makes it harder for us to free ourselves from the struggle against sin."

Paul's Opening Illustration

Paul opens this discussion by showing that we can't handle the sin problem with the Law standing over our shoulders. We must be free from the Law to be free from sin—but we don't know how to handle such freedom. It is human nature to want rules, regulations, and instructions rather than freedom. That is the problem Paul addresses in the opening section of Romans 7:

> Do you not know, brothers—for I am speaking to men who know the law—that the law has authority over a man only as long as he lives? For example, by law a married woman is bound to her husband as long as he is alive, but if her husband dies, she is released from the law of marriage. So then, if she marries another man while her husband is still alive, she is called an adulteress. But if her husband dies, she is released from that law and is not an adulteress, even though she marries another man. (Romans 7:1–3)

Paul uses an illustration taken from marriage. Paul begins by saying that this illustration is addressed to those who know the Law—that is, to the Jews. In Paul's illustration, a woman marries and she is bound to her husband as long as he lives. This may seem strange in these days of easy divorce, but according to the Law of Moses, and according to God's intentions, marriage is for life.

In the marriage ceremony, people today usually vow to take each other "for better or for worse, until death do us part." Today, however, most people seem to marry "for better or else." As one woman put it, "I took him for better or worse, but he's worse than I took him for!" So in our culture, divorce is commonplace, but in God's sight marriage is for life.

That is the background for Paul's illustration at the beginning of Romans 7. Remember, Paul is not making a point about marriage; he is using marriage to make a point about the Law. Marriage is just an illustration, and here is the concept Paul illustrates:

The woman who is married is helpless to change her situation until her husband dies. Any attempt to change her marital status while her husband is alive is a violation of the Law. She becomes an adulteress if she tries to marry another man while her first husband still lives.

In Paul's illustration, the woman is a picture of the believer—you and me. What, then, does the first husband represent? Some Bible commentators say the first husband represents the Law. I disagree. The Law in the illustration is what binds the man and the woman together, and I believe the Law in the illustration simply represents the Law. The first husband represents something else altogether.

If you follow Paul's argument through the first six chapters of Romans, I think it becomes clear that the first husband represents *our old humanity in Adam.* In other words, the old husband is the sinful human nature, the old self that we inherited from Adam. We are bound to it as a wife is bound to her husband. We don't like our old sinful self, but we are stuck with it—apart from Christ.

I think it is important, at this point, to make a distinction. What we are calling "our old self" should more accurately be called a "false self." The Scriptures tell us that the sin heritage from Adam is actually an alien invasion of human nature. Sin invaded the human spirit when Adam fell, and it was passed along to the rest of the human race, with the single exception of Jesus Christ. Sin reigned unchallenged in the human race until it was challenged by Christ Himself.

We have lived so long with this "false self" that we identify it with our real selves; we think it is *us.* Even so, we still feel the Spirit of God stirring a hunger within us for true righteousness. We think, "I wish I were not what I am; I wish I could choose to always do good." We admire true righteousness, which is why the life of Jesus is so attractive to us.

Despite our hunger to be good as Jesus was, all our efforts to do good fail because in Adam we are bound to the sinful self, the false self. That brings us back to Paul's illustration from marriage.

When we try to be good while we are bound by the Law to our old self, the result is a false facade of goodness. Deep inside, we know we are bound to sin, but we try to create a false front of goodness, an image or reputation of goodness—and the result is that we are hypocrites. Though we try outwardly to be good, we inwardly know that we are still the same old self-centered creatures we always were.

Paul describes this hypocritical self as an "adulterer." Under the Law, all our attempts to marry ourselves to an image of goodness makes adulterers of us, for we are still married by the Law to the old life within.

But then Christ comes into our lives. He fulfills the Law through His death on the cross. When we authentically receive Him as Lord and Savior, we identify with His life, death, and burial. Our sinful self—the old, false self in Adam—is officially declared dead. In his illustration, Paul describes the death of the old sinful self in these terms: "But if her husband dies, she is released from the law of marriage."

When Jesus hung on the cross and became sin for us (as Paul describes in 2 Corinthians 5:21), He became what we were in Adam. He became the old husband, and he died. So when Christ died, our old husband, that false self, died. At that moment, we were set free from the Law. Now, in the terms of Paul's illustration, we are free to marry another. There is now no hypocrisy, no adultery. The new marriage is holy and righteous—and the new husband is the risen Lord Jesus Christ. Just as He became our old sinful self upon the cross, He now lives to become our new, true self.

This is the amazing declaration of Scripture: Jesus Christ, entering your life and mine by grace through faith, overthrows the alien invader, sin. He takes His rightful place in the very core of our being. Sin is now on the outside, calling to us, trying to seduce us. We can hear its siren call, but we do not have to answer it. So we must live in reliance upon Jesus—not the Law—to give us the power to remain faithful to Him.

Love Does What the Law Could Not

In the next few verses, Paul expands on his illustration from marriage:

> So, my brothers, you also died to the law through the body of Christ, that you might belong to another, to him who was raised from the dead, in order that we might bear fruit to God. For when we were controlled by the sinful nature, the sinful passions aroused by the law were at work in our bodies, so that we bore fruit for death. But now, by dying to what once bound us, we have been released from the law so that we serve in the new way of the Spirit, and not in the old way of the written code. (Romans 7:4–6)

When Paul says, "you also died to the law through the body of Christ," he is referring to what the Scriptures say in many places: On the cross, the Lord Jesus was made sin for us. He took our place on the cross and became sin for us. When He died, we also died—we died to sin and we died to the Law. The Law has nothing to say to us anymore. We are free to be married to another, to the risen Lord Jesus Christ. Our first husband is Christ crucified; our second husband is Christ risen from the dead.

When we were married to sin, we were controlled by our sinful nature and our lives produced the fruit of sin and death. But now, through Christ, we have died to the Law that bound us, so that we serve God in a new way. Because we share in the death and resurrection life of Jesus, we are free from any condemnation of the Law. Clearly, we will stumble, we will fail—but the Law no longer condemns us. That, after all, was the purpose of the Law: to condemn.

But now we have a new identity. We are no longer bound to our sin. When we stumble and fail, we can go to God, confess it, then forget it. That is the power of God's love and grace.

So it is not the Law that makes it possible for us to live righteously before God; it is love and grace. Love can do what the

Law could never do. It can help us to live righteously before God. The Law filled us with guilt and fear of condemnation whenever we sinned. Love fills us with gratitude whenever we are forgiven. When we truly understand how Jesus sacrificed for us, when we begin to grasp the love He has shown to us, we *want* to serve and obey Him out of genuine gratitude and love.

Is the Law Evil?

The Law condemns us—but we are no longer under Law if we are resting in Christ. Therefore, the Law does not serve any useful purpose in delivering us from sin. The Law can expose our sin and drive us back to Christ, but it cannot deliver us from sin. Only our love-relationship with God can do that.

What, then, is the purpose of the Law in a Christian's life? Should we simply dispense with it?

Some Christians say, "I'm a Christian, saved by grace. The Law was given to Moses for the Israelites, but it doesn't apply to a Christian. So I simply ignore the Law." Christians who make such claims do not understand the biblical view of the Law and grace. Paul never says that we should dispense with the Law; nor does Jesus. In fact, Jesus told us in the Sermon on the Mount that if anyone disparages the Law or waters it down, that person is under the curse of God. The Law abides forever.

So we need to understand what Paul teaches about the Law and grace in Romans 7. The remainder of Romans 7 divides into two sections. In verses 7–13, Paul discusses how the Law exposes sin. In verses 14–25, Paul discusses what it feels like when the Law exposes sin. He writes:

What shall we say, then? Is the law sin? Certainly not! Indeed I would not have known what sin was except through the law. For I would not have known what coveting really was if the law had not said, "Do not covet." But sin, seizing the opportunity afforded by the commandment, produced in me every kind of covetous desire. For apart from law, sin is dead. Once I was alive apart from law; but when the commandment came, sin sprang to life and I died. I found that the very commandment that was intended to bring life actually brought death. For sin, seizing the opportunity afforded by the commandment, deceived me, and through the commandment put me to death. (Romans 7:7–11)

Paul is clearly describing his own experience with the Law. He employs the past tense throughout this passage, which suggests that he is describing his life before he became a Christian. We know that Paul was raised in a devoutly religious Jewish home. He was taught the Law from birth. So when he says he lived "apart from the Law," he doesn't mean that he didn't know what the Law was. He simply means that there came a time when the Law came home to him. This is what he refers to when he writes, "When the commandment came, sin sprang to life."

In the home in which he was raised, Paul was protected and sheltered from exposure to serious temptations. He was raised in the Jewish culture, where everyone around him was sheltered as well. So Paul grew up relatively untroubled by problems of sin. As a boy, he probably thought, *Keeping the Law? That's not hard! I hardly ever face temptation.*

But then came a time when he was no longer sheltered, when he went out into the world and was exposed to temptations he never imagined before. Suddenly, for the first time in his life, young Paul felt the full force of the prohibition of the Law. The Law says, "Do not covet, commit adultery, murder, steal." Yet the world said, "Do whatever feels good." And he began to feel the prohibition of the Law.

What was the specific prohibition Paul encountered? It was the tenth commandment, "Do not covet." He writes: "I would not have known what coveting really was if the law had not said, 'Do not covet.' But sin, seizing the opportunity afforded by the commandment, produced in me every kind of covetous desire." Suddenly, Paul found himself awakened to this commandment.

He was a Pharisee before he became a Christian, and perhaps he began to covet the success, fame, and possessions of many of other Pharisees. In any case, he became aware of the Law's prohibition of coveting, and his own covetous desires and ambitions were awakened by it.

Paul is telling us that sin lies silent within us. We don't even know it's there. We think we are handling life without difficulty. Then, without warning, we discover all kinds of sinful desires awakening within us. We find ourselves filled with vengeful thoughts, feelings of lust, covetous desires and ambitions. It is as if the engine of sin has been quietly idling until the leaden foot of the Law suddenly tromped on the accelerator, causing sin to come roaring to life inside us.

Does this mean that the Law is at fault? Is the Law a bad thing, producing evil in our lives? Paul answers this question in the next two verses:

> So then, the law is holy, and the commandment is holy, righteous and good.
>
> Did that which is good, then, become death to me? By no means! But in order that sin might be recognized as sin, it produced death in me through what was good, so that through the commandment sin might become utterly sinful. (Romans 7:12–13)

No, the Law is not evil. It is holy, righteous, and good. It exposes the evil force of sin within each of us. The Law shows sin to be what it is—something powerful and dangerous, something that has greater strength than our willpower.

The Law Is Spiritual

In verses 14–25, Paul describes the same experience in terms of how we feel when the Law exposes the evil within us. There is only one major difference between verses 7–13 and verses 14–25: Paul switches to the present tense. That is significant because it means that he is now describing his experience at the time he wrote this letter to the Romans. The next few verses, then, describe the Law as it touches the life of a Christian—a believer who is deceived by the sin that still resides in him. Paul writes:

> We know that the law is spiritual; but I am unspiritual, sold as a slave to sin. I do not understand what I do. For what I want to do I do not do, but what I hate I do. (Romans 7:14–15)

The key to this whole passage is the statement in verse 14: "The law is spiritual." Paul says, in effect, "The Law deals with my spirit. It gets right at the very heart of my being." Human beings are essentially spirits, so the Law affects us in the spiritual dimension of our being.

"But I am unspiritual," Paul goes on to say. In other words, "I can't respond to the Law because I am sold as a slave to sin." Compare this with Romans 6:17–18, where Paul speaks of slavery to sin, saying, "But thanks be to God that, though you used to be slaves to sin, you wholeheartedly obeyed the form of teaching to which you were entrusted. You have been set free from sin and have become slaves to righteousness."

How could Paul write that he had become a slave to righteousness in Christ, then just a few paragraphs later write, "I am unspiritual, sold as a slave to sin"? Isn't this a contradiction?

No. Any apparent contradiction can easily be explained in that Paul is describing what happens when a Christian tries to live under the Law. When a Christian, by his willpower and determination, tries to do what is right in order to please God, he is living under the Law. When we try to live under the Law, the result is that we become inwardly conflicted: What we want to do, we don't do; and we hate the things we do.

The Never-Ending Struggle

Next, Paul moves right to the heart of the struggle we all face:

And if I do what I do not want to do, I agree that the law
is good. As it is, it is no longer I myself who do it, but it
is sin living in me. I know that nothing good lives in me,
that is, in my sinful nature. For I have the desire to do what
is good, but I cannot carry it out. For what I do is not the
good I want to do; no, the evil I do not want to do—this I
keep on doing. Now if I do what I do not want to do, it is
no longer I who do it, but it is sin living in me that does it.
(Romans 7:16–20)

Paul says that as a Christian, redeemed by the grace of God,
there is now something within him that agrees with the Law and
wants to do good. But at the same time, there is something else
within him that rises up and says "No!" Even though Paul wants
to do good, his resolve collapses and he sins. I'm sure you can
identify with Paul's confession.

How does Paul explain this contradiction between what he
wants to do and what he ends up doing? He says, "It is no longer I
who do it, but it is sin living in me that does it." Isn't that a strange
explanation? Paul says that there is a conflict within our humanity. There is the "I" that wants to do good, and there is the sin that
dwells in "me"—a "me" that is different from the "I."

Human beings are complex creatures. We have within us a
spirit, a soul, and a body. These are distinct from each other. Paul
suggests that the redeemed spirit never wants to do what God has
prohibited. The redeemed spirit, the "I" of this statement, agrees
with the Law and says that the demands of the Law are good. Yet
an alien power, a self-willed beast lies dormant within us until it
is awakened by a commandment of the Law. The beast springs to
life, and we do what we do not want to do.

Jesus agrees with this assessment. On one occasion He said, "If
your right hand causes you to sin, cut it off," (see Matthew 5:30).
He did not mean that you should literally amputate your hand. He
was speaking metaphorically to underscore the seriousness of sin.
He was also showing us that there is a "me" within us that gives

orders to our hands, feet, eyes, tongue, brain, and sex organs—a "me" that is at odds with the "I." The "I" is often offended and aghast at what the "me" does. So Jesus was telling us that the "I" must take desperate measures and cut off the sinful "me."

Next, Paul looks at the other side of this problem:

> So I find this law at work: When I want to do good, evil is right there with me. For in my inner being I delight in God's law; but I see another law at work in the members of my body, waging war against the law of my mind and making me a prisoner of the law of sin at work within my members. (Romans 7:21–23)

This is another view of the same problem: You want to do right, and your inner "I" delights in God's Law—yet another principle is at work in the body. That principle wages war against your inner "I." It holds you hostage, forcing you to do what you don't want to do. The result: defeat, discouragement, and self-condemnation. You hate yourself for doing what you keep trying not to do. You think, "What's the matter with me? Why can't I do what is right? Why am I so weak?" This is our never-ending struggle.

Voicing the discouragement and frustration we all feel, Paul cries out:

> What a wretched man I am! Who will rescue me from this body of death? (Romans 7:24)

We mistakenly think that resisting sin is a simply matter of having enough willpower. We think we can defeat sin in our lives by simply determining to do so. God stands by and allows us to battle sin in our own strength. Finally, we come to the end of ourselves and cry out, "What a wretched man I am! Who will rescue me from this body of death?"

Sin deceives us—and the Law comes in, opens our eyes, and exposes sin for what it truly is. Once we finally see how wretched sin makes us, we are ready to receive God's prescription for sin. At that point, we can say with Paul:

> Thanks be to God—through Jesus Christ our Lord! (Romans 7:25)

Who will deliver us from this body of death? Thanks be to God, the Lord Jesus has delivered us! Once the Law forces us to recognize our wretchedness and failure, we are ready to turn to God for our deliverance.

We are no longer under the Law. That is the fact. We must stop thinking, *I need to battle these sinful urges and obey the Law in my own power!* Instead, we must think, *I am a free child of God! I am dead to sin and dead to the Law because I am married to Christ. His power enables me to walk away from sin, free in Christ.*

There is one more sentence to Romans 7:25, but that sentence actually belongs to the topic Paul explores in Romans 8, so we will save that for the next chapter. Meanwhile, let me tell you a story that encapsulates the reality that Paul speaks of in that final, triumphant statement: "Thanks be to God—through Jesus Christ our Lord!"

Some years ago, before the fall of Soviet communism, I met a pastor from Russia who was living in Canada. He had a burden to take the Word of God into the Soviet Union, even though the Bible was forbidden there. This pastor told us about his first experience of crossing the Soviet border with a load of Bibles in the trunk of the car. He didn't want to smuggle the Bibles in or use any other dishonest tactic. He simply counted on God to help him get the Bibles into the Soviet Union somehow.

He and a friend loaded the boxes of Bibles into the car and drove toward the border. The closer they came to the border, the more anxious they felt. Just a mile from the checkpoint, the pastor's friend said, "How do you feel?"

"Scared," said the pastor. "Let's stop and pray."

So they pulled to the side of the road and poured out their hearts to God. "Lord," they said, "we're scared. We're afraid of being arrested. But we know that You have led us to do this because You want Your Word to reach the people of the Soviet Union. We're willing to take this risk, but You've got to see it through. We don't have the wisdom to handle any problems that may come up, so if You want Your Word to go into that country, You have to make it possible."

As he prayed, the pastor felt totally helpless and dependent upon God—but he also had a sense of peace. The two men got back on the road and drove to the checkpoint. There, the guard examined their car and said, "What do you have in the trunk?"

"Some boxes," the pastor answered truthfully.

"Let me see them," said the guard.

The pastor opened the trunk. There, in plain sight, were the boxes of Bibles. The pastor waited for the guard to open the boxes and find the Bibles. Instead, the guard simply said, "Very well." Then he slammed the trunk and waved them on.

The pastor and his friend drove on into the Soviet Union and they distributed the Bibles to the spiritually hungry people there.

This is the way God wants us to live. We must acknowledge that we are powerless to do God's will. We are powerless—but we serve an all-powerful God. What is impossible for us is easy for God. If we acknowledge our own inability, we can rest in His infinite ability.

The Law exposes the sin and wretchedness in us so that we, in abject poverty of spirit, will cry out to God, "This is Your problem! I can do nothing! Lord, You take it!" And He will do so.

We need the Law. We need it every time sin deceives us. But the Law will not deliver us from sin. The purpose of the Law is to bring us to the feet of our mighty Deliverer.

CHAPTER 9

NO CONDEMNATION

Romans 8:1–17

Alcoholics, smokers, and drug addicts all know this struggle: They want to quit, they determine to quit, but they can't. The addicted person knows he may lose his family, his reputation, his career, and even his life—yet he is powerless in the grip of sin and addiction.

Those who struggle with homosexuality or other sexual sins feel the same way. They find it hard to say "No" to their old life-style, even though they desperately want to.

Those who struggle with anger and rage experience the same struggle. So do those who struggle with habits of overeating or gambling or some other destructive behavior.

No matter what our area of sin or habit, we are weak. We are helpless to change by will-power alone. That is the struggle Paul describes. That is the struggle of the Christian life.

Many Christians resent the fact that we have to struggle against ourselves throughout this life. They think that God should take this struggle away and remove temptation so they will never have to struggle again. When the struggle goes on and on, some people become disappointed with God because He doesn't take them out of the struggle.

We all identify with that struggle. But as we come to Romans 8, we see that Paul does not leave us there. He wants us to know that struggle does not have to defeat us. It can be resolved—and he is going to tell us how. In the last verse of Romans 7, Paul gave this triumphant cry of relief:

> Thanks be to God—through Jesus Christ our Lord! (Romans 7:25)

The verse does not end there, of course—but the next sentence of that verse actually belongs at the beginning of Romans 8. Paul writes:

> So then, I myself in my mind am a slave to God's law, but in the sinful nature a slave to the law of sin. (Romans 7:25)

That statement serves as an important transition. It summarizes all that Paul has been saying in Romans 7, and it introduces the theme of Romans 8. In fact, there should not even be a period at the end of that sentence. It should run on into, and become part of, the first sentence of Romans 8. Here's how the entire statement should read:

> So then, I myself in my mind am a slave to God's law, but in the sinful nature a slave to the law of sin, [but] there is now no condemnation for those who are in Christ Jesus, because through Christ Jesus the law of the Spirit of life set me free from the law of sin and death. (Romans 7:25–8:2)

Notice the place where I have inserted in brackets the word *[but]*. The New International Version starts a new sentence there with the word *therefore*. The only reason this sentence is interrupted is that the chapter division is arbitrarily and inaccurately made at that point. Keep in mind, the chapter and verse divisions of the Bible are not divinely inspired. When Paul wrote his letter to the Romans, there were no such divisions. Those were added hundreds of years later, and there are numerous instances, such as this one, where they interrupt the flow of the text in unfortunate ways. So we need to ignore the chapter division here as we try to grasp Paul's original intent in these verses.

What is Paul saying in this passage when it is all taken together? First, it is clear that there is a struggle in the Christian life—a struggle between what Paul calls "the sinful nature" and the Spirit of life. (To be precise, the word that is translated "sinful nature" literally means *flesh* in the original language; as used in Scripture, the word *flesh* refers not only to the physical body but to the sin that reigns in the body.)

The body or "sinful nature" is our link to our father, Adam. Genetically, all that we have in our bodies is traceable through history to a single human being, Adam. God made a body for Adam that is like ours—with two eyes, two ears, a nose, and so forth. We have these characteristics because Adam had them. We have also inherited from Adam this principle of sin that is in us.

We could describe the principle of sin as the access that the devil has to our humanity—the means by which Satan is able to implant in our minds "the flaming arrows of the evil one" (see Ephesians 6:16). This refers to subtle satanic attacks in the form of obscene and lustful thoughts, selfish attitudes, spiritual arrogance and pride, bitterness and hate, and other sinful thoughts that come suddenly into our minds when we least expect them. They come from this root of sin that is in our bodies, inherited from Adam.

How can we break this hold that Satan has on us, this principle of sin? We break it, Paul says, by seeing ourselves in a new way—by learning to view ourselves as we truly are in Jesus Christ. That is the theme of Romans 8: There is an eternal struggle, and that struggle can cease only when we discover who we truly are in Christ.

What we truly need is a new self-image. That is our only path of deliverance. When we see who we truly are, we can say "No" to the flesh and "Yes" to the Spirit—and we can discover a whole new walk of life.

What Is Meant by "No Condemnation"?

"There is now no condemnation for those who are in Christ Jesus," Paul says. The reason there is no condemnation is given in just one little phrase: "in Christ Jesus." In other words, we are no longer condemned because we are justified by faith. Though we came from Adam, we are now in Christ. God will never condemn those who are in Christ—never!

Condemnation means *rejection by God*. So if we are no longer condemned, then we know that God will never turn us away. We have been reborn into the family of God by faith in Jesus Christ. The Holy Spirit has come to dwell within us and He will never leave us.

One of the most beautiful stories of the Bible is the parable of the prodigal son. The prodigal son left home, wasted all that he had in sinful living, and ended up slaving away in a pigpen. The insightful Bible teacher, Dr. Vernon McGee, once asked, "Do you know the difference between the son in that pigpen and the pigs? The difference is that no pig ever said to himself, 'I will arise and go to my father.'" Dr. McGee is right. Only a son says that. The son got up, left that pigpen, and returned to his father. When he arrived, the son was not condemned by his father, not rejected, not tossed out of the family. He was loved and accepted.

That is a picture of our relationship to God, once we have been justified by faith. We are part of God's family, and there is now no condemnation, only love and acceptance.

"No condemnation" also means that God is not angry with us when we struggle with temptation and moral dilemmas. He knows that we want to be good, we want to stop doing bad. He knows that we feel shame when we fail. He grieves with us over our sins. Though we condemn ourselves for our failures, God does not. He knows that, as the Scriptures reveal to us, we are children in His family, and we are learning to walk. A loving father does not beat his children for stumbling as they take their first steps. Rather, God encourages us and teaches us how to take the next step without falling.

"No condemnation" also means that there is no punishment. God will never take us to the woodshed because of our struggles. We may punish ourselves and cry out, "What a wretched person I am!" But God will never say that, and He will not punish us.

This is not to say that God will never discipline us if we deliberately rebel against Him. The Bible is clear that our loving Father disciplines those He loves, so that He can correct us and rescue us from a self-destructive lifestyle of sin and rebellion. But He will never punish us if we are sincerely struggling to walk as He wants us to walk.

The Way to Victory

Not only is there now no condemnation for the believer, says Paul, but God has also made a provision for victory. "Through Christ Jesus," he says, "the law of the Spirit of life set me free from the law of sin and death." That is why Paul voices this shout of triumph at the conclusion of Romans 7: "Thanks be to God—through Jesus Christ our Lord!" (Romans 7:25).

When we tell ourselves, "I'm a hopeless wretch," God says, "You have the wrong view of yourself. You are not a hopeless wretch. You are married to Christ, and you have been set free. Accept His forgiveness, thank God for it, and move on in the confidence that your struggle has ended."

Of course this does not mean that God has ended the reign of the flesh in our lives. The law of sin and death, like the law of gravity, goes on working all the time. But the moment you believe that what Jesus Christ says about you is true, a new law comes in. That new law is stronger than the law of sin and death.

God has given us a new image of ourselves. It may be hard for us to accept that new image of ourselves, because it doesn't agree with the way we feel about ourselves. Unfortunately, many of us trust our feelings more than we trust the Word of God. Feelings are fickle and unreliable. God's Word is eternal and dependable. His image of us is the truth upon which we can always rely.

Next, Paul explains to us the basis for victory:

For what the law was powerless to do in that it was weakened by the sinful nature, God did by sending his own Son in the likeness of sinful man to be a sin offering. And so he condemned sin in sinful man, in order that the righteous requirements of the law might be fully met in us, who do

not live according to the sinful nature but according to the
Spirit. (Romans 8:3–4)

This is a beautiful description of the good news in Jesus Christ.
Paul says the Law is powerless to produce righteousness. It can
demand and condemn, but it cannot make us good.

That is why nagging somebody never helps them to do good.
Nagging is a form of law, and it only makes the behavior worse. If
you try to nag your spouse or child, you will find this principle at
work. Nagging only makes them worse. Why? Because, says Paul,
the Law only stirs up the power of sin. It unleashes the beast of
sin within us. Paul puts it this way elsewhere in the New Testament: "The sting of death is sin, and the power of sin is the law"
(1 Corinthians 15:56).

To break through this vicious circle, God did an astounding
thing: "What the law was powerless to do . . . God did by sending
his own Son in the likeness of sinful man." There is a beautiful
tenderness in the phrase "His own Son." God did not send an
angel or some other lesser being. He sent His own Son, a part of
His own nature and being. He sent His Son as a man, in the likeness of sinful flesh. Jesus had a real physical body, like yours and
mine. Since sin has been done in the body, it must be judged and
broken in the body.

The body of Jesus was in the likeness of sinful flesh. It was
like our sinful bodies, so it was subject to human infirmities. Jesus
could become weak, tired, and hungry; Jesus could even die. But
there was no sin in Him. In that body of flesh, without sin, Jesus
became sin for us. As Paul puts it, God sent His Son "to be a sin
offering" for us. In the mystery of the cross, which we can never
understand no matter how long we live, the Lord Jesus somehow
gathered up all the sins of the world so that they could be crucified
in His own body.

God's view of us becomes real in our lives when we choose
to live according to the Spirit, not according to our sinful nature.
When we believe what God says about us and we see ourselves in

a new way, then our behavior can't help but change. This is God's way of deliverance.

Hal Lindsey tells the story of the daughter of one of the royal families of Europe. She saw herself as unlovely and unlovable because of one feature—her large, bulbous nose. Her family hired a plastic surgeon to change the contour of her nose. After the operation, he removed the bandages and held up a mirror so that the girl could see that the operation was a complete success. Everyone around the girl gasped in amazement: Her nose was completely changed. She was beautiful.

The girl saw herself and gasped—not in wonder but in horror. "It's no different!" she cried. "I'm still ugly! I knew it wouldn't work!"

For months afterwards, the doctor and the girl's family worked with her, trying to convince her that she was beautiful. Everyone else could see the change, but the girl herself could not. After months of therapy, she finally accepted the fact that she was changed and beautiful. Only when her view of herself changed did her behavior finally began to change.

We are like that girl. We have been changed. We have been made beautiful in God's sight. But for some reason, we are unable to believe and accept God's truth about ourselves. We still see ourselves as hopeless wretches—and we behave accordingly.

Once we realize that we are truly free, we can act as free human beings, made in the image of God. Sin shall not have dominion over us, for we are under grace. By His grace, God affirms that we have been changed and made new. Now all we have to do is believe it!

The Mind Controlled by the Spirit

Next, Paul presents us with two possible ways that a Christian can live: We can (1) walk according to the flesh or the sinful nature; or (2) we can walk according to the Spirit. The New International Version of the Bible is a reliable translation, but it is not so accurate and helpful in this next section of Romans 8.

So, from time to time, we will look at this passage in both the New International Version and in the "Ray Stedman translation." Paul writes:

> Those who live according to the sinful nature [literally, *the flesh*] have their minds set on what that nature desires; but those who live in accordance with the Spirit have their minds set on what the Spirit desires. (Romans 8:5)

These two possibilities are set before us as Christians: Will we walk according to the flesh or according to the Spirit? The choice we make determines whether or not we manifest the righteousness that the Law demands.

Notice that it all depends upon what we set our minds on. Do we set our minds on what the Spirit desires? Or do we set our minds on what the flesh desires? That's the deciding factor—what you do with your thinking.

The mindset of this world saturates our entertainment media, our news media, and the conversations of the people around us. What do most people focus on in life? Money, status, power, comfort, pleasure, fun. People desire these things because they mistakenly think that they bring fulfillment. These are the things the people of the world live for.

You may say, "What's wrong with that?" Answer: Nothing. It is perfectly reasonable for sincere, dedicated Christians to devote a part of their lives to making money (providing for their families), to achieving positions of influence (which can be used for Christian leadership and witnessing), to making comfortable homes (where Christian hospitality can be practiced), to enjoying nature and entertainment (even Jesus took time to rest, relax, and enjoy Himself).

But when these things become the focus of our lives, when we seek our fulfillment in wealth, possessions, status, and pleasure instead of finding our satisfaction in God, then these perfectly good pursuits become destructive to our souls. God never intended that we should become Christian ascetics, living in caves, having no fun, doing nothing but memorizing Scripture and thinking about God all day. He gave us the whole world to enjoy, but He intends to be at the center of our lives.

To have our minds set on the Spirit means that, in the midst of providing for our families and enjoying life, we are primarily concerned with loving God, loving others, and living to glorify our Lord and Savior, Jesus Christ. Living with our minds set on the Spirit does not remove us from the mainstream of life, it places us in the middle of it—and it gives us God's point of view.

Paul goes on to describe the results that flow from these two ways of living that he has set before us:

> The mind of sinful man is death, but the mind controlled by the Spirit is life and peace. (Romans 8:6)

That is how the New International Version renders this verse. I think a more accurate rendering would read this way:

> The thinking of the flesh is death, but the thinking of the Spirit is life and peace. (Romans 8:6, author's translation)

What happens when you, as a Christian, let yourself live as the world lives, never bringing God's perspective into your life? You are living according to the flesh—and the thinking of the flesh is death. Death is not something waiting for you at the end of your earthly existence; it is something you experience *now*, whenever you live according to the flesh.

The Scriptures tell us that death, in this present experience, always comes down to four basic things: fear, guilt, hostility, and emptiness. These forms of death result when your mind is set on the thinking of the flesh—on making money, having fun, seeking status, seeking to gratify the self. If that is all you want out of life, you will also have fear, guilt, hostility, and emptiness.

Fear is experienced as worry, anxiety, dread, or timidity. Guilt is experienced as shame, self-hatred, self-righteousness, or perfectionism. Hostility manifests itself as hate, resentment, bitterness, revenge, or cruelty. Emptiness is experienced as loneliness, depression, discouragement, despair, or meaninglessness. These are all symptoms of death—the "living death" that comes from living according to the flesh.

What, then, is living with the mind set on the Spirit? It is placing God at the center of our lives. It means making Him the Lord of our careers and finances, our pleasure and fun, our fulfillment and joy, our ambitions and influence. We do not make it our goal in life to be powerful and famous; our goal is to serve God, and if He chooses to give us a position of influence so we can better serve Him, then we humbly accept it; if He chooses to use us in a place of anonymity, then we accept that position graciously and gratefully. We allow God to be the Lord of our lives.

The Body Is Dead

Paul goes on to explain why the mind set on the flesh produces death:

> The sinful mind is hostile to God. It does not submit to God's law, nor can it do so. (Romans 8:7)

Here is the crux of the problem: The mind set on the flesh brings death because it is hostile to God and it can't obey the law of God. As James 4:6 says, "God opposes the proud but gives grace to the humble." If we live only to please, gratify, advance, and exalt ourselves, then we are opposed to God and God is opposed to us!

God gives grace to the humble. He advances and exalts those who place their confidence in Him, not in the self.

The next few verses form a parenthetical statement in which Paul shows us the difference between a Christian who lives "according to the flesh" and a non-Christian who is "in the flesh." There is a great difference between these two states, and we need to carefully recognize that difference:

Those controlled by the sinful nature cannot please God. You, however, are controlled not by the sinful nature but by the Spirit, if the Spirit of God lives in you. And if anyone does not have the Spirit of Christ, he does not belong to Christ. (Romans 8:8–9)

Paul is literally saying:

Those who live in the flesh cannot please God. You, however, are not in the flesh but in the Spirit, if the Spirit of God lives in you. And if anyone does not have the Spirit of Christ, he does not belong to Christ. (Romans 8:8–9, author's translation)

Many Christians miss the plain sense of that passage. Paul says that if anyone does not have the Spirit of Christ, that person does not belong to Christ. You cannot tell if a person is a Christian by what that person does at one given moment. You might take a snapshot of a Christian at a moment of failure, and his actions might be indistinguishable from the actions of a non-Christian. You might catch that person committing an act of sin that looks exactly like the act of a non-Christian. But there is a difference, says Paul. The Christian has the Spirit of Christ in him (and that ultimately makes a huge difference in that person's overall behavior); the other does not have the Spirit, and he will continue in sin, and his sinful condition will predictably worsen.

You may know non-Christians who are kinder, more thoughtful, and more gracious than most Christians. You may say, "Look at those non-Christians! If their behavior is so gracious and pleasant, surely they must belong to God!" But that is not necessarily so. If anyone does not have the Spirit of Christ, he does not belong to Christ. Many people seem decent and pleasant when life is proceeding smoothly, without pressure or testing. The difference shows up in the ultimate tests of life. When the crunch comes, the one who does not have the Spirit will collapse; the one who has the Spirit will rise and ultimately conquer.

A Christian can live "according to the flesh" even though he is not "in the flesh." This is a crucial distinction.

Paul continues, giving us an important insight into the nature and function of the Holy Spirit in our lives:

> But if Christ is in you, your body is dead because of sin, yet your spirit is alive because of righteousness. And if the Spirit of him who raised Jesus from the dead is living in you, he who raised Christ from the dead will also give life to your mortal bodies through his Spirit, who lives in you. (Romans 8:10–11)

That is a profound statement. In verse 9, Paul referred to the Holy Spirit as "the Spirit of God" and "the Spirit of Christ." Here, Paul makes it clear that the Spirit is the means by which Jesus Christ Himself is in us. By means of the Spirit, Christ is in you. And if Christ is in you, your body is dead because of sin. Does that seem like a shocking statement to you?

The problem is, our bodies are yet unredeemed. As a consequence, our bodies are the source of the sin that troubles us so. That is why the body lusts; that is why our minds react with hate and hostility. Sin finds its source in the body. That is why our bodies grow old and die. The sin that pervades our unredeemed bodies is killing us.

If you are not a Christian, death is your entire story. You are still in Adam, you are not in Christ. Your body is dead, and so is your spirit. Everything about you is falling apart, and will continue to do so.

But if you are a Christian, only your unredeemed body is in death. Your spirit is alive because of the gift of righteousness. Christ has come in and you are linked with Him. As Paul so beautifully puts it, "Though outwardly we are wasting away, yet inwardly we are being renewed day by day" (see 2 Corinthians 4:16). The Spirit of God within us is stronger than the sin that is in our bodies. So even though our bodies are wasting away, the Spirit is increasingly giving us strength to control the body. That is the point Paul makes as he continues:

> And if the Spirit of him who raised Jesus from the dead is living in you, he who raised Christ from the dead will also give life to your mortal bodies through his Spirit, who lives in you. (Romans 8:11)

Some commentators say that this verse refers to the promise of the resurrection at the end of life, when God will make our bodies alive once more. But that is not what Paul is saying. He is talking about the Spirit in us, giving life to our mortal bodies in the here and now. He is telling us that, though the sin in our mortal bodies tempts us, our human spirit has been made alive in Jesus Christ, and the Spirit of God dwells in us. The Spirit gives us the strength to say "No!" to temptation.

We cannot reverse the processes of death—no one can. Our bodies are going to die. But we can refuse to let the members of our bodies become the instruments of sin. We can refuse, by the power of the Spirit, to let our eyes, hands, tongues, brains, and sexual organs be used for evil purposes.

Next, Paul explains tells us how to truly *live*:

> Therefore, brothers, we have an obligation—but it is not to the sinful nature, to live according to it. For if you live according to the sinful nature, you will die; but if by the Spirit you put to death the misdeeds of the body, you will live, because those who are led by the Spirit of God are sons of God. (Romans 8:12–14)

When Paul says, "If you live according to the sinful nature, you will die," he literally means that your present experience becomes an experience of waking death. You may *think* you are alive, but all your living is really a form of death.

But if you live by the Spirit and put to death the sins of the body, you will truly live. You will experience authentic *life*, with all that life means in terms of security, fulfillment, vitality, joy, and peace. Paul stresses that authentic living takes place only by means of the Holy Spirit, by believing what the Spirit of God has said. That is how you live by the Spirit—by faith. When you believe that the sins of the body can be controlled by the power of the Spirit, then you can say *no* to sin.

A person who lives by the Spirit can make money, have fun, gain fame, and find fulfillment in life, and through it all, God will be glorified. The righteousness which the Law demands is fulfilled in those who walk not after the flesh, but after the Spirit.

The Sons of God Among Men

In the next section, Paul uses a term he has not used before in this letter:

> . . . Those who are led by the Spirit of God are sons of God.
> For you did not receive a spirit that makes you a slave again
> to fear, but you received the Spirit of sonship. And by him
> we cry, "Abba, Father." (Romans 8:14–15)

First, we should clearly understand that "son" is a generic term that includes both sexes. All genuine believers in Christ, whether male or female, are "sons of God." The human spirit is sexless. What is true of the spirit is quite apart from what is true of the body.

Next, it is important to recognize that every human being is not automatically a "son of God." People often speak broadly of the human race as being "the children of God," and there is a real sense in which all human beings are the creatures of God, and therefore the offspring of God. But Paul is making a clear distinction here between people who are led by the Spirit of God and people who are not. Only those who are led by the Spirit of God are genuinely the "sons of God."

This is an important distinction. In your struggle against temptation and sin, you need to know that you are not a slave to sin. You are a son of the living God, with the power and authority to overcome evil and sin. At times, you may be temporarily overcome but you are never defeated. Sin cannot defeat you, because you are a son of God.

Paul goes on to say, "For you did not receive a spirit that makes you a slave again to fear, but you received the Spirit of sonship." Literally, Paul says "you received the Spirit of adoption." You became a son of God by being adopted into God's family.

You may be thinking, *What do you mean, I've been adopted into the family of God? I thought the Scriptures taught that I was born into the family of God when I was born again.* Actually both concepts are accurate: As a Christian, you were both adopted and born into the family of God. As Jesus said on another occasion, "With man this is impossible, but with God, all things are possible" (Matthew 19:26). You can't be both adopted and born into a human family, but you can in God's family.

God has taken us out of our natural state in Adam, and has legally made us sons of God. But He reminds us that we are in His family by adoption so that we might never take His grace for granted. This is not to say that we should feel insecure. We are as much a part of God's family as if we had originally been born into it. He will never disown us or reject us.

The next logical question is: "How can I be *sure* that I am a son of God?" Paul has been leading up to this question throughout this letter. This is the most important question that you and I must settle. Our joy and fulfillment in this life depend on it; so does our ultimate destiny in the next life. So the apostle Paul gives us three very practical tests—three levels of assurance—so that we can know for sure whether or not we are sons of God.

First, Paul says that if you are led by the Spirit of God, you are a son of God. To be led by the Spirit means that you are under the control of the Spirit. The evidence for this test is found in your own experience. As you look back over your life, do you see that your thoughts, behavior, responses, and goals have been submitted to God for His leadership? Is your life marked by a growing love for the Scriptures and an increasing understanding of the Scriptures? Is your life marked by a growing desire to spend time alone with God in prayer, both speaking to God and listening for His leading within your spirit? Do you see growing signs of victory over temptation and sin? Are you growing in your love for fellow Christians? Do you have a growing hunger for God and His righteousness? If you can see that you are being led by the Spirit of God, then you have passed the first test.

Second, Paul says that if you are led by the Spirit of God, you will have a growing assurance of your sonship before God. "You received the Spirit of sonship," he writes in verse 15. "And by him we cry, 'Abba, Father.'" Abba is the Aramaic word for *father*. By means of the Spirit, we experience an emotional response to God in which we become keenly aware of His fatherhood. In that awareness, our souls cry out within us, "Abba! Father!" Abba is a baby's word; it is like the sound a baby would make to his daddy: "Da-Da!" It is the word Jesus used in the Garden of Gethsemane when He begged the Father, His heavenly daddy, to let the terrible cup of the cross pass from Him.

The eminent Bible scholar, Dr. Alan McRae, tells the story of when his little son was learning to speak. His little boy came up to him with outstretched arms, saying, "Abba, Abba!" Dr. McRae turned to his wife and said, "Look! He's already learning to speak Aramaic!"

The closest and most trusting relationship you can have is a relationship with a loving father. It gives you a wonderfully secure feeling to experience the embrace of those strong, protective arms and to hear the sound of that deep, warm voice of love. Children crave the affection of a father's heart, the guidance of a father's wisdom, the security of a father's arms. If you have ever sensed the fatherhood of God and the brotherhood of Jesus, it is because the Spirit of God has awakened your heart to an awareness of your place in the family of God.

Third, Paul shares with us another level of assurance that we are the sons of God:

The Spirit himself testifies with our spirit that we are God's children. (Romans 8:16)

This is the deepest level of assurance. The Spirit of God testifies with our spirit—a testimony that goes far deeper than emotions. It is a deep conviction born of the Spirit of God Himself—an underlying awareness that makes it impossible to deny that we are part of God's family.

Looking back, I can see this deep conviction of the Spirit in my own life. I made a decision for Christ when I was about eleven years old. While attending a Methodist brush arbor meeting, I responded to the invitation, went forward, and received Jesus as my Lord and Savior. I had a wonderful time of fellowship with the Lord that summer and the next winter. There were times when I was overwhelmed with a sense of the reality of God in my life. I would sing hymns until tears came to my eyes. I felt called to preach, and I would go out to the pasture and preach to the cows. Those cows were a good audience—they never went to sleep on me.

The next fall, we moved to a small Montana town that didn't have a church. Gradually, because of a lack of Christian fellowship, I drifted away from that close relationship with God. I fell into behavior that I am ashamed of today. I developed some false attitudes toward God and the Scriptures. I ceased to believe in the inspiration of the Bible, and I argued against it during my high school and college years. I developed a reputation as a skeptic.

But during those seven lean years in my relationship with God, I found it impossible to deny God or turn my back on Him. Somehow I knew, deep down inside, that I still belonged to Him. I knew there were certain things I could not bring myself to do, even though I was tempted. I could not do them because I knew I had an unbreakable tie with God. That is the witness of the Spirit.

We may not always feel like genuine Christians—but feelings can betray us. The Holy Spirit, however, can never betray us. As 1 John 3:20 says, "If our heart condemn us, God is greater than our heart" (see 1 John 3:20 KJV). There is a witness, born of the Spirit, which we cannot shake or deny. When we genuinely and sincerely receive Jesus as Lord and Savior, God's Spirit bears witness with our spirit that we are God's own children.

And because we are God's own children, we are also God's heirs, as Paul explains:

> Now if we are children, then we are heirs—heirs of God and co-heirs with Christ, if indeed we share in his sufferings in order that we may also share in his glory. (Romans 8:17)

This verse introduces the climax of Paul's letter to the Romans. Here, Paul calls us "heirs of God and co-heirs with Christ," and he speaks of the glory that awaits us. He also connects that glory with the sufferings we are going through now—which ties this passage to Romans 5, where Paul encourages us to rejoice in our sufferings.

This is a good place to see where Paul has led us in this discussion. He tells us that we had our beginning in Adam, from whom we inherited a body of sin. Now, by faith in Christ, we are justified by faith. There is now no condemnation for us, because we are in the Spirit. If we are in the Spirit, we are led by the Spirit. If we are led by the Spirit, we are the sons of God. If we are the sons of God, we are heirs of God. All that God owns will be entrusted to us—what a staggering thought!

This is what we must remember when we face temptation and struggle with guilt. This is how God views us. This is who we are. If we remember who we are, then we will act according to who we are. When we do, we will find that there is power available to us—the power to say *no* to the flesh, the power to say *yes* to the Spirit, the power to walk in the way God created us to walk.

CHAPTER 10

IF GOD BE FOR US

Romans 8:18–39

In February 1947, a young missionary named Glenn Chambers waited to board a plane for Quito, Ecuador. Once he got aboard that plane, he would be on his way to fulfilling a dream of becoming a missionary broadcaster at Radio HCJB, "the Voice of the Andes."

While he waited at the Miami airport, he decided to dash off a quick letter to his mother—but he had no stationery with him. So he flipped through a magazine until he found a page with a lot of white space on it. He ripped out the page—an advertisement that had a single word WHY? printed in the middle of the page and some smaller print at the bottom.

Writing quickly, Glenn Chambers wrote down his thoughts in the white spaces of the page, including some words of affection and thanks to his mother for her prayerful support of him while he was in missionary training. Then he folded the page, sealed it in an envelope, purchased a stamp from a vending machine, and addressed it to his mother. As the boarding call sounded, he dropped the letter in a mailbox. Then he boarded the plane.

Hours later, as his plane flew over the rugged mountains of Colombia, something went terribly wrong. The plane crashed into a mountain peak, leaving no survivors.

Two days later, Glenn Chambers' grieving mother received the letter her son had written at the Miami airport just hours before his death. She opened the envelope and unfolded the paper. There, in huge black letters, was the one word that had been haunting her since she heard the news of her son's tragic death: *WHY?*

Though she was grateful to have this last message of love from her late son, that question—WHY?—continued to trouble her for days and weeks afterward. Glenn was so young, so talented, so full of promise, so eager to serve the Lord. Why did God allow him to die?

In time she came to a conclusion that gave her a measure of comfort amid her pain. She expressed that comfort in an interview. "I don't know why Glenn died," she said, "but I do know this: God is too kind to do anything cruel. God is too wise to make a mistake. And God is too deep to explain Himself."

That is the theme Paul brings us to in the closing verses of Romans 8—the theme of Christian suffering. Paul talked about rejoicing in suffering in Romans 5; then, in Romans 8, he returned to the subject of suffering when he wrote:

> Now if we are children, then we are heirs—heirs of God and
> co-heirs with Christ, if indeed we share in his sufferings in
> order that we may also share in his glory. (Romans 8:17)

In that verse, Paul links two concepts that we generally do not associate: suffering and glory. It seems a bit like pouring ketchup on ice cream, or like adding maple syrup to a tuna sandwich. The idea of linking suffering and glory, hurts and hallelujahs, makes no sense to the human mind. Yet we find suffering and glory joined together in almost every passage of Scripture that deals with the suffering of the Christian. For example, Paul links suffering and glory together in this passage:

> For our light and momentary troubles are achieving for us
> an eternal glory that far outweighs them all. (2 Corinthians
> 4:17)

Clearly, then, suffering and glory do go together in God's eternal plan. Our sufferings as believers are directly linked with the glory that is coming.

The Privilege of Suffering

God's Word continually presents both the sufferings and the glory as *privileges* that are given to us. As Paul has plainly stated:

For it has been granted to you on behalf of Christ not only to believe on him, but also to suffer for him. (Philippians 1:29)

We should not get the idea that we *earn* glory by our sufferings. The Bible does not teach that those who suffer the most earn the greatest degree of glory. We cannot earn God's glory. Rather, God's glory is given to us as part of our inheritance in Christ. It is a gift, a privilege granted by His grace. Suffering, too, is our inheritance in Christ. It is a privilege that we have to share in the sufferings that Jesus underwent on our behalf.

Paul underscores the theme of the latter part of Romans 8 in this verse:

I consider that our present sufferings are not worth comparing with the glory that will be revealed in us. (Romans 8:18)

The theme of this verse and verses that follow is the incomparable glory that awaits us as believers—a glory beyond description, greater than anything we can imagine. Throughout the Old Testament and into the New Testament runs a thread of hope, a rumor of approaching glory. This rumor speaks of a day that is coming when all the pain, heartache, and injustice of this world will be explained, justified, and absorbed into a time of incredible blessing and glory upon the earth. The whisper of this approaching glory actually increases in intensity throughout the Old Testament, as the New Testament approaches.

That whisper becomes a shout in the writings of Paul, where he makes this astounding statement that our present sufferings are not even worth comparing with the coming glory. That statement would ring hollow if not for one important fact: The man who made that statement was a man who had suffered greatly!

The apostle Paul endured beatings with leather whips, beatings with fists, and stonings in which he was practically buried beneath a pile of brick-sized rocks. He was chained and imprisoned for the "crime" of preaching the love of Christ. He was shipwrecked, starved, naked, and cold. And the man who endured all of this and more tells us, "Our present sufferings are not worth comparing with the glory that will be revealed in us."

I am not making light of your sufferings. I have seen people go through physical illness and injury or emotional distress that seems beyond human endurance. I would never minimize such suffering, nor would Paul. His message is not that our sufferings are trivial; his message is that the glory to come is so utterly beyond our comprehension that our sufferings will one day seem insignificant. C. S. Lewis gives us a glimpse of this coming glory in his book *The Weight of Glory*:

> The door on which we have been knocking all our lives will open at last. . . . We are to shine as the sun. We are to be given the Morning Star. I think I begin to see what it means. In one way, of course, God has given us the Morning Star already: you can go and enjoy the gift on many fine mornings if you get up early enough. What more, you may ask, do we want? Ah, but we want so much more— something the books on aesthetics take little notice of. But the poets and mythologies know all about it. We do not want merely to *see* beauty, though, God knows, even that is bounty enough. We want something else which can hardly be put into words—to be united with the beauty we see, to pass into it, to receive it into ourselves, to bathe in it, to become part of it.[1]

Those words fill us with a yearning to plunge into the incredible glory that God has prepared for those who love Him—yet even those words, as beautiful as they are, do not come close to doing justice to that glory. Even though we can't imagine it, we can accept on faith the fact that this glory will be ours to bathe in and enjoy, because we are heirs of God and co-heirs with Christ.

Meanwhile, we suffer. If you are a follower of Jesus Christ, you *will* suffer. It is a privilege, though it hardly feels like one. Yet we can endure the suffering, and even triumph in it, because we know the glory that is to follow.

Creation Suffers and Waits

Next, the apostle Paul offers two proofs that confirm this hope of glory. The first proof is that nature itself testifies to the coming glory. He explains it this way:

> The creation waits in eager expectation for the sons of God to be revealed. (Romans 8:19)

The original Greek word that is translated "eager expectation" offers an interesting insight. It is a word used to depict a man waiting for something to happen, craning his head eagerly forward. The Phillips translation captures this imagery when it renders this verse in these words: "The whole creation is on tiptoe to see the sons of God coming into their own."

Paul continues his discussion of his proof from nature:

> For the creation was subjected to frustration, not by its own choice, but by the will of the one who subjected it, in hope that the creation itself will be liberated from its bondage to decay and brought into the glorious freedom of the children of God. (Romans 8:20–21)

Paul says that creation awaits the coming climax of history because the history of creation is linked with the history of the human race. Creation fell when the human race fell in Adam. Not only did our whole race fall into the bondage of sin and death (as we have earlier seen in Romans), but the entire physical universe fell, too. It was human sin that put thorns on roses, and that put hostility and blood-thirst in the hearts of carnivorous beasts. The human world and the natural world (including the animal world) all testify to the fall of Adam. The universe has been subjected to frustration, bondage, and decay.

The phrase Paul uses, "its bondage to decay," is an accurate description of what scientists call "the second law of thermodynamics," or "the law of entropy." This law of physics states that everything is decaying; the universe is running down; order is becoming disarranged and disordered. Everything that lives eventually dies. All of this is the result of the fall of humanity, the sin of Adam.

One of my favorite vacation spots is the beautiful High Sierra region of California, where the great sequoia trees grow. Today, only a few small sequoia groves remain. Sequoias are the oldest living things in the world; a few are up to 3,000 years old, which means they were a thousand years old when Jesus was born.

Tragically, many of these great trees were destroyed a century ago by loggers. The first white men to discover these precious sequoia groves didn't realize how rare these trees had become and how old they were. All they saw was a forest of massive trees and the possibility of huge profits. So they cut down hundreds of those ancient trees and cut them into boards, only to discover that the wood of the sequoia tree is so soft that you can't build anything out of it.

If you go to those groves today, you will see a few remaining trees, still incredibly tall and majestic—but they are surrounded by blackened stumps and rotting logs. Hundreds of ancient trees are simply gone, wasted—and nobody made even a dime on all of that destruction. Most of the trees that were cut were never removed, but were simply left to rot.

That is what man does to God's creation wherever he goes. He despoils, ruins, and pollutes. This is just a small part of the overall bondage to decay that we see in the creation around us, the result of human sin and rebellion.

But Paul tells us that when humanity is finally delivered from decay, nature will be delivered as well. A time is coming when the sons of God will be revealed—when what God has made us in our spirits will be visible before the world. In that hour, nature will be set free from its bondage to decay. The universe will burst into bloom, demonstrating a beauty we cannot possibly imagine right now. The desert will blossom like the rose, the prophet says, and the lions will lie down with the lambs. No one will suffer any harm on God's holy mountain. Rivers will run free and clear and sweet again (see Isaiah 11:9; 35:1–10).

In anticipation of that day, Paul says, nature groans—but it groans in hope and eager expectation:

> We know that the whole creation has been groaning as in the pains of childbirth right up to the present time. (Romans 8:22)

Nature groans in the hope that the creation itself will be brought into the glorious freedom of the children of God. Someone once observed that all the sounds of nature are in a minor key. Listen to the sighing of the wind. Listen to the roaring of the tide. Even the warblings of songbirds are in a minor key. All nature sings—but it sings a song of bondage. Yet nature also sings a song of hope, looking forward to that day of the glory of the children of God.

Next, Paul tells us that our present experience confirms that this day of glory is coming:

> Not only so, but we ourselves, who have the firstfruits of the Spirit, groan inwardly as we wait eagerly for our adoption as sons, the redemption of our bodies. For in this hope we were saved. But hope that is seen is no hope at all. Who hopes for what he already has? But if we hope for what we do not yet have, we wait for it patiently. (Romans 8:23–25)

Here Paul says here that though we are redeemed in spirit, our bodies are not yet redeemed; as a result, we, too, are groaning. Here we see a contrast as well as a parallelism between our present groaning and our future glory. Nature groans; we groan. Yet this groaning will one day result in glory. Our present trials, as Paul says, "are achieving for us an eternal glory that far outweighs them all" (2 Corinthians 4:17). Do you think of suffering that way? Do you reflect on the fact that your sufferings are *working* for you? Every groan is a reminder of the promise of glory. As you reflect on this truth, it will transform your sufferings.

Our lives consist of groans. We groan because of the ravages of sin in our lives. We groan over lost opportunities. We groan over lost loved ones. We remember that, as Jesus approached the tomb of His friend Lazarus, He groaned in His spirit because of His grief; He groaned even though He knew that He would soon raise Lazarus from the dead. We groan in disappointment, in bereavement, in sorrow, in pain. Life consists of a great deal of groaning.

But Paul reminds us that in our groaning there is hope. Nature groans in expectation of future glory, and so should we. As believers, we are saved in hope, and by that hope we live. Paul tells us that hope is the earnest, confident expectation of something unseen: "But hope that is seen is no hope at all. Who hopes for what he already has? But if we hope for what we do not yet have, we wait for it patiently."

The waiting is made bearable by the fact that we already have the firstfruits of the Spirit. We know that the Spirit of God is able to give joy in the midst of heartache. He is able to give us peace in the midst of turmoil. This is what Paul calls the firstfruits of the Spirit—the power of God to make a heart calm and peaceful despite turbulent, painful circumstances.

Moreover, Paul says, the Spirit is alongside us as we wait for the coming glory:

In the same way, the Spirit helps us in our weakness. We do not know what we ought to pray for, but the Spirit

himself intercedes for us with groans that words cannot
express. And he who searches our hearts knows the mind
of the Spirit, because the Spirit intercedes for the saints in
accordance with God's will. (Romans 8:26–27)

Here Paul tells us that even the Holy Spirit is groaning. He
mentions three groanings in this passage: nature is groaning, we
are groaning, and the Spirit is groaning with words that cannot be
uttered. This passage helps us to understand prayer. Paul says that
we do not know what we ought pray for. We lack wisdom.

This does not mean (as I have actually heard some people
claim!) that since we don't know how to pray as we ought, and
since the Spirit is going to pray for us anyway, then we don't need
to pray. Such a claim contradicts everything else the Scriptures
have to say about prayer.

God wants us to pray, but at the same time, we have to
acknowledge that we often do not know how to pray adequately,
nor do we know what to pray for. At times when we feel an urging to pray, we sense that something is wrong, but we don't know
what we should pray for. So we lift our souls to God, expressing
our bewilderment and our lack of wisdom. We ask God through
His Spirit to make the request of the Father that ought to be made.
That prayer is always answered because the Spirit always prays in
agreement with the will of God the Father.

God Works for Good in All Things

Next, Paul tells us what happens when the Spirit intercedes
in prayer:

And we know that in all things God works for the good
of those who love him, who have been called according to
his purpose. (Romans 8:28)

This verse is often plucked out of context by well-meaning
believers. But it is important to see it within the overall flow of

Romans 8. This verse should never be interpreted separately from the previous two verses. Paul says that what the Spirit prays for is what happens. The Spirit prays according to the mind of God, and the Father answers by bringing into our lives the experiences we need.

This means that even the trials and tragedies that occur in our lives are the Father's answer to the prayer of the Spirit. All the events in our lives, the pleasant things and the painful, the ease and the pressures, happen according to the plan of God. The Spirit prays for us with groanings too deep for words; the Father answers those prayers and allows certain events to happen. Why? We can't fully know why, but we do know that God knows best. He permits those events because either we or someone close to us needs this to happen. God weaves these events into a perfect plan, so that good will come out of even the worst suffering and tragedy.

This verse never tells us that everything we experience will be good and pleasant. This verse says that, whether an occurrence is bad or good, pleasant or painful, it will ultimately work together for good if you are called by God to play a part in His eternal plan and purpose. This perspective makes a great difference for us as we await the coming glory! God does not guarantee that we will never suffer, but He does guarantee that our suffering brings us closer to the coming glory.

We are being prepared for something beyond our ability to imagine or comprehend. One of these days, when we reach the end of life (if not before!), we will step out of time into an incredible eternity of glory. It is the glory that Jesus Christ had before the beginning of the world, a glory that we will one day shall share with Him.

As we face our sufferings, we are blessed and comforted by the privilege of being considered worthy to suffer for the name of Jesus, so that we may share in His glory.

Five Steps to Glory

If there is one verse that serves as the high point of the book of Romans, it is certainly Romans 8:28: "And we know that in all things God works for the good of those who love him, who have been called according to his purpose." Note that important statement: As Christians, we are called according to God's purpose.

Think of it! You and I have a God-given purpose in life. What seems to be a meaningless jumble of events is actually a complex schematic diagram in the mind of God. Everything that happens is an interlocking piece of a vast puzzle. All the events in our lives, and the lives of people all around us, are moving toward a desired end, a grand and glorious conclusion.

God's purpose, as we saw in Romans 8:14, is to have many sons who will be led by the Spirit and who will love Him with all their hearts. That is why Jesus reminds us of God's great commandment: "'Love the Lord your God with all your heart and with all your soul and with all your mind.' This is the first and greatest commandment" (see Matthew 22:37–38).

To accomplish this purpose, God called the entire universe of time and space into existence. He spun the world in its orbit. He populated the world with human beings and permitted them to be tempted, to sin, and to fall. He sent His own beloved Son into this sin-ridden world. He accomplished the sacrifice of His Son on the cross, then effected the resurrection of the Son. Now, Paul says, God is intricately working all things together for the good of those who love Him, who have been called according to His purpose.

That is what life is all about. That is what the universe is all about. That is the meaning of it all. God's purpose is to have a race of people, His own children, who will love Him. Love is the aim of life.

Now, in the next verses, Paul looks back over the first eight chapters of his letter to the Romans, and he sums up in five brief steps the process that God takes:

For those God foreknew he also predestined to be conformed to the likeness of his Son, that he might be the firstborn among many brothers. And those he predestined, he

also called; those he called, he also justified; those he justified, he also glorified. (Romans 8:29–30)

Here are the five steps that God has taken in millions of lives,
stretching from eternity to eternity: (1) He foreknew; (2) He predestined; (3) He called; (4) He justified; and (5) He glorified.

At this point, it is important to note that Paul is not addressing
the question of why some people believe and some do not. That is
the problem of the doctrine of election, which we will examine in
Romans 9. In that chapter, Paul clearly states everything that can
possibly be understood about God's election of the believer. But
that is not what Paul is talking about in Romans 8:29–30. He is
simply describing the process God uses to bring people to a place
of belief. Let's look at these five steps in detail:

First step: God foreknew us. Some people take this to mean
that God foreknew that we would believe in Christ, so He chose
us to be part of His elect. But as I previously noted, this verse
does not deal with the doctrine of election. Paul says, "*those* God
foreknew," which is a reference to people, not events. In other
words, this verse does not refer to God foreknowing what would
happen in the future; it refers to God knowing that a great number
of individual human beings would one day be born. Before the
foundation of the earth, God foreknew that you and I and millions
of other believers would one day come into existence.

Second step: God predestined us. "Ah," you may say, "I know
what *that* means! God looked over all of humanity and said, 'That
one, that one, and that one will go to hell, and this one, this one,
and that one will go to heaven.'" That is not a biblical view of predestination. In God's Word, predestination has nothing to do with
who is going to hell. Predestination is concerned only with believers, not unbelievers. It simply tells us that God made a decision
ahead of time about the goal toward which He will move everyone
who believes in Jesus Christ. That goal is clearly stated in Romans
8:29: conformity to the character of Christ. Paul writes: "Those
God foreknew he also predestined to be conformed to the likeness

of his Son." Everything that happens in our lives is focused on that one supreme purpose.

God's primary concern is for the shaping and molding of our character. He knows that we can never develop the character He wants without times of trial and suffering. That is why suffering is an inevitable part of the picture. It helps us to remember that God's primary objective is not that we be happy all the time, but that we will be molded and shaped into the likeness—the character—of His Son, Jesus. He is designing our lives in such a way that we will be more loving, gracious, gentle, bold, courageous, and obedient, just as Jesus was. In the glorious future that awaits us, there will be many sons of God, many believers who reflect the qualities of Jesus Christ. And the firstborn among them will be Jesus Himself.

Third step: God called us. God drew us to Himself. Jesus said, "No one can come to me unless the Father has enabled him" (see John 6:65). We may think that we choose God, but the reality is that we only respond to the call of the Spirit of God. This is not to say that we have no choice in the matter; we certainly do. But it is also true that before we chose God, He drew us in ways that we do not even recognize.

Some, like the apostle Paul himself, are called by God in brilliant, dramatic, ground-shaking ways. Paul was a hardened, Christian-hating Pharisee named Saul when he heard the call of God. He was traveling on the road to Damascus on a mission to persecute Christians when the glory of the Lord shone upon him, more brilliant than the sun itself. He heard a loud voice say, "Saul, Saul, why do you persecute me? It is hard for you to kick against the goads" (see Acts 26:14). That last statement meant that Saul/Paul was fighting and struggling against God's will, which was goading him like a cattle prod, trying to move the stubborn Pharisee toward a relationship with Jesus Christ. When God called Paul, He did so with a shout and a light from heaven.

In most cases, however, the call of God is quiet and imperceptible, made up of hundreds, even thousands of seemingly insignificant events and unnoticed turning points. Dr. Harry Ironside used to tell about a young man who gave his testimony at an evangelistic meeting. This young man spoke about how God sought him and called him, loved him and delivered him, cleansed him and saved him—a tremendous testimony to the glory of God. After the meeting, an older man came up to the young man with a criticism.

"You know," the older man said, "I appreciate everything you said about what God did for you, but you didn't say anything about your part in it. Salvation is really part us and part God, and you should have mentioned your part."

"Oh," the younger man said, "You're right. I should have said what my part in my salvation was. You see, my part was to run away from God as hard as I could. His part was chasing after me, calling to me, until He finally caught me."

So it is with all who come to Christ. Can any of us truly say that we chose God without receiving any nudging, prodding, or calling from Him? Of course not. Those God foreknew, He also predestined; and those He predestined, He also called.

Fourth step: God justified us. Throughout the book of Romans, we have been exploring the meaning of justification. We know that justification is God's gift of righteousness and worth. Those who are justified are valuable in His sight. They are forgiven, cleansed, loved, and accepted in the sight of God. Justification is something we could never do ourselves; only Jesus could justify us through His sacrifice upon the cross.

Had God given us His righteousness apart from the atoning sacrifice of Jesus on the cross, He could have been accused of simply excusing and indulging sin. But the cross freed God to give us the gift of His righteousness while satisfying the debt of our sin.

Fifth step: God glorified us. Paul writes this in the past tense, as if our glorification has already taken place. And it is true: our glorification has already begun. Glorification is what Paul refers to as the revelation of the sons of God (see Romans 8:19). All of creation anticipates the moment when God suddenly pulls back the curtain on what He has been doing through the human race. The glorification is going on now, behind the scenes of history; on that day, the process will be complete, and the sons of God will stand out in glory.

Theologians call this process of glorification by another name: *sanctification.* This is the process by which the inner worth that God imparts to us gradually changes our attitudes, habits, speech, and conduct. As we become sanctified in Christ, people around us notice that we are changing, becoming more Christlike. The process of sanctification and glorification is inevitable in the life of an authentic believer. God has begun the process, and He is going to carry it through to completion at the day of the revelation of the sons of God.

No one is ever lost in the process. Those whom God foreknew before the foundation of the world, He also predestined to be changed into the likeness and character of His Son. Those He predestined, He called; those He called, He justified; those He justified, He glorified and sanctified. No one could ever be lost in that process, because God alone is responsible for it—and God does not make mistakes. For you and me, that process will involve pain and toil, sorrow and loss, stumbling and failure, falling and forgiveness, and even death—but incredible glory waits at the end of that road.

More Than Conquerors!

Next, Paul poses a series of questions:

> What, then, shall we say in response to this? If God is for us, who can be against us? He who did not spare his own Son, but gave him up for us all—how will he not also, along with him, graciously give us all things? (Romans 8:31–32)

These questions summon forth a response of love. That is what God truly wants from us: our unforced, unfeigned love. He wants to know that, whatever problems and heartaches we go through, we will love Him and we will receive His love. After all, God loved us so much that He did not spare His own son, but gave up His Son for us all. What can we do in response to such a great love but love Him endlessly in return?

If you truly grasp what God has done for you, your first response of love is to say, "If God is for me, who can be against me?" When we truly love God, our fear is removed. Yes, we will have sorrows to endure, problems to solve, enemies to face. But if God is for us, can any sorrow destroy us, any problem defeat us, any enemy conquer us? No, we are fearless! Even death holds no sting for us. If God is for us, victory is inevitable, glory is assured.

The psalmist understood this truth. "The LORD is my light and my salvation," he wrote. "Whom shall I fear? The LORD is the stronghold of my life—of whom shall I be afraid?" (Psalm 27:1). That is our message of comfort and courage whenever trouble or opposition come our way. "God loves me, and I love God. If God is for me, who can be against me?" So the first sign that we love God is that our fear is removed.

Next, Paul asks:

Who will bring any charge against those whom God has chosen? It is God who justifies. Who is he that condemns? Christ Jesus, who died—more than that, who was raised to life—is at the right hand of God and is also interceding for us. (Romans 8:33–34)

The second sign that we love God is that we are secure in God's completed work of salvation. God has justified us; who now condemns us? Justification means that no charge can be leveled against us, and no one can accuse us before God.

The devil, of course, is the accuser of the brethren. He will accuse us and make us feel condemned and unworthy. But Paul is saying to us, "Don't listen to the voice of the accuser. It is God who justifies you—so no one has any right to accuse you. Jesus Christ has already borne our guilt. So confess your sin to God, accept His forgiveness, and move on."

Paul's next question brings into focus the third sign that we love God:

> Who shall separate us from the love of Christ?
>
> (Romans 8:35)

Can any person, any being, any force, any power come between you and Jesus? Here, Paul confronts a question many Christians ask: "Is there any way I can lose my salvation? Once I come to Christ, is there anything that can remove me from Him?" So Paul poses this question, then says, in effect, "Let's look at all the possibilities." He writes:

> Shall trouble or hardship or persecution or famine or nakedness or danger or sword? As it is written:
>
> "For your sake we face death all day long;
>   we are considered as sheep to be slaughtered."
>
> (Romans 8:35–36)

Here, Paul considers the worst events that life can throw at us—the most gruesome horrors that anyone can face, from natural disasters to the persecution of oppressors to the bloody sword of war and terrorism. Even in the face of such frightening events, Paul's answer is:

> No, in all these things we are more than conquerors through him who loved us. (Romans 8:37)

These things cannot separate us from the love of Christ. Even amid the worst this world can do to us, Paul says, we are super-conquerors. Why? Because instead of dividing us from Christ, these forces actually move us closer to Him, they make us more dependent upon Him. The closer we cling to Jesus, the more victorious we shall be.

Next, Paul addresses the possibility of supernatural forces—angels, demons, powers and events that we can't even imagine. He writes:

> For I am convinced that neither death nor life, neither angels nor demons, neither the present nor the future, nor any powers, neither height nor depth, nor anything else in all creation, will be able to separate us from the love of God that is in Christ Jesus our Lord. (Romans 8:38–39)

Paul has left nothing out of that list. He has accounted for everything: demons and dark powers, black magic and angels, truth and error, death and life. He has even accounted for terrors that might come from some science-fictional alternate dimension, for when he writes, "nor anything else in all creation," his original wording is actually "nor anything even in a different creation"! Paul wanted to be sure that he omitted nothing. He has listed every conceivable (and inconceivable!) danger to our souls—and he firmly concludes that nothing, nothing, nothing can separate us from the love of God.

If that doesn't convince us, what will? More to the point, as Paul asked in verse 31, what, then, shall we say in response to this? How can we respond other than to love Him with all our hearts, souls, minds, and strength?

Christian poet and author Ruth Harms Calkin has expressed the grateful, loving heart of a believer who has truly grasped the truth of Romans 8. "Nothing can separate me from Your measureless love," she writes. "Pain can't, disappointment can't, anguish can't. Yesterday, today, tomorrow can't. The loss of my dearest love can't. Death can't. Life can't. Riots, war, insanity, unidentity, hunger, neurosis, disease—none of these things nor all of them heaped together can budge the fact that I am dearly loved, completely forgiven, and forever free through Jesus Christ Your beloved Son."

May that be our grateful prayer as we stand awestruck before God, amazed by His love.

CHAPTER 11

LET GOD BE GOD

Romans 9

A man once said to his friend, "I hear you fired your pastor. Why were you unhappy with him?"

"Well," said the other man, "he kept telling us we were going to hell."

"What does your new pastor say?"

"Our new pastor says we're going to hell, too. But we like him."

"Really? If your new pastor tells you you're going to hell, just like the old one, why do you like him?"

"Because," the man said, "when our old pastor said it, he sounded glad of it. When our new pastor says it, he sounds like it's breaking his heart."

In Romans 9, Paul talks about his Jewish brothers and their eternal fate. And when Paul speaks, we know that his heart is breaking.

At this point in our journey through Romans, we have arrived at a major division in the book. This division separates Roman 1–8 from Romans 9–11. The first eight chapters of Romans form a brilliantly logical explanation of God's plan of grace and redemption. The next three chapters deal with the same themes, but take the form of a vivid depiction of those themes, as dramatized in the story of the nation of Israel. Paul's purpose in Romans 9–11 is to make these themes more vividly real in our minds.

At the same time, we should remember that Paul is about to tackle some of the deepest and most difficult questions ever contemplated by the human mind. I'm reminded of a story in the Old

Testament, in which the prophet Jeremiah comes to God with a complaint about some false brethren who are plotting against him. Jeremiah expects God to give him a word of comfort; instead, the Lord tells Jeremiah,

> "If you have raced with men on foot
>   and they have worn you out,
>   how can you compete with horses?
> If you stumble in safe country,
>   how will you manage in the thickets by the Jordan?"
>   (Jeremiah 12:5)

In Romans 1–8, we have been racing with men on foot. We have been in a safe country. Now, as we enter Romans 9, we are about to run with horses. We are entering the thicket of Paul's discussion of God's plan of grace and redemption. In Romans 9, Paul squarely confronts all of the bitter and hostile accusations that people level against God.

One of the most perplexing issues of all is the apparent paradox involving human free will and God's election or predestination. In Romans 1–8, Paul clearly stated that we human beings are helpless and powerless to save ourselves. True, we are free to choose God or reject Him, and we must make a choice—yet Paul says that God also chose us! Our limited intellects can't grasp how those two concepts interlock—our freedom and God's sovereign election. So Paul turns the spotlight on Israel to demonstrate how it all works.

This is one of the most fascinating chapters in all of Scripture. If we grasp what Paul wrote in Romans 9, we will gain a profound insight into the mind of God.

Paul's Broken Heart

In this chapter, Paul lays out a sad and sobering story of the nation of Israel. The people of Israel viewed themselves as having an inside track with God, in view of their standing as God's chosen people. Truly, Israel enjoyed spiritual advantages that no other nation had.

Yet Paul begins this section by describing Israel as a nation that is far from God. He doesn't state this fact with accusation or anger, but with anguish. His opening words are painful to read:

> I speak the truth in Christ—I am not lying, my conscience confirms it in the Holy Spirit—I have great sorrow and unceasing anguish in my heart. For I could wish that I myself were cursed and cut off from Christ for the sake of my brothers, those of my own race, the people of Israel. (Romans 9:1–4)

To the Jews of his day, Paul undoubtedly seemed like an enemy, because of his teaching and preaching of Jesus as the promised Messiah. Paul's ministry stirred the antagonism of the Jews wherever he went. But Paul makes it clear that he is not an enemy of the Jewish people. He is a Jew himself, and he dearly loves his people. His heart breaks for them.

Paul does not come to the Jewish people shedding "crocodile tears," as people often do. You've probably heard someone say to you, "It hurts me to tell you this, and I only say it because I love you"—and then that person proceeds to shred you with glee! No, Paul's anguished sincerity is plain in every word, particularly when he says, "I could wish that I myself were cursed and cut off from Christ for the sake of my brothers."

Few experiences in life are more painful than to watch helplessly as someone you love drifts down a path of self-destruction. Paul's love for his people is so great that he would be willing to take their place in hell if it would bring them to Christ. Such a deep love for others is rare in all humanity.

Paul's love for his countrymen reminds us of the account of Moses in Exodus 32. After meeting with God on the mountain, Moses came down and found the people engaged in idolatry, dancing around a golden calf. Though he was angry with his people, Moses loved them, so he prayed to God, "Please forgive their sin—but if not, then blot me out of the book you have written" (see Exodus 32:32).

I am moved by the prayers of Paul and Moses. I have loved ones for whom I would gladly die if it would help them find eternal life in Jesus Christ—but it is hard to imagine wishing myself condemned in hell for the sake of another soul. Yet Paul and Moses would willingly place their own eternal souls on the altar for the people they love. Though Paul knows that such a thing is impossible, he sincerely would if he could.

So Romans 9 begins with a revelation of Paul's anguished heart for his people. What a lesson this is to us. As we approach others with the gospel, we must not approach them with denunciations and accusations. Instead, we must approach them as Paul approached his Jewish brothers—with a heart that is broken for the lost.

Eight Jewish Advantages

The reason for Paul's anguish comes into focus as he continues.

> Theirs is the adoption as sons; theirs the divine glory, the covenants, the receiving of the law, the temple worship and the promises. Theirs are the patriarchs, and from them is traced the human ancestry of Christ, who is God over all, forever praised! Amen. (Romans 9:4–5)

Here Paul lists advantages that the nation of Israel possessed.

First, the people of Israel were chosen by God to be His special people. "Theirs," writes Paul, "is the adoption as sons." God separated this nation from all the other nations. The people of Israel were the descendants of Abraham and the twelve sons of Jacob. God Himself said of them, "Israel is my firstborn son" (see Exodus 4:22). Gentiles have not always understood the special place Israel has in the mind and heart of God. Perhaps some non-Jewish people resent that special relationship. But there can be no question that God truly did choose the people of Israel. To this day, their position in history is different from that of any other nation in the world.

Second, God gave His glory to the Jews. Theirs, Paul writes, is "the divine glory," which is a reference to the Shekinah, the bright cloud that followed Israel through the wilderness and which later entered the Holy of Holies in the tabernacle. The Shekinah glory marked the presence of God Himself among His people. Centuries later, when King Solomon built the first Temple in Jerusalem, the cloud of glory filled the Holy of Holies and the people knew that God had come to live among them.

Third, the Jews also had the covenants, the remarkable agreements that God made with Abraham, Isaac, Jacob, Moses, and David. In the covenants, God committed Himself to do certain things for the nation of Israel, and He has never gone back on those covenants.

Fourth, the Jews had the Law. This was their dearest and greatest treasure, and it still is. In his novel *In the Beginning*, Chaim Potok describes how even contemporary orthodox Jews love the Torah, the scrolls of the Law. They have a service set aside in which the men of the congregation take the scrolls of the Law and dance with them. Afterwards, one of the young men of the congregation asks himself, "I wonder if the *Goyim* [the Gentiles, the non-Jews] ever feel this way about the Word of God?" God gave the Law to Moses, and to this day the Jews treasure and revere the Law.

Fifth, the Jews had the Temple worship. God told the Jewish people how they should conduct themselves when worshiping in the Temple. He told them the kinds of offerings to bring and the rituals to perform. The Jews had the Temple itself, one of the most beautiful structures ever built by men. The Temple was the glory of Israel. The Temple of Herod (successor to the Temple of Solomon) still stood in all its splendor at the time Paul wrote the letter to the Romans.

Sixth, the Jews had the promises. Those promises are still found in the pages of the Old Testament—promises of a time when the Jews would lead the nations of the world, promises of a coming

Messiah who would reign as the King over all the world, promises that Jerusalem would be the center of the earth. The government of God would flow from the city of Jerusalem, and extend across the entire planet. Those promises will one day be fulfilled by God.

Seventh, the Jews had the patriarchs—fathers of the nation, great leaders such as Abraham, Moses, Jacob, and David.

Eighth, the Jews had the Messiah. The ancestry of Jesus Christ is traced through the Jews. Though Jesus the Messiah belongs to the entire world, He came from the house of Israel.

Even though the Jews possessed these eight advantages, they opposed the early Christian movement. They could not see that Jesus was the Messiah that their own Scriptures had promised. That is why Paul says, "I have great sorrow and unceasing anguish in my heart . . . for the sake of my brothers, those of my own race, the people of Israel." Even at this early stage in the life of the first-century church, Paul could see an approaching crisis between the Jews and their Roman oppressors that would result in the destruction of Jerusalem as a judgment against the nation.

Paul was well acquainted with the dire predictions Jesus had made about the coming destruction of the Temple in Jerusalem and the terrible events that would fall upon the people of Israel (see Mark 13:1–2; Matthew 24:1–2; Luke 19:41–44; 21:5–6). Paul's sorrowing words suggest that he was aware that the Jewish people would soon be scattered among the nations of the world, and they would remain dispersed for centuries to come. Paul wrote the letter to the Romans in AD 62, and events were already moving to bring about a final confrontation. That confrontation would occur in AD 70, when the armies of Rome under General Titus would lay siege to Jerusalem, break through the city walls, level the Temple to the ground, take the Jewish people captive and disperse them among the nations—all in fulfillment of Jesus' prophecy.

Despite the tremendous advantages the Jewish people possessed, the nation of Israel had proved faithless and had overwhelmingly rejected the promised Messiah. Because of this, Paul's heart was broken for his fellow Jews.

Is God Unfair?

Having expressed his broken heart for his brother Jews, having listed eight advantages that the Jewish people possessed, Paul raises a question that goes to the heart of his theme in Romans 9: Did the failure and faithlessness of Israel mean that God had failed? Was God faithless? Did Israel's failure result from God's inability to save His people? Paul writes:

> It is not as though God's word had failed. For not all who are descended from Israel are Israel. Nor because they are his descendants are they all Abraham's children. (Romans 9:6–7)

Some people had probably suggested that it was God's fault that Israel had largely rejected Jesus the Messiah. If God had called the Jewish people, why didn't they respond? Paul answered this question with a strong statement of the faithfulness of God. His statement, however, is written in terms that cause many to struggle with his message.

I might as well warn you right now that you are probably going to question Paul's argument all the way through Romans 9. The concepts in this chapter trouble our thinking because, as God once said to the prophet Isaiah, "'For my thoughts are not your thoughts, neither are your ways my ways,' declares the LORD" (Isaiah 55:8). At times God acts in ways that we don't understand and don't agree with, and many of the truths of Romans 9 fall into this category.

Here Paul introduces three principles regarding how God carries out His plan in history. The first principle: The special privileges God grants to nations or individuals do not imply that those people will be saved. Salvation is never based on natural advantages or privileges.

Paul mentions two patriarchs in this passage, Jacob (Israel) and Abraham. (Israel is the name God gave Jacob after Jacob wrestled with His angel; Israel means "a prince with God.") When Paul writes, "For not all who are descended from Israel are Israel," he is saying that not all physical descendants of Jacob are spiritual descendants. So we must conclude that salvation is not based on natural advantages; salvation cannot be inherited like one's eye color or family name.

The second principle: God's salvation is always based on a divine promise. Paul writes:

> On the contrary, "It is through Isaac that your offspring will be reckoned." In other words, it is not the natural children who are God's children, but it is the children of the promise who are regarded as Abraham's offspring. For this was how the promise was stated: "At the appointed time I will return, and Sarah will have a son." (Romans 9:7–9)

Here Paul refers to Genesis 18, in which God said to Abraham and Sarah, "I will surely return to you about this time next year, and Sarah your wife will have a son" (Genesis 18:10). Sarah was well past the age of child-bearing, so to fulfill that promise, God had to act in a supernatural way.

Abraham already had another son, Ishmael, who was born to Hagar, Sarah's Egyptian servant. Sarah had urged Abraham to impregnate her servant as a means of hurrying God's promise along. When Ishmael was born, Abraham took the boy to God and said, in effect, "Here is my son. Will you fulfill your promises through him?" God's answer: "No, I won't. This is not the son I promised you. The promise must be fulfilled by the son I send you." This story illustrates futility of trying to force God into acting according to our timetable.

This is a biblical principle that never goes out of date. We often think we know better than God exactly how and when our prayers should be answered. We cannot force God's hand. He is faithful to His promises and to His own timetable.

The third principle is perhaps the most difficult of all for us to accept. Paul writes:

Not only that, but Rebekah's children had one and the same father, our father Isaac. Yet, before the twins were born or had done anything good or bad—in order that God's purpose in election might stand: not by works but by him who calls—she was told, "The older will serve the younger." Just as it is written: "Jacob I loved, but Esau I hated." (Romans 9:10–13)

The third principle is that salvation never takes any notice of whether we are "good" people or "bad" people. This may seem shocking, but it is true. It could be argued that Esau was a "better" person than his twin brother Jacob, yet God chose Jacob and passed over Esau.

The quotation "Jacob I loved, but Esau I hated" comes from Malachi 1:2–3. Many people struggle with these harsh-sounding words. All Paul is saying in quoting those words is that ancestry does not make a person righteous before God. The twin sons of Isaac and Rebekah had the same father, the same mother, and they were born minutes apart. Yet one is accepted by God and the other is not. Why? Because the choices they made were totally different.

Paul is saying that their choices—not their parentage—were the deciding factor in God's view of them. One of these twins, Jacob, was granted a place of honor in human history; the other, Esau, was not.

Why would God say "Esau I hated"? Is God harsh, cruel, and arbitrary? In reality, the more difficult statement to understand is, "Jacob I loved"! Jacob was a conniving, scheming man of weak character for most of his life. His brother Esau was a rugged individualist and seemingly the more admirable of the two. Looking over the course of their lives, it was Jacob who was brought to faith in God while Esau was not. Thus Jacob became a symbol of how God works in human lives.

It is important to realize that the word *hated* here is not as strong in the original language. It is our best attempt to capture a sense of the original Hebrew word that simply means "to love less." God is not saying that He despised Esau. Rather, God had chosen to make Jacob the father of the great nation which would bring forth the Messiah, the Redeemer of the world. Even so, God clearly had a regard for Esau, because He blessed Esau and made a great nation of Esau's descendants.

It may surprise you to learn that the final confrontation between Jacob and Esau took place in the New Testament, when Jesus stood before Herod the king, just hours before the crucifixion. Herod was an Idumean, or Edomite, a descendant of Esau. Jesus was a descendant of Jacob through King David. There, standing face-to-face, were Jacob and Esau! Herod had nothing but contempt for the King of the Jews, and Jesus would not open His mouth in the presence of Herod. This is God's strange and mysterious way of dealing with humanity. His ways are not our ways, and His thoughts are not our thoughts.

Paul is teaching that God has a sovereign, elective prerogative that He exercises on His own terms: (1) Salvation is never based on natural advantages. (2) Salvation is always based on God's promise. (3) Salvation is never based on whether we are "good" or "bad." How do you react to those three terms of God's sovereign election? Perhaps something within you wants to cry out, "That's unfair!"

If that is your reaction, you are not alone. When I have preached sermons on this passage, I have seen people walk out in disgust. It is normal to feel that God is unfair when we look at this passage. His ways are not our ways.

At the same time, we know that God never acts in a way that is inconsistent with His character. And what is God's character like? As we have already seen, the God of the Bible is a God who did not spare His own son, but gave Jesus over as a sacrifice for our sin. Our God is a God of love. So how can we reconcile the love of God with the apparent unfairness of God that we have seen so far in Romans 9? Let's continue our journey through the thicket of this chapter and see if we can make sense of these strange and mysterious actions of God.

No Checks or Balances

There was a time when almost everyone on earth believed that the earth was flat. It was a comfortable, safe theory—but believing it did not make it true. As evidence began to accumulate that the earth was round, not flat, people got very upset—and religious people were the most upset of all! They believed that the Bible taught that the earth was flat. They could even quote Scripture passages that seemed to substantiate this "fact." It took many years and much conflict for religious people to realize that the earth was round and the Scriptures, in fact, affirm this to be true.

I think many people have a similar problem with Romans 9. They have grown up with a "flat," two-dimensional view of God. It is comfortable and safe to view God in a certain way, to fit God into a neat little theological box. But Paul, in Romans 9, comes along and kicks the sides out of our box. He tells us that God is infinitely greater than our theological categories. If we want to understand the reality of God, we must set aside our preconceived notions.

The central question of Romans is this: "What is the basis of God's election of the believer?" We know that God does not choose us on the basis of our good works or natural advantages. So what is the basis of God's election?

Paul's answer may shock you: The basis of God's election is simply His sovereign right to choose. That's it: *God has a right to choose.* Paul writes:

> What then shall we say? Is God unjust? Not at all! For he says to Moses,
>
> > "I will have mercy on whom I have mercy,
> >   and I will have compassion on whom I have
> >   compassion."
>
> It does not, therefore, depend on man's desire or effort, but on God's mercy. For the Scripture says to Pharaoh: "I raised you up for this very purpose, that I might display my power

in you and that my name might be proclaimed in all the earth." Therefore God has mercy on whom he wants to have mercy, and he hardens whom he wants to harden. (Romans 9:14–18)

That statement could not be more clear: God chooses whom He chooses.

This may well be the one truth about God that people dislike the most. We rebel at the notion of God as a completely sovereign being. We do not like it that He is not accountable to anyone for His actions. He is sovereign, and His sovereignty seems tantamount to tyranny. We don't trust anyone with absolute power. That is why we have checks and balances in the U.S. Constitution—and it offends us that there are no checks and balances on God.

In order to understand God and trust His love for us, we must do something that is very hard for us to do: We must rid ourselves of the idea that God's sovereignty is a threat to us. We must accept the fact that God can be trusted with absolute sovereignty. In fact, the sovereignty of God is our only hope!

Paul reminds us that God declares His own sovereignty. As God told Moses, "I will have mercy on whom I will have mercy, and I will have compassion on whom I will have compassion" (Exodus 33:19). Moses is an excellent example of God's sovereign right to choose. Who was Moses that God should bless him and use him? Moses was a murderer; on one occasion, in a fit of temper, he had killed a man. He fled to the desert, a fugitive from justice for forty years. But God in His sovereignty selected Moses to be His messenger. God made Moses famous throughout history and gave him supernatural authority over the king of Egypt.

Why did God choose Moses? Because He had the sovereign right to do so. That is the only explanation we are given.

God also demonstrated His sovereignty in regard to Pharaoh, the king of Egypt. God took a man who was no better than Moses and gave him power over all of Egypt. God often places power in the hands of the most base and evil men. Why? Because He chooses to do so. Moreover, God allowed Pharaoh to do what all men do by nature—resist God. Pharaoh hardened his heart so that God might demonstrate His power and authority before the world.

That aspect of God bothers many people. It almost seems as if God is a braggart and feels compelled to show the world how great He is. When we see such tendencies in the people around us, we are repelled.

The problem is that we think of God as no more than a human being on a grand scale. We attribute human motives and human frailties to God. We fail to account for the fact that His ways are not our ways, nor are His thoughts our thoughts. We forget that God is above all a God of love, and everything He does is necessary to the welfare of His beloved creatures. The more we understand His goodness and greatness, the richer our lives will be.

God's Sovereignty—Our Only Hope

Having concluded that God is sovereign, Paul anticipates our objection:

> One of you will say to me: "Then why does God still blame us? For who resists his will?" (Romans 9:19)

That brief statement encompasses all the bitter accusations that people bring against God: "God is responsible for all human evil. If God is sovereign, then He is ultimately to blame, not us!" This accusation has taken many forms through history, but it all boils down to this: Humanity always seeks to shift the blame for human evil to God.

People frame the argument this way: "God uses human beings any way He chooses, and human beings cannot resist Him. God used Pharaoh, and Pharaoh was like a marionette in the hands of God. So God uses people to do evil acts, then He turns around and blames them for the evil He made them do! It's not right to make someone do something evil, then punish them for it! God is unjust!"

How do you answer such a charge? Paul responds with a four-point reply, beginning with point number one:

But who are you, O man, to talk back to God? "Shall what
is formed say to him who formed it, 'Why did you make me
like this?'" (Romans 9:20)

Paul's first point is this: "Man is a finite and limited creature;
God is the infinite and limitless Creator. Man is frail, short-lived,
and error-prone; God is all-powerful, eternal, and faultless. How
does a mere man dare to challenge the wisdom and judgment of
the infinite God? Our reasoning and logic are hopelessly inad-
equate, because there are mysteries to God and His creation that
we can't begin to understand." Paul continues:

Does not the potter have the right to make out of the same
lump of clay some pottery for noble purposes and some for
common use? (Romans 9:21).

Paul's second point is this: Even human beings exercise sovereignty over their own creations. Nobody blames the potter for
making sovereign choices with regard to a lump of clay. Nobody
says, "What an unfair potter! He divides the lump of clay and
makes a beautiful ornamental vase with one lump and a lowly
chamber pot with the other! What about the rights of the clay?"
The question is utterly absurd.

You might say, "That's a bad analogy! Human beings are not
clay!" But we could extend the analogy to living things, to plants
and animals. We could replace the potter with a gardener who
sovereignly selects and places plants, uproots weeds, slaughters
bugs with pesticides, and so forth. Or we could replace the potter with a poultry farmer who raises chickens or turkeys, who
slaughters birds without any concern for their rights and feelings,
converting living creatures into a plastic-wrapped commodity in
a supermarket. The fact remains: Human beings exercise this kind
of sovereignty all the time. If we feel entitled to do so as human
beings, how can we deny the sovereignty of the One who created
the universe?

But Paul is not finished. He continues his argument:

> What if God, choosing to show his wrath and make his power known, bore with great patience the objects of his wrath—prepared for destruction? What if he did this to make the riches of his glory known to the objects of his mercy, whom he prepared in advance for glory—even us, whom he also called, not only from the Jews but also from the Gentiles? As he says in Hosea:

> "I will call them 'my people' who are not my people;
> and I will call her 'my loved one' who is not my
> loved one,"

and,

> "It will happen that in the very place
> where it was said to them,
> 'You are not my people,'
> they will be called 'sons of the living God.'"

Isaiah cries out concerning Israel:

> "Though the number of the Israelites
> be like the sand by the sea,
> only the remnant will be saved.
> For the LORD will carry out
> his sentence on earth with speed and finality."
>
> (Romans 9:22–28)

Paul's third point is this: God may have purposes and objectives that we cannot see. And doesn't He have the right to keep His own counsel regarding His plans? What if one of His objectives is not only to display His power and wrath by allowing human beings to oppose Him, but also to display His patience? God has listened to all the slander that people speak against Him, and He patiently puts up with humanity. Perhaps His patience is designed to make the riches of His mercy known so that the fairness and righteousness of His wrath will be made evident.

Paul suggests that without the display of God's wrath, no Gentiles would ever be saved, only an elect remnant of Israel. Because God's wrath has been demonstrated, many Gentiles have turned to God through Jesus Christ, fulfilling the prophecy of Hosea that those to whom God says, "You are not my people," will be called "sons of the living God."

To put it bluntly, for some to be saved, others must be lost. This is a mystery, and I don't claim to understand it. Someday in eternity, I'm sure it will all make sense, but for now, it remains a mystery that must be accepted by faith alone.

Next, Paul makes his final argument:

> It is just as Isaiah said previously:
> "Unless the Lord Almighty had left us descendants,
> we would have become like Sodom,
> we would have been like Gomorrah." (Romans 9:29)

Paul's fourth point is this: If God had not chosen to call us to Himself by an elective decree, none of us would have been saved. The problem is that we look at the whole issue of election from a faulty premise. We begin with the false assumption that all human beings come from a neutral position. From this neutral position, we choose either good or evil—but that is not the case.

The truth is, we were *born* lost. Our starting position was never neutral. We were lost in Adam before we drew our first breath. We start life in a state of rebellion against God. We do not have the slightest hope of salvation unless God makes a sovereign decision to call us. If God is not sovereign, then we are lost indeed—as lost as Sodom and Gomorrah.

Having visited the sites where Sodom and Gomorrah once stood, I can tell you that this is the perfect metaphor to describe what utter desolation is like. In that region, nothing lives, nothing grows. Only by the sovereign will of God have you and I escaped such a fate!

As Paul told us earlier in Romans, "There is no one righteous, not even one; there is no one who understands, no one who seeks God." Now, perhaps, it becomes clear that God is in no way guilty of shutting anyone out without a chance. His sovereign grace is necessary to our salvation. Without His grace, no one would ever be saved. The entire human race would be lost.

Salvation is God's sovereign choice—and that is where we must leave the matter. Our limited understanding can penetrate no further than this into the Mystery—at least for now.

Jesus, the Stumbling Stone

In the final verses of Romans 9, Paul anticipates one last question that is on our minds: If God is sovereign and chooses whomever He will, how can we tell if we are chosen or not? Here is Paul's reply:

> What then shall we say? That the Gentiles, who did not pursue righteousness, have obtained it, a righteousness that is by faith; but Israel, who pursued a law of righteousness, has not attained it. Why not? Because they pursued it not by faith but as if it were by works. They stumbled over the "stumbling stone." As it is written:

> "See, I lay in Zion a stone that causes men to stumble and a rock that makes them fall, and the one who trusts in him will never be put to shame." (Romans 9:30–33)

How can you tell if you are chosen or not? The answer is astonishingly simple: You can tell by what you do with Jesus. God has placed a stone in the midst of human history. The name of that stone is Jesus. When you encounter that stone, you are confronted with a choice: You can stumble on it—or you can stand on it. There is no other alternative. What will you do with Jesus?

If you stumble over Jesus, then clearly you have not been chosen. But if you stand on Jesus, you are among the elect of God. When you choose Jesus, then you prove that God has chosen you.

Jesus is the crisis of humanity. What will you do with Him? Jesus Himself put it this way: "No one can come to me unless the Father who sent me draws him, and I will raise him up at the last day" (John 6:44). He also said, "All that the Father gives me will come to me, and whoever comes to me I will never drive away" (John 6:37).

If you want to make sure that God has called and elected you, then all you have to do is simply respond to Jesus, place your trust in Him, and receive Him into your life. As you do so, give thanks to God the Father who called you and rescued you by His sovereign love and mercy.

CHAPTER 12

HOW TO BE SAVED

Romans 10

I once sat in a crowded movie theater, waiting for the picture to begin. A stranger stood in the aisle, pointing to the empty seat next to me. "Excuse me," he said, "is that seat saved?"

"No," I replied cheerily, "but I am."

He gulped, then departed to find a seat on the other side of the aisle.

There is something about the word *saved* that threatens and upsets people. Yet, when you open the Scriptures, you find that this word is simply unavoidable. The reason Christians have to talk about being *saved* is that so many people in the human race are *lost*. The Bible clearly teaches that the human race is a lost race, and the only hope for lost people is that they be saved.

"I am the gate," Jesus said. "Whoever enters through me will be *saved*" (John 10:9, italics added). His disciple, Peter, agrees. "Salvation is found in no one else," Peter said, "for there is no other name under heaven given to men by which we must be *saved*" (Acts 4:12, italics added). To which Paul adds, "For the message of the cross is foolishness to those who are perishing, but to us who are being *saved* it is the power of God" (1 Corinthians 1:18, italics added).

We can do nothing to save ourselves. Salvation is 100 percent grace, zero percent human effort. As Paul wrote, "For it is by grace you have been saved, through faith—and this not from yourselves, it is the gift of God—not by works, so that no one can boast" (Ephesians 2:8–9). The grace of God reaches down and lifts us out of our lostness. Christ did not die to improve us or fix us or make us better people; He died to *save* us. No word better describes what God has done for us through His Son, Jesus Christ.

As we come to Romans 10, Paul confronts the most fundamental and essential question of the Christian faith: How can we be saved?

Christ Is the End of the Law

In Romans 10, Paul again uses Israel as a model for understanding how God's plan works. Paul begins by addressing the question of why some people who have little knowledge of God are saved while others who have much religious knowledge are not saved. Part of the answer is found in Romans 9, in which Paul delved into the mystery of God's sovereign choice to elect whomever He will. God has the sovereign right to choose some and not choose others.

Now, in chapter 10, Paul looks at this same issue from the other side. He turns from God's sovereignty to human responsibility. While it is true that God chooses and calls people to Himself, it is also true that no one comes to God unless he or she responds to God's call.

To the finite human mind, this seems like a contradiction. We cannot resolve this mystery because our level of understanding is too limited. We cannot grasp even a fraction of the workings and purposes of God. So even though God's sovereignty seems to contradict human free will from our perspective, from God's perspective there is no contradiction. God calls human beings by an elective decree that is irresistible—yet human beings respond to His call by a decision of their own free will.

Here is how Paul introduces us to this fascinating and profound mystery:

> Brothers, my heart's desire and prayer to God for the Israelites is that they may be saved. For I can testify about them that they are zealous for God, but their zeal is not based on knowledge. Since they did not know the righteousness

that comes from God and sought to establish their own, they did not submit to God's righteousness. (Romans 10:1–3)

It is important to note that, despite Paul's profound conviction that God saves whomever He will according to His sovereign elective choice, Paul still prays and yearns over his fellow Jews. The fact that God makes sovereign choices does not cancel out the need for prayer and evangelism. We should never use the sovereignty of God as an excuse for inaction, as if to say, "God will choose whom He will, so there's no point in praying or witnessing." God sovereignly calls whomever He will—but He usually issues that call through the preaching, witnessing, and prayers of Christians.

In this passage, Paul also takes note of the zeal of the Jewish people. "I can testify about them," he says, "that they are zealous for God." Indeed they are. Orthodox Jews take God seriously. The Jewish way of life is built around God. Gentiles—non-Jewish people—certainly have religious experiences and religious thoughts, but most Gentiles keep God on the periphery of life. To most non-Jewish people, God is confined to one small category of life labeled "religion." But for the serious Jew, God is the center of everything.

Yet, as Paul goes on to note, the Jews, in spite of all their zeal, fail to find peace and forgiveness. They are zealous for God, Paul says, but their zeal is not based on knowledge. They do not know the righteousness that comes from God—that is, the atoning sacrifice of Jesus on the cross. So they have attempted to establish their own righteousness, based on religion, rituals, and works. In the process, they have missed the free gift of God, which is of faith, not of works.

The problem with the Jews, Paul says, is that they try to obey the Law of Moses. They try to be "good enough" to please God, which is humanly impossible. There are many people today, both Jews and Gentiles, who live the same way. Such zeal, no matter how well-intentioned, is ultimately futile. Anyone who seeks to come before God on the basis of good works and religious effort is doomed to failure.

Paul goes on to say:

Christ is the end of the law so that there may be righteousness for everyone who believes. (Romans 10:4)

Christ is the end of the Law—but that does *not* mean that
Christ has abolished the Law. The purpose of the Law is to make
us aware of our shortcomings. If we didn't have a standard to live
up to, we would not realize how lost we are. The Law makes us
aware of the sin that is destroying us, and that awareness drives
us to Christ.

But once we have turned to Christ and have received the righteousness from God, what good is the Law? It can do nothing more
for us. That is why Christ is the end of the Law. Once we are in
Christ, we have reached the destination that the Law was designed
to move us toward. It is as if the Law were a road and Christ is at the
end of that road. That is the sense in which He is the end of the Law.

Next, Paul applies his relentless logic, quoting Moses to prove
what the Law is for:

Moses describes in this way the righteousness that is by
the law: "The man who does these things will live by them."
(Romans 10:5)

Paul is quoting the words of Moses from Leviticus 18:5. There
Moses said that those who keep the Ten Commandments would
be blessed by God. When you read the Ten Commandments, you
can't help noticing that they seem so simple that it would be easy
to obey them. Yet when you try to put those ten simple rules into
practice, you soon discover a rebellious spirit welling up inside
you. That rebellion keeps us from following its simple decrees.

Moses said that the person who keeps the Law will live—but
no one can keep the Law! As we have seen throughout Romans,
the Law doesn't help us to live a righteous life. It merely reveals
the evil in our lives.

If You Confess "Jesus Is Lord"

Now Paul goes on to quote Moses again, this time from Deuteronomy 30:14, and he contrasts the way of the Law against the way of faith:

> But the righteousness that is by faith says, "Do not say in your heart, 'Who will ascend into heaven?'" (that is, to bring Christ down), or "'Who will descend into the deep?'" (that is, to bring Christ up from the dead). But what does it say? "The word is near you; it is in your mouth and in your heart," that is, the word of faith we are proclaiming. (Romans 10:6–8)

This is crucial to understand. Paul is saying that Moses taught salvation by grace through faith, just as much as Paul taught. Moses knew that the Law would not work to make people righteous. Even as Moses was bringing the Ten Commandments down from the mountain, the people were busily breaking all ten of them! So Moses taught that God had provided a true way of deliverance and salvation, so the people could be made righteous in God's sight even though they had failed to keep the Law.

Paul tells us that Moses knew that God would lay the foundation for salvation through a coming Savior. God had revealed to Moses that Christ would one day come down from heaven, and that He would be raised from the dead. The apostle wants us to understand that God planned all along for people to be saved through faith in Christ.

The death and resurrection of Jesus was not a change in the way God saved human beings. Throughout the Old Testament, salvation was *always* by grace through faith in a Savior who was yet to come. His sacrifice was symbolically depicted in the sacrifices of innocent animals. The arrival of Jesus in human history was the fulfillment of the basis on which God had already been saving people for centuries.

The Law never saved anyone. Animal sacrifices never saved anyone. Only faith in the atoning sacrifice of Jesus saves; in Old

Testament times, that faith was directed toward a future event; in New Testament times, that faith was directed toward an event that was already accomplished on the cross. The common denominator between Old Testament salvation and New Testament salvation is *faith in Jesus.*

Paul wants us to understand that faith in Jesus has always been God's plan for salvation. That is why Paul quotes these words of Moses: "The word is near you; it is in your mouth and in your heart." The mouth represents our intellectual understanding of God's program of salvation, expressed in words. The heart represents our inner being—the will, the spirit deep within us, which understands at a deep level the basis on which God saves. To make sure no one misses his point, Paul adds these clear words:

> That if you confess with your mouth, "Jesus is Lord," and believe in your heart that God raised him from the dead, you will be saved. For it is with your heart that you believe and are justified, and it is with your mouth that you confess and are saved. (Romans 10:9–10)

It could not be stated more clearly than that. This is a simple, straightforward explanation of how to be saved. Salvation begins, Paul says, with the confession of the mouth that "Jesus is Lord." That doesn't mean you have to stand up in a public place and make an announcement in order to be saved. There is certainly nothing wrong with doing so, but that is not what Paul is saying here. He is using the mouth as a symbol of the conscious acknowledgment of what we believe. It means that we recognize that Jesus has the right to lordship over our lives. Prior to this point, we have been lord of our own lives, but now we have decided to let Jesus take over the throne of our lives.

Jesus is Lord of our past, forgiving our sins. He is Lord of our present, indwelling us and controlling every aspect of our lives. He is Lord of our future, leading us into our approaching glory. He is the Lord of life, the Lord of death, the Lord over all things.

You cannot read the book of Acts without recognizing that the basic creed of the early Christians was "Jesus is Lord." When Peter preached on the day of Pentecost, his theme was, "Jesus is Lord." Paul tells us here that Jesus is Lord.

If you believe in your heart that He is risen and you are ready to say, "Jesus is my Lord," then God will act. At that moment, you are instantly removed from among the lost and you take your place among the saved. Your sins are forgiven, you have righteous standing before God, and you have the Holy Spirit living within you. You have the power of Jesus Himself available to you—power over evil, over the flesh, over Satan himself. That is what happens when you confess with your mouth that Jesus is Lord, and when you believe in your heart that God raised Him from the dead.

There is no place in Scripture that says we should receive Jesus as our *Savior*. Throughout Scripture, we are told to believe in Him as *Lord*. When you believe in Him as Lord, He becomes your Savior. But you don't accept Christ as a Savior apart from accepting Him as Lord.

Is Jesus the Lord of your life? Have you enthroned Him in your heart? The moment you do is the moment your redemption begins, as Paul confirms in these verses:

As the Scripture says, "Anyone who trusts in him will never be put to shame." For there is no difference between Jew and Gentile—the same Lord is Lord of all and richly blesses all who call on him, for, "Everyone who calls on the name of the Lord will be saved." (Romans 10:11–13)

The statement, "Anyone who trusts in him will never be put to shame," is a quotation from Isaiah 28:16, showing that it is not on the basis of works but on the basis of faith—trust in God—that salvation takes place. The next quotation, "Everyone who calls on the name of the Lord will be saved," is from Joel 2:32, and this Scripture quotation makes the same point. Paul is painstakingly making his case that the doctrine of salvation by grace through faith is not a new concept, but is the same doctrine that the Scriptures have taught for thousands of years.

Five Steps to Salvation

The rest of Romans 10 deals with one of the most frequently asked questions about the gospel. We especially hear this question from non-Christians, who often raise it as an objection. But it is also a question that troubles many sincere believers. The question is this: "What happens to all the people who have never heard about Jesus? Isn't it unfair for God to condemn someone who has never even heard of Jesus?" Paul writes:

> "Everyone who calls on the name of the Lord will be saved."
> How, then, can they call on the one they have not believed in? And how can they believe in the one of whom they have not heard? And how can they hear without someone preaching to them? And how can they preach unless they are sent? As it is written, "How beautiful are the feet of those who bring good news!" (Romans 10:13–15)

Here, Paul outlines five steps that enable people to be saved, and he presents them in reverse order. In verse 13, he quotes the prophet Joel: "Everyone who calls on the name of the Lord will be saved." That is the fifth and final step: In order to be saved, people must see their need and call upon the name of Jesus the Lord.

Then, in verse 14, Paul asks: "How, then, can they call on the one they have not believed in?" That is the fourth step: Belief. The heart must be involved—that place of inner awareness and conviction.

Then Paul asks, "And how can they believe in the one of whom they have not heard?" That is the third step: Hearing. Before belief takes place, a person must hear the truth of the gospel.

Then Paul asks, "And how can they hear without someone preaching to them?" The second step: Preaching. Someone must take the gospel to people so they will hear and believe.

Then Paul asks, "And how can they preach unless they are sent?" The first step: Sending. Preachers, teachers, evangelists, and everyday Christians must be sent out into the world, equipped to share the gospel wherever they go.

So, in chronological order, these are the steps to bringing people to salvation: (1) We send out preachers. (2) Those preachers spread the gospel. (3) People hear the gospel. (4) They believe on the basis of what they hear. (5) They call upon the name of the Lord and are saved.

Dr. Lewis Sperry Chafer, who was one of my teachers at Dallas Seminary, told us, "Remember, you have not preached the gospel until you have given people something to believe—something God has done that their minds can grasp, something they can use as a basis for understanding what God has offered to them—their salvation." In other words, we should not present Christianity as a feeling, an experience, or a philosophical idea. The message of Christianity is a fact of history, an objective truth.

The Christian message is that Jesus was born as a baby in Bethlehem; that He lived a sinless life as the Son of God; that He was crucified on a cross outside of Jerusalem; and that He rose from a tomb—an actual, historical resurrection. The Christian faith is grounded in events that cannot be explained away. Those historical events have a profound meaning for every human life, a meaning that Jesus Himself summed up in these words: "For God so loved the world that he gave his one and only Son, that whoever believes in him shall not perish but have eternal life" (John 3:16).

That message has transformed millions of lives down through the centuries. It is a message that demands a messenger—indeed, every Christian should be a messenger, carrying this message around the neighborhood, the office, the mall, the playground, the car pool, everywhere we go. We must ask God to give us opportunities to share that message with the people all around us. As Jesus said, "The harvest is plentiful, but the workers are few. Ask the Lord of the harvest, therefore, to send out workers into his harvest field" (Luke 10:2). It is God who sends messengers out into the world. He calls men and women and sends them to the far reaches of the earth with the message of salvation.

Paul quotes Isaiah 52:7, saying, "How beautiful are the feet of those who bring good news!" Those who allow God to use them to share the gospel of salvation, healing, and deliverance, are beautiful to God. And there are usually many people with beautiful feet who participate in the process of bringing one person to a place of believing in Jesus.

The conversion process is much like turning on a light. You flick the switch on the wall and the light goes on. It seems so simple—yet behind that simple act of turning on a light, there is a very complicated process. There is power house many miles away, generating power from coal or nuclear fuel or water passing through turbines at a dam. The electricity is transmitted from the power house by a series of high-tension lines, substations, transformers, and other equipment that brings the current into your house, all so that you can flick a switch and turn on a light.

In the same way, we often only see "the light come on" when a person comes to Christ, yet there is always a complex process behind that moment of conversion. There was the birth at Bethlehem, the amazing life and death of Jesus, the miracle of the resurrection, the sending forth of the Holy Spirit on the Day of Pentecost. There was the writing of Scripture, the centuries of church history, and the various reformations, reawakenings. and evangelistic movements. There were moments in each individual life where a friend spoke a word of witness, where a snippet of the gospel message was heard and had an impact, where a sermon or a radio message nudged the heart in the direction of faith. There are so many processes and influences that work together in every individual life to produce that moment of illumination.

And behind the entire process, there is the sovereign will of God. He began the process, He oversees the process, He completes the process in the life of every person He calls to Himself.

What About Those Who Have Never Heard?

But what if, after all that God has done to call people to Himself, some people still do not respond, but hold back in unbelief? Here Paul faces that question, with a focus on Israel:

> But not all the Israelites accepted the good news. For Isaiah says, "Lord, who has believed our message?" Consequently, faith comes from hearing the message, and the message is heard through the word of Christ. (Romans 10:16–17)

Here Paul describes what I call "the puzzle of unbelief." It is puzzling that people are so suspicious and self-willed that they resist even good news!

I know a man who had amassed considerable wealth by the time he came to know Jesus as his Lord and Savior. He was so enthusiastic about his newfound faith that he immediately began telling all his friends about Jesus Christ. He was surprised and disappointed when his good news fell on deaf ears—none of his friends wanted to hear how Jesus had changed his life.

Then he had an idea for a way to dramatize the good news of Jesus Christ. He sat down and wrote a check for a million dollars, payable to "CASH." The check was valid; the million (and much more) was sitting in the bank. All anyone had to do was endorse the check and become an instant millionaire. He went around and offered this check to anyone who would take it. Some people thought he was joking. Others thought there had to be a catch. Still others were too proud to accept his money. In the end, no one accepted this man's offer, though he had every intention of giving away a million dollars to the first person who accepted the check!

There is something deeply embedded in our nature that doesn't want to accept good news, that refuses to believe in a genuinely free gift. God, through Jesus Christ, offers the entire human race the infinite riches of His grace. But when people hear the good news of the gospel—the best news the world has ever heard!—many of them simply turn their backs and walk away.

The prophet Isaiah encountered this same resistance hundreds of years before Christ. In Isaiah 53, he wrote:

Who has believed our message
    and to whom has the arm of the LORD been revealed?
He grew up before him like a tender shoot,
    and like a root out of dry ground.
He had no beauty or majesty to attract us to him,
    nothing in his appearance that we should desire him.
He was despised and rejected by men,
    a man of sorrows, and familiar with suffering.
Like one from whom men hide their faces
    he was despised, and we esteemed him not.
Surely he took up our infirmities and carried our sorrows,
yet we considered him stricken by God,
      smitten by him, and afflicted.
But he was pierced for our transgressions,
    he was crushed for our iniquities;
the punishment that brought us peace was upon him,
    and by his wounds we are healed.
We all, like sheep, have gone astray,
    each of us has turned to his own way;
and the LORD has laid on him
    the iniquity of us all. (Isaiah 53:1–6)

Isaiah gave the nation of Israel an amazing preview of the coming Messiah, Jesus Christ—yet the nation rejected the prophet's message. As Paul says in verse 16, "But not all the Israelites accepted the good news. For Isaiah says, 'Lord, who has believed our message?'"

The message of the gospel demands a response. If you hear this message, you must either accept it or reject it. Those who receive this message with gladness will come to faith—but our message must be Christ-centered. Paul is very clear on this point: Saving faith comes only from the message of Christ. "Faith comes from hearing the message," he says in verse 17, "and the message is heard through the word of Christ."

But what about those who have not heard the word of Christ? And if they haven't heard, how can God condemn them for unbelief? Here, Paul takes up this issue:

> But I ask: Did they not hear? Of course they did:
> "Their voice has gone out into all the earth,
>   their words to the ends of the world."
>
> (Romans 10:18)

Here, Paul quotes Psalm 19, a psalm that tells how all of nature bears witness to the reality of God. Paul's meaning becomes obvious if we look at the lines he quoted in their context:

> The heavens declare the glory of God;
>   the skies proclaim the work of his hands.
> Day after day they pour forth speech;
>   night after night they display knowledge.
> There is no speech or language
>   where their voice is not heard.
> Their voice goes out into all the earth,
>   their words to the ends of the world. (Psalm 19:1–4)

The psalmist tells us that the gospel has been universally proclaimed through nature. Clearly, that is not as detailed a revelation of God's truth as can be found in Scripture. But the "gospel according to nature" provides enough evidence of God that no one can say, "I didn't know." Remember Paul's words in the first chapter of Romans:

... since what may be known about God is plain to them, because God has made it plain to them. For since the creation of the world God's invisible qualities—his eternal power and divine nature—have been clearly seen, being understood from what has been made, so that men are without excuse. (Romans 1:19–20)

So the answer to the question, "What about those who have never heard about God?," is: "There aren't any people who have never heard. God is revealed in nature. A universal proclamation has gone out." That is why Hebrews 11 makes this beautifully simple declaration of how people come to God:

And without faith it is impossible to please God, because anyone who comes to him must believe that he exists and that he rewards those who earnestly seek him. (Hebrews 11:6)

There must be faith, the acknowledgment that God exists and that He rewards everyone who sincerely and genuinely seeks Him. Everyone everywhere is responsible to seek the God who is revealed in nature. If people are obedient to that responsibility, God will reward them and give them more light, more insight, more understanding.

And there is still another level of God's revelation of Himself. God in His grace often gives more light even when people refuse the light of nature. For example, America is filled with churches, Christian publications, Christian radio, and Christian TV shows. Christians appear on secular news and entertainment shows, talking about their faith in Christ. Christians witness to their faith in workplaces, neighborhoods, shopping malls, and sporting events all across America. The light of the gospel has been seen by most Americans at one time or another—yet there is still an enormous level of unbelief in America.

God has given us much light—but more light does not necessarily mean more belief. Unbelief can reject bright light as well as dim light. That is why this nation, awash in the brilliant light of the gospel, is still a nation filled with unbelievers.

Paul continues:

> Again I ask: Did Israel not understand? First, Moses says,
> "I will make you envious by those who are not a nation;
> I will make you angry by a nation that has no
>   understanding."
> And Isaiah boldly says,
> "I was found by those who did not seek me;
> I revealed myself to those who did not ask for me."
>
> (Romans 10:19–20)

God sent the prophets to Israel—Moses, Samuel, Elijah, Elisha, Isaiah, Jeremiah, and all the other prophets in the Old Testament. He sent them to arouse the people to jealousy through the fact that, though Israel had often rejected the prophets, the Gentile nations around would believe. These prophecies have been fulfilled in these days, as faith in Jesus the Messiah has taken root largely among Gentile populations while Jewish people have largely rejected the Christian faith. Paul singles out the emotion of jealousy as a means by which God provokes belief.

You can see how the principle of jealousy works by watching children at play. When a child tires of a toy and tosses it aside, another child will usually pick it up and start to play with it. Seeing another child playing with his toy, the first child will become jealous and snatch the toy away, declaring, "It's mine!"

Jealousy is a principle of our fallen human nature. God uses this principle to wake people up, to arouse in people an interest in the gospel. Sometimes one member of a family will come to Christ and experience an abundance of joy and blessing in his or her life. That will make the other family members jealous to know what they are missing. When they become sufficiently jealous, they ask, "What are *you* so happy about?" And that is a perfect opening for witnessing.

Paul says that God is using this same principle on a grand scale, using world events to provoke feelings of jealousy so that the people of Israel will become ready to hear the gospel. First, Paul notes that Moses predicted that God would use nations that were far less educated and cultured than the Jews. "I will make you angry by a nation that has no understanding," said Moses.

One of the striking things about Jewish culture is the undeniable intellectual brilliance of the Jews. The descendants of Abraham, Isaac, and Jacob dominate the fields of science, philosophy, literature, art, and music today. Fully 20 percent of the Nobel laureates have been Jewish. Yet these brilliant people look around and see other ethnic groups with far fewer intellectual accomplishments, and these groups are finding God and experiencing blessings. Why? Because God wants to awaken His chosen people, Israel, to faith in Jesus the Messiah.

God is also using nations and people who are less zealous to awaken the Jewish people, as He said through the prophet Isaiah: "I was found by those who did not seek me; I revealed myself to those who did not ask for me." As we have already seen, the Jewish people are zealous for the Law of God. They almost seem haunted by the God of Abraham, Isaac, and Jacob. Yet among the Gentiles, who show little zeal compared to an orthodox Jew, there are many who receive enormous blessing and abundant grace from God through Jesus Christ. This, too, God does to arouse the Jewish people to jealousy, so that He can draw them to Himself. God wants to awaken His people, Israel, so that they will turn to Him through faith in Jesus and be saved.

Paul concludes this chapter by describing the final stage of divine pursuit:

> But concerning Israel he says,
>   "All day long I have held out my hands
>   to a disobedient and obstinate people."
>   (Romans 10:21)

This is a beautiful picture of the character of God. He displays amazing patience and forbearance: "All day long I have held out my hands to a disobedient and obstinate people." That phrase "all day long" encompasses a period of some 4,000 years—the period of time since Abraham set out from Ur in obedience to God. Forty centuries later, God is still patiently, lovingly holding out His hands to Israel, waiting for them to return to Him by faith.

Romans 10 closes with this picture of God standing with His arms open, longing to draw all people, Jews and Gentiles, to Himself. The most amazing truth we discover is that God never sends anyone to hell without a chance. In order to be condemned by God, you must resist and ignore the patient pleas of a loving God. The entire universe bears witness to the existence of God, and no one ends up separated from God purely because he or she has not had a chance to hear. The world has heard, and the world is without excuse.

Now, the most important question of all is a personal question: Have you settled the issue of your salvation with God? Paul has told you, simply and clearly, how to be saved:

> That if you confess with your mouth, "Jesus is Lord," and believe in your heart that God raised him from the dead, you will be saved. For it is with your heart that you believe and are justified, and it is with your mouth that you confess and are saved. (Romans 10:9–10)

If you have never made that confession, if you have never received Jesus as the Lord of your life, I urge you to stop resisting His plea. He stands, patiently and lovingly, waiting to wrap you in His strong, protective arms. Don't wait another day. Open your heart to Him now, and be saved.

CHAPTER 13

THE CHURCH AND THE CHOSEN PEOPLE

Romans 11

Hanukkah and Christmas are celebrated at the same time of the year—and with good reason. These two celebrations, one Jewish and one Christian, have something in common. Hanukkah is a celebration of the cleansing of the Temple in preparation for the arrival in Israel of the long-awaited Messiah. Christmas is the celebration of the coming of that same Messiah to a waiting world. The connection between these two celebrations symbolizes the close relationship that the nation of Israel has with the church of Jesus Christ.

Romans 11 deals with that connection between Israel and the church. Unfortunately, the church and Israel have historically behaved like two relatives who can't get along with each other. Through the centuries, disagreement and even outright persecution have prevailed. But in Romans 11, Paul—a Jew among Jews—shares valuable insights into how we should live with our Jewish friends and neighbors.

Twice in this passage, the apostle Paul asks the question, "Did God reject His people?" In other words, has God washed His hands of the people of Israel because of Israel's rejection of Jesus Christ? Does Israel no longer have a place in God's plan? Each time he raises the question, Paul answers resoundingly, "By no means!" God is definitely not through with the Jews; the people He chose so long ago remain at the center of His love and His plan for human history.

There are some who teach that the church has inherited all of the Old Testament promises that once pertained to Israel. They claim that God has washed His hands of Israel and has put the church in Israel's place. Those who teach such notions should take a closer look at God's Word, and especially Romans 11. I find it amazing that some Bible teachers are so quick to take all of the blessings and glories that were promised to Israel in the Old Testament and apply them to the church—but they still apply all the curses and punishments to Israel! If we want to understand the mind of God, we must interpret the Scriptures fairly and objectively.

So let's turn to Romans 11 and see what God's Word truly says about God's chosen people, Israel. Paul begins with the first of two questions:

> I ask then: Did God reject his people? By no means! I am an Israelite myself, a descendant of Abraham, from the tribe of Benjamin. God did not reject his people, whom he foreknew. (Romans 11:1–2)

Paul uses himself as an example of the fact that those Jews whom God foreknew, He did not reject. Clearly, God did not set aside the Jews as a race, because the Jews are still welcomed by God with respect to individual salvation. At its beginning, the early church was made up primarily of Jewish people, and down through the centuries there has always been a remnant of Christian Jews—Jews who have accepted Jesus as their Messiah.

Notice how Paul refers to himself as one of those whom God foreknew. In other words, Paul says that he is one of God's elect, one whom God has called to be saved. In his letter to the Galatians, Paul reminds us that he was foreknown and chosen by God from his mother's womb. Even while he opposed Jesus and persecuted Christians, Paul was one of the elect. Though Paul struggled and resisted, God was calling him and drawing him inexorably to Himself.

Again and again in his New Testament letters, Paul marvels at the grace of God. He is continually amazed that God would call a blaspheming persecutor of the church to Himself, and that God would lovingly remake him into a new creation in Christ. Paul is just one example of many millions of Jews who have believed in Jesus as their Lord, Savior, and Messiah.

A Faithful Remnant

Paul goes on to remind us that God has always maintained a faithful remnant of believing Jews, even during times when it seemed that the entire nation had fallen away from God:

> Don't you know what the Scripture says in the passage about Elijah—how he appealed to God against Israel: "Lord, they have killed your prophets and torn down your altars; I am the only one left, and they are trying to kill me"? And what was God's answer to him? "I have reserved for myself seven thousand who have not bowed the knee to Baal." So too, at the present time there is a remnant chosen by grace. And if by grace, then it is no longer by works; if it were, grace would no longer be grace. (Romans 11:2–6)

There was a time in the life of the prophet Elijah when he thought he was the only person left in Israel who remained faithful to God. This happened soon after Elijah's triumphant defeat of the priests of the false god Baal, when Elijah called fire from heaven to consume all of the sacrifices. Following Elijah's triumph, the wicked Queen Jezebel began a persecution against the prophets of God, including Elijah. As a result of that persecution, Elijah reached a point where he felt all alone, as if there were no other faithful Jews in the land (see 1 Kings 18 and 19).

In that lonely moment, Elijah prayed, "I have been very zealous for the LORD God Almighty. The Israelites have rejected your covenant, broken down your altars, and put your prophets to death with the sword. I am the only one left, and now they are trying to kill me too" (1 Kings 19:14). But God answered, "I reserve seven thousand in Israel—all whose knees have not bowed down to Baal" (1 Kings 19:18). Elijah thought he was alone, but God told him to count again—there were 7,000 other righteous, faithful Jews.

Elijah had forgotten two things: (1) his own limited knowledge, and (2) God's unlimited power. For the believer, the situation is never as bleak as it seems because God is always more powerful than we realize.

Paul's point is this: God is sovereign, and by His grace, He chooses whom He will—and He always chooses to reserve a faithful remnant for Himself. We easily become discouraged because we do not see all that God is doing behind the scenes of the world. But God is always working to accomplish His eternal plan, and that means He is choosing whom He will choose, saving whom He will save. It all comes down to God's grace, which He exercises by His sovereign choice.

Grace is God at work. Works is man at work. If salvation is by grace, then it can't be by works. And if salvation is by works, then it can't be by grace. You can't mix works and grace. If God calls you and saves you, then your salvation has nothing to do with works. In His grace, completely apart from works, no matter how rebellious and unfaithful the general population may be, God always keeps a faithful remnant of believers.

In Paul's day and in our own day, there are probably some (and perhaps many) Jews who have never heard about Jesus, yet they have a saving faith. What they know about God comes from observing nature and studying the Jewish Scriptures (what Christians call the Old Testament). They may have read the many Old Testament prophecies that relate to the coming Messiah, and that have been fulfilled in Jesus. They are earnest, devout, humble souls, and they have just never been told enough about Jesus that they would recognize Jesus of Nazareth as the living fulfillment of the prophecies from Genesis to Malachi. There are probably hundreds of thousands of Jews who are faithful to the fragmentary knowledge they have of Jesus.

In any case, Paul makes it abundantly clear that God does not reject any individuals who come to Him from the nation of Israel. But even though there have always been individual Jews who have trusted Jesus as their Lord and Savior, it is a tragic fact that the people of Israel have overwhelmingly rejected Jesus, as Paul here observes:

> What then? What Israel sought so earnestly it did not obtain, but the elect did. The others were hardened, as it is written:
> "God gave them a spirit of stupor,
>   eyes so that they could not see
> and ears so that they could not hear,
>   to this very day."
> And David says:
> "May their table become a snare and a trap,
>   a stumbling block and a retribution for them.
> May their eyes be darkened so they cannot see,
> and their backs be bent forever."
>
> (Romans 11:7–10)

These are harsh words, but this is the response that God has determined shall accompany unbelief. When we hear truth, we should always act on it. If we don't, we lose our capacity to recognize truth. Our eyes become darkened so that we can no longer see the truth. If we harden our hearts against God's truth, then even our own table, our own food, will become a snare and a trap, leading us into slavery.

The table and food symbolize the Law. Jewish people highly prize the Law, even though many today are not strongly religious and are not well versed in the Old Testament. The Jewish rabbis, who make an intensive, life-long study of the Law, seem to

focus on legalism, ritualism, and endless debates over interpretation—yet they have missed the most important dimension of
the Old Testament: Jesus the Messiah, whose coming is predicted
throughout the Old Testament.

Once, when Jesus was contending with His opponents, the
scribes and Pharisees, He told them, "You diligently study the
Scriptures because you think that by them you possess eternal
life. These are the Scriptures that testify about me, yet you refuse
to come to me to have life" (John 5:39–40). Two thousand years
later, little has changed.

Beyond Recovery?

Next, Paul addresses the second question:

> Again I ask, Did they stumble so as to fall beyond recov-
> ery? Not at all! (Romans 11:11)

This question deals with the promises God made to the nation
of Israel. As individuals, anyone can come to Jesus and be saved,
whether that person is a Jew or a Gentile. But God made certain promises that were directed toward Israel as a whole. Paul's
question is: Has the nation of Israel forfeited those promises God
made? His answer: Not at all! By no means!

Paul then offers five logical arguments to prove that Israel will
ultimately be a godly nation once more. In fact, Israel will become
the leading nation of all the earth. His first argument:

> Rather, because of their transgression, salvation has come to
> the Gentiles to make Israel envious. (Romans 11:11)

Paul says that the salvation of the Gentiles was intended by
God to make the Jews envious of salvation, so that Israel would
also turn to God. In the book of Acts, we see that Paul's ministry of
evangelism was initially to the Jews. It was only when the Jews in
the synagogues refused to hear his message that Paul turned and

preach to the Gentiles. In city after city, the Gentiles were blessed by the gospel of Jesus Christ after the Jews had refused it. Gentiles were allowed to enter the kingdom of God by grace through faith. As a result, the lives of these believing Gentiles were transformed— and the Jews were envious of the change they saw in them.

This statement of Paul's speaks volumes to us about how we should live our lives as Christians. It tells us that we should be so enthusiastic, joyful, and loving toward one another that every Jewish person who sees us will say, "What do they have that I don't?" One of the great tragedies of the church is that, down through the centuries, we have not demonstrated much to attract the jealousy of Israel! If we are to witness to the Jewish community as God intended, then our lives should demonstrate the vibrant joy that comes from a relationship with Jesus Christ.

Next, Paul's second argument to prove that Israel will one day be a godly nation again:

> But if their transgression means riches for the world, and their loss means riches for the Gentiles, how much greater riches will their fullness bring!
>
> I am talking to you Gentiles. Inasmuch as I am the apostle to the Gentiles, I make much of my ministry in the hope that I may somehow arouse my own people to envy and save some of them. For if their rejection is the reconciliation of the world, what will their acceptance be but life from the dead? (Romans 11:12–15)

Paul's second argument is that Israel must ultimately return to God because worldwide blessing will come only when that return takes place.

I once attended the Congress for World Evangelization at Lausanne, Switzerland, and I was awed to see that every nation on earth was represented there. This meant that the gospel had penetrated to some degree in every nation on the face of the earth. The riches of the gospel had spread throughout the world, producing *freedom*, the liberation of the human spirit. Wherever the gospel is freely proclaimed, people live free from oppression and tyranny. This is because human freedom comes by means of the gospel.

Paul says that the gospel has gone out to the Gentile world because the gospel was rejected by the Jews. "Their rejection," he says, "is the reconciliation of the world." Those of us who are Gentile Christians should give thanks to God for the spiritual riches we have received because of Israel's rejection of the gospel.

At the same time, we grieve for Israel—and I speak here not of the political entity that is geographically located in the region of Palestine, but that special nation of people that is spread across the globe, the physical descendants of Abraham, Isaac, and Jacob. We grieve for these people who are so zealous for the Law, yet they failed to recognize the long-awaited Messiah whom their Scriptures foretold.

Even so, a bright and glorious future awaits Israel. Paul writes, "For if their rejection [of the gospel] is the reconciliation of the world, what will their acceptance [of the gospel] be but life from the dead?" A day is coming when Israel will return to God in faith and trust. When that happens, it will be as dramatic an event as a dead body coming back to life! According to the Old Testament prophets, the restoration of Israel will be a time when the earth will blossom like the rose, when there will be no more war (see Isaiah 11). The restored nation of Israel will be a source of blessing throughout the earth.

As Christians, we need to keep our eye on this remarkable nation of people—and we should pray for God's blessing on the Jewish people and nation. "Pray for the peace of Jerusalem," writes David in Psalm 122:6. "May those who love you be secure." And God promised Israel through Abraham, "I will bless those who bless you, and whoever curses you I will curse; and all peoples on earth will be blessed through you."

Next, Paul's third argument to prove that Israel will one day be a godly nation again:

> If the part of the dough offered as firstfruits is holy, then the whole batch is holy; if the root is holy, so are the branches. (Romans 11:16)

This statement may be confusing to you, but an orthodox Jew would instantly understand Paul's meaning, because he is referring to the offerings and sacrifices in the tabernacle. For the offering of the firstfruits, a pile of dough was made up, and someone would take a handful of it and present it to God. Paul's argument is that if that first handful was acceptable and holy before God, the rest of the dough would be too.

In this passage, the firstfruit symbolizes Abraham, the father of the nation of Israel. Abraham was accepted before God; therefore his descendants will be too. They are not cut off from God or from a relationship with Him; they are claimed by God.

Paul's fourth argument to prove that Israel will one day be a godly nation again:

> If some of the branches have been broken off, and you, though a wild olive shoot, have been grafted in among the others and now share in the nourishing sap from the olive root, do not boast over those branches. If you do, consider this: You do not support the root, but the root supports you. You will say then, "Branches were broken off so that I could be grafted in." Granted. But they were broken off because of unbelief, and you stand by faith. Do not be arrogant, but be afraid. For if God did not spare the natural branches, he will not spare you either. (Romans 11:17–21)

Here Paul uses an olive tree to symbolize Abraham. He is addressing both Jews (the natural branches of the "tree" of Abraham) and Gentiles (the grafted branches). When a Gentile becomes a Christian, he becomes a son of Abraham, an adopted Israelite, grafted into the Abrahamic tree. But when a Jew becomes a Christian, he doesn't have to become a Gentile. The Jews are the natural branches of the tree; the Gentiles are grafted in.

C. S. Lewis once said, "In a sense, the converted Jew is the only normal human being in the world. Everyone else is, from one point of view, a special case dealt with under emergency conditions." It's true. God opened the back door and let the Gentiles into His kingdom as an emergency case; the ones who really belong are the Jews. It is healthy for Gentile Christians to remember that and be grateful to God for the privilege of being grafted into the tree of Abraham.

Paul's fifth and final argument to prove that Israel will one day be a godly nation again:

> Consider therefore the kindness and sternness of God: sternness to those who fell, but kindness to you, provided that you continue in his kindness. Otherwise, you also will be cut off. And if they do not persist in unbelief, they will be grafted in, for God is able to graft them in again. After all, if you were cut out of an olive tree that is wild by nature, and contrary to nature were grafted into a cultivated olive tree, how much more readily will these, the natural branches, be grafted into their own olive tree! (Romans 11:22–24)

The olive tree represents the faith of Abraham. By being grafted into that faith, we have received blessing from the God of the earth through His grace, without any works or merit on our own part. Paul is saying that the Gentiles are like a wild olive tree with hard, shriveled fruit; the Gentiles have been grafted into a cultivated tree that brings forth rich fruit.

Then Paul describes a result of grafting that is contrary to nature. For example, if you graft a nectarine branch into a peach tree, the grafted branch grows nectarines, not peaches. The branch produces fruit according to its own nature, not the nature of the tree that now supports it. But in his analogy, Paul suggests something very different. He is saying that when we are grafted, a miracle takes place. We are wild olive branches that produce hard, shriveled, bitter fruit—but once we are grafted into a cultivated tree, we begin to produce the rich, juicy, fat fruit of the cultivated tree. Paul's argument is that if God can do such a miracle with the fruit of grafted Gentile branches, how much more will He produce a rich, juicy, fat harvest from the true branches, the Jews?

Paul also speaks of the kindness and the severity of God. We don't like to think about the severity of God, but it is important that we be reminded from time to time. Paul's point is this: If you come to God with an attitude that is grateful, humble, and repentant, you will always find Him loving, gracious, forgiving, and openhearted, ready to give you all that you need. But if you come to God with an attitude of complaining and justifying yourself, you will find God as hard as iron and as merciless as fire.

That is the key to the mystery of Israel and its present blindness to God's truth. As long as the Jews come to God on the basis of works and self-justification, they will find God stern and iron-willed. When they come in repentance, they will find God standing with open arms, like the father in the story of the Prodigal Son. Zechariah describes the moment when Israel returns to God and His crucified and risen Son, Jesus:

> "If someone asks him, 'What are these wounds on your body?' he will answer, 'The wounds I was given at the house of my friends.'" (Zechariah 13:6)

Jesus, speaking through the Old Testament prophet, also says:

> "And I will pour out on the house of David and the inhabitants of Jerusalem a spirit of grace and supplication. They will look on me, the one they have pierced, and they will mourn for him as one mourns for an only child, and grieve bitterly for him as one grieves for a firstborn son." (Zechariah 12:10)

The whole nation of Israel will mourn and repent of its rejection of Jesus the Messiah. And God will comfort and restore Israel, and He will make that nation a fountain of blessing to replenish the earth. This will surely come to pass, because God's promises cannot fail.

A Supernatural Mystery

In the next section, Paul talks about the mystery of Israel's rejection of Jesus and of Israel's coming spiritual restoration:

> I do not want you to be ignorant of this mystery, brothers, so that you may not be conceited: Israel has experienced a hardening in part until the full number of the Gentiles has come in. And so all Israel will be saved, as it is written:
>
> "The deliverer will come from Zion;
>   he will turn godlessness away from Jacob.
> And this is my covenant with them
>   when I take away their sins."
>
> As far as the gospel is concerned, they are enemies on your account; but as far as election is concerned, they are loved on account of the patriarchs, for God's gifts and his call are irrevocable. (Romans 11:25–29)

Paul calls the Jews' resistance to the gospel a mystery. He doesn't mean that it is obscure and difficult to understand. The word *mystery* has a special meaning in Scripture, and it refers to an occurrence that is supernatural, that cannot be understood through normal human observation and logic.

If you have ever attempted to talk to a Jewish person about Jesus Christ, you may have a sense of what Paul is talking about. You usually encounter a solid wall of indifference and objection to your message—a hardened resistance to the gospel that seems to go beyond mere indifference.

Jews are probably the most religious people on earth, yet there is a remarkable resistance among Jewish people to the preaching of the gospel of Jesus Christ. Sometimes this resistance is accompanied by an anger that seems out of proportion to the "annoyance" of being asked to listen to the good news of Jesus Christ.

Jewish resistance to the gospel seems all the more remarkable in that Jesus is everywhere regarded as a great Jewish teacher who affirmed the Jewish Scriptures. There are many leading Jewish thinkers who have expressed a high regard for Jesus. Jewish physicist Albert Einstein said, "As a child I received instruction both in the Bible and in the Talmud. I am a Jew, but I am enthralled by the luminous figure of Jesus the Nazarene." Jewish novelist John Cournos observed, "Jesus was a Jew—the best of Jews. . . . Jesus was not only a Jew. He was the apex and the acme of Jewish teaching."

Rabbi Leo Baeck, a Jewish religious leader and Holocaust survivor, said, "Jesus is a genuine Jewish personality. All his struggles and works, his bearing and feeling, his speech and silence, bear the stamp of a Jewish style, the mark of Jewish idealism, of the best that was and is in Judaism. He was a Jew among Jews." Zionist leader Rabbi Stephen S. Wise, founder of the Jewish Institute of Religion, said, "Jesus was not only a Jew, but he was *the* Jew, the Jew of Jews. . . . In that day when history shall be written in the light of truth, the people of Israel will be known not as Christ-killers, but as Christ-bearers; not as God-slayers, but as the God-bringers to the world."

Despite these statements of renowned Jewish leaders, there remains a widespread antipathy toward Jesus and resistance to the gospel among the Jewish people as a whole. Paul calls this phenomenon a mystery because it defies natural explanation.

Paul goes on to say, "Israel has experienced a hardening in part until the full number of the Gentiles has come in." What does he mean by "a hardening *in part*"? He means that not all Jews will be resistant to the gospel. He does not tell us if "in part" means 10 percent, 50 percent, or 90 percent. All we are told is that there will be some Jews who simply will not listen to the gospel.

Understand that if you are witnessing to a Jewish person and that person rebuffs you, it does not mean that this person is "hardened." Sometimes a person who seems hardened against the gospel simply needs to be patiently loved in the name of Jesus over a long period of time. It is not for us to decide who is "hardened" and who is not. Only God knows the actual state of any human heart. Our job is to simply be witnesses to everyone we meet.

Not only does Paul say that this hardening is partial, but it is limited in duration—it will not go on forever. The hardening of the Jewish heart will last "until the full number of the Gentiles come in." What does "the full number of the Gentiles" mean? The original Greek word translated "full number" is *pleroma*, which literally means "fullness." So this phrase should literally be translated "the fullness of the Gentiles." Some interpret that to mean that a certain number of Gentiles will become converted to Christ, and when that number is reached He will intervene and end the spiritual blindness of Israel.

After studying this passage and related texts, I don't think that "the fullness of the Gentiles" refers to a particular number of Gentiles. This is the second time in Romans 11 where the word *fullness* (Greek *pleroma*) is used; the first time, in verse 12, refers to Israel: "But if their transgression means riches for the world, and their loss means riches for the Gentiles, how much greater riches will their fullness [*pleroma*] bring!" Here, this word means "that which fills," and Paul uses it in direct contrast to the words "their loss." The phrase "their loss" does not refer to a diminished number of Jews, but to diminished spiritual riches, the result of their rejection of Jesus the Messiah. Though they have the outward trappings of faith and they have the Law of Moses, they have lost the richness of a living, radiant relationship with God.

So, when Paul uses this phrase, "the fullness of the Gentiles," he is talking about a Gentile church that will become so full in spiritual riches that it will awaken the envy and spiritual hunger of Israel. Anyone who reads church history knows that there has not always been much about Gentile Christian churches that would awaken envy and spiritual hunger among the Jews! Throughout much of Christian history, the Jews have seen Gentile Christians as enemies—and with good reason. Tragically, the Jews have often been persecuted and oppressed in the name of Jesus Christ.

If the interpretation I am suggesting is correct, then this passage is a message of hope to those who are Gentile Christians. It means that a day is coming when the Gentile churches will be so enriched with spiritual blessing that the Jews will say, "We want that blessing for ourselves! We want Jesus to be our Lord and Messiah!" In that day, the Jews will be receptive, as never before, to the gospel.

I think we are catching a glimpse of that moment already. We are seeing Jews turning to their Messiah in greater numbers than at any other time in history. Paul says that the prophets have foretold the spiritual restoration of Israel, and he quotes from Jeremiah 31:33–34. The deliverer is coming and forgiveness will be granted to Israel. The Jews are loved by an unchanging God, and He will abide by His unchanging promises. The people of Israel are still God's chosen people.

God's Unsearchable Judgments

Next, Paul deals with God's principle of salvation for all people, whether Jew or Gentile:

> Just as you who were at one time disobedient to God have now received mercy as a result of their disobedience, so they too, have now become disobedient in order that they too may now receive mercy as a result of God's mercy to you. For God has bound all men over to disobedience so that he may have mercy on them all. (Romans 11:30–32)

This is an amazing glimpse of the strange workings of the mind of our God. Again we have to acknowledge that His ways are not our ways. Here is the answer to the question Paul first raised at the beginning of Romans 9: "Has God failed?" Since God was trying to reach the Jews, since He sent His own Son and the

Jews rejected Him, doesn't that mean that God's plan has failed? The answer is now clear: No, God hasn't failed. He used the Jews' rejection as a means to reach the Gentile world—and, of course, that was His objective all along.

Only the mind of an infinite God could have conceived such a surprising plan—but that is not all! God still has more surprises in store. Having shown mercy to the Gentiles, God now uses the very mercy He has shown to the Gentiles to make the Jews rebellious so that they, too, will receive mercy. Paul is saying that unless you realize how rebellious your heart is, there is no chance for you to receive mercy. So God works in human history to make us aware of our basic, inherent rebellion against Him. Paul concludes that everyone is a rebel, and God desires that everyone recognize and admit that fact, so they can receive mercy.

What blocks any individual or nation from receiving God's mercy? Invariably, it is an attitude of self-sufficiency: "I don't need help. I can handle my own problems without any help from God." This attitude cuts people off from the mercy of God. Those who insist on asserting their own righteousness cannot receive the righteousness that comes by faith.

Paul closes this section with a doxology—a burst of praise and adoration for the wisdom and greatness of God:

> Oh, the depth of the riches of the wisdom and
>   knowledge of God!
>   How unsearchable his judgments, and his paths
>   beyond tracing out!
> "Who has known the mind of the Lord?
>   Or who has been his counselor?"
> "Who has ever given to God,
>   that God should repay him?"
> For from him and through him and to him
>   are all things.
>   To him be the glory forever! Amen.
>   (Romans 11:33–36)

God's judgments are unsearchable, His thoughts are beyond our understanding, His wisdom is light-years deeper than human wisdom. There is no way we can fathom God. All of our efforts to define Him, confine Him, and reduce Him to our level are doomed to failure. He is not accountable to us. He owes us no explanation. He is God.

We cannot begin to grasp His eternal plan. The moment we try to figure out what He is doing in human history, we bump into mystifying paradoxes that boggle our finite minds. For example, we know from Scripture that God has given human beings free will, and that God never interferes with human responsibility. Nothing God has ever said or done will ever infringe on our ability to make free moral choices. Yet—and this is the paradox—nothing we do as human beings can ever frustrate God's sovereign plan! It seems like a contradiction to us, yet from God's infinite, eternal perspective, it all makes perfect sense. That is the kind of God we have.

When we look at Jesus, we catch a glimpse of the subtle brilliance of the mind of God. The enemies of Jesus were constantly trying to trap Him by maneuvering Him into an either/or, no-win situation. For example, they asked Him if it is right to pay taxes to Caesar. If Jesus said "Yes," He would anger the Jews, because they hated the Roman oppressors; if He said "No," He would be advocating disobedience to the Roman government, and the Romans would arrest Him. His enemies thought they had Him trapped.

But Jesus evaded their trap by applying a logic that transcends human thinking. He called for a coin, which He held up in front of His enemies. "Whose image is on this coin?" He asked. His enemies replied, "Caesar's." Jesus said, "In that case, give to Caesar what belongs to Caesar, and give to God what belongs to God." And His enemies could not argue with Him. They discovered that the wisdom and judgment of Jesus was unsearchable, and beyond their ability to fathom.

There is a subtle point that Jesus makes when He holds up that coin. He says that we should give to Caesar whatever bears

Caesar's image. This implies that we should give to God whatever bears God's image. God has stamped His image on each of us. What, then, do we owe God? Answer: Ourselves. We owe God everything we are.

Paul asks: Who has been God's advisor? In other words, who has ever suggested something to God that He hasn't thought of? You have probably *tried* to advise God; I know I have. There have been times when I looked at a problem and I saw a way to solve it, so I prayed and suggested to God a way that He could work it out. I thought I was very helpful to God, but it invariably turned out that He knew things that I didn't. His solution was always infinitely better than anything I could think of.

Paul also asks: Who has ever given to God, that God should repay him? Is there anything we can give God that didn't come from Him in the first place? God is the originator and sustainer of all things. Your very existence—the next breath you take, the next beat of your heart—depends entirely on Him. All things begin with God and end with God. So Paul says, "To him be the glory forever! Amen."

An Unfortunate Chapter Division

At this point we come upon the most unfortunate chapter division in the entire Bible. The division between Romans 11 and Romans 12 separates Paul's conclusion from the tremendous arguments that have led up to it. Paul's next word is "Therefore . . ." This is a word that clearly signals a major summation. At the beginning of Romans 12, Paul writes:

> Therefore, I urge you, brothers, in view of God's mercy,
> to offer your bodies as living sacrifices, holy and pleasing to
> God—this is your spiritual act of worship. (Romans 12:1)

That phrase, "this is your spiritual act of worship," is a mistranslation. Literally, Paul says, "this is your logical service" or "your reasonable service." Paul is saying that it is only reasonable and logical for us to present ourselves unreservedly to God. It is, in fact, our only logical reason for existing. It is why God made us. If we do not present ourselves to God as living sacrifices, then we cannot achieve our purpose and meaning in life.

If you are a Christian, then your spirit is already surrendered to God. Now it is only logical that you should offer your body as well as your spirit. You should allow God to use your body as an available, surrendered instrument for His purposes. If you do so, then God—this great God of unsearchable wisdom and infinite riches—will fill your body with His own amazing power and life. He will launch you on an amazing adventure—the adventure of a lifetime, the adventure of faith.

CHAPTER 14

WHO AM I, LORD?

Romans 12

Jerome Hines enjoyed a forty-year career as a bass soloist with the Metropolitan Opera Company in New York. Standing six and a half feet tall, he was an imposing man whose deep voice was matched by a deep musical talent. He was a rarity among opera singers, in that he could perform not only in Italian and French, but in German and Russian as well. He was also a deeply committed Christian who authored his own opera, *I Am the Way*, about the life of Jesus, as well as several books including his autobiography of faith, *This Is My Story, This Is My Song*. Jerome Hines lived out Paul's appeal in Romans 12:1 to offer ourselves as living sacrifices to God.

Hines grew up in southern California and wanted to sing opera from an early age. Before he became a Christian, his only goal was to find fame and fortune on the operatic stage. He trained and sacrificed throughout his early life. He achieved his dream at age twenty-five when he joined the Met in 1946, replacing the distinguished soloist Ezio Pinza. He was a star—yet he was surprised to find that stardom was not what he expected. Instead of feeling satisfied and fulfilled, he felt empty.

One day, he attended a concert featuring George Beverly Shea, the longtime soloist for the Billy Graham crusades. Hines was impressed by the power of Shea's voice—a voice that could easily have taken Shea to Broadway or the operatic stage. Hines wondered why Shea had dedicated his life to singing at evangelistic crusades. Listening to George Beverly Shea sing "I'd Rather Have Jesus," Hines was struck by the message of the song:

I'd rather have Jesus than silver or gold,
I'd rather be His than have riches untold,
I'd rather have Jesus than houses or land,
I'd rather be led by His nail-pierced hands
Than to be the king of a vast domain,
And be held in sin's dread sway.
I'd rather have Jesus than anything
This world affords today.

Listening to those words, Hines realized why his life seemed so empty. He had set his heart on fame and fortune—but only Jesus brings satisfaction and fulfillment. So Jerome Hines turned his life over to the Lord Jesus.

As a Christian, Hines continued to sing opera, but now he sang for the glory of God. Years after his conversion, he was placed in a position of having to pay a high price for his decision to live for Christ.

After months of training for an opera role he had always wanted to sing, he went to a rehearsal. He was shocked to see several performers engaging in a lewd and offensive dance. Hines went to the director and asked, "What are those dancers doing?"

"That," said the director, "is the choreography that introduces the opera."

"But there's no such choreography in this opera!" Hines said. "It has never been performed that way!"

"We're modernizing it," the director said, "bringing it up to date for today's audiences. It'll be a big hit. Audiences love this kind of innovation."

"It's pornographic!" Hines said. "I won't lend my talent to such a lewd performance."

"Well," said the director, "you'll have to talk to Mr. Bing about that."

So Jerome Hines went to Rudolph Bing, the general manager of the Metropolitan Opera Company. After Hines explained his objections, Bing replied, "We have a contract. If you don't sing, you'll never perform again."

"You may break my career," said Hines, "but you won't change my mind. If that dance is in the opera, I will not sing."

Finally, Bing relented—but only partly. "All right, Jerome," Bing said, "I can see you're serious about this. You don't have to sing—but the opera will go on as planned, including the dance. We'll just have to put another singer in the role."

So Jerome Hines gave up the role he had dreamed of—a decision that cost him at least a hundred thousand dollars. But Jerome Hines remained faithful to his Lord. At considerable cost to himself, he had offered his body and his voice as a living sacrifice, holy and pleasing to God.

What Will You Do with Your Life?

At the end of Romans 11, Paul gave us a stirring doxology, praising God for His unsearchable wisdom and the wonders of His marvelous plan. In his original manuscript, Paul continued right on into a conclusion, signaled by the word "Therefore. . . ." In Romans 12:1, he says, in effect, "Therefore, because God is so amazingly rich in wisdom, glory, love, and mercy, I urge you, brothers, to offer yourselves as living sacrifices, holy and pleasing to God, which is only your logical, reasonable act of worship."

Paul's message in this verse is captured beautifully in these lines from the hymn "When I Survey the Wondrous Cross" by Isaac Watts:

Love so amazing, so divine,
Demands my soul, my life, my all.

That is what Paul urges us to do as our reasonable service to God. When he says "offer your bodies as living sacrifices," Paul uses the aorist tense, which refers to an action that is taken once and for all. It is not something you do over and over again. Once you offer your body to God as a living sacrifice, you do so for life, and the rest of your life is lived on that basis.

It amazes me that God would even want our bodies. Earlier, Paul told us that the body is the seat of what he calls "the flesh," that rebellious nature within us that does not want to do what God wants. The body is the source of our temptation to sin; it is the part of us that grows weak and wobbly with age. Yet God wants us to offer our bodies to Him; when we do so, our bodies become holy and pleasing to God.

Paul is not saying that we must get our lives cleaned up before we offer ourselves to God. Instead, God says to us, "Come as you are. I am the answer to your problems, so start with Me. You can't solve your problems by yourself; let Me come into your life and I will make you clean."

Let's put verse 1 together with verse 2 so that we can see what God does with the living sacrifice we offer to him:

> Therefore, I urge you, brothers, in view of God's mercy, to offer your bodies as living sacrifices, holy and pleasing to God—this is your spiritual [reasonable] act of worship. Do not conform any longer to the pattern of this world, but be transformed by the renewing of your mind. Then you will be able to test and approve what God's will is—his good, pleasing and perfect will. (Romans 12:1–2)

Paul says that we must do the rational, sensible thing with our bodies and present them to the Lord, once and for all. In response, God says, "Very good, I accept this sacrifice you have given me. It is holy and pleasing to Me. Now there are two things you must do on an ongoing and continual basis. First, you must make sure, on a daily, continual basis, that you no longer conform yourself to the pattern of this world. Second, you must allow yourself to be transformed by the daily, continual renewing of your mind."

Whereas Paul's urging to offer our bodies to God was stated in the once-and-for-all aorist tense, his command to not conform but be transformed is stated in the present tense. We are to do this continually and daily. You bring your body to God once and you base the rest of your life on that commitment. But you refuse conformity with the world and seek transformation by the renewing of your mind in an ongoing way.

The phrase "the pattern of this world" literally means "the schemes of this world"—the blueprint, the purposes, and the values that ungodly people use as their game plan for living. God tells us, "Don't live as the world lives. Don't think as the world thinks. Don't live your life by the dead and meaningless values of the culture around you."

Some people think that this command refers to certain activities that "worldly" people engage in. They see it as a command to not smoke, drink, swear, gamble, and so forth. It may well be that such activities are included in this command, but it actually goes far deeper than that. When Paul says, "Do not conform any longer to the pattern of this world," he was not setting up a list of taboos. He was saying, "Don't let the dead values, goals, and philosophies of this world squeeze you into their mold. Don't become caught up in the spirit of this dying age."

The spirit of the age is always the same. It never changes from generation to generation. The basic pattern of this world is the gratification and advancement of the self. People everywhere, and in all times, live for the self. They are ambitious to exalt themselves in the world, to accumulate wealth and power for themselves, to make themselves look good, to make themselves the envy of everyone around them. That is the spirit of this age and of ages past.

God says, "Don't get caught up in the self-centered thinking of the world around you. If you let it, the selfish spirit of this age will drag you down and destroy your usefulness to Me. If you wish to save your soul, then you must sacrifice your self. You must become conformed to My Son, Jesus Christ, the selfless servant—and you must not be conformed to the self-gratifying ways of this dying world."

The pressure to conform pervades all of society. Even in the church, we find ourselves talking, thinking, and living according to the ways of this world. Our dying culture shouts at us through our TV sets and magazines, our neighbors and co-workers: "Conform!" Though we must invariably pay a price for resisting the pressure of the world to conform, we must not yield. In order to stand up against the pressure that is trying to squeeze us into a worldly, self-centered mold, we must obey the next command: "Be transformed by the renewing of your mind."

The only way to keep from being conformed to the world is by being transformed by the renewing of your mind. Your thinking must change. You can't go on thinking the way the world thinks; if your thinking doesn't change, you will inevitably find yourself becoming conformed to the pattern of this world.

What kind of transformation does Paul mean? How should our thinking change? There is only one way to acquire the kind of mind that will see through the destructive schemes of the world: we must have what the Scriptures call "the mind of Christ," (see 1 Corinthians 2:16). That means we must learn to think and perceive as Jesus did. We must focus on what is truly important, eternally important—not on the meaningless, temporary things that the world prizes so highly: money, status, fame, power, and pleasure. The mind of Christ seeks to advance God's kingdom, not the kingdom of the self. The mind of Christ says, "Not my will, Lord, but Yours be done." You can't have the mind of Christ unless your mind is being renewed every day.

How do we renew our minds? Through fellowship with other Christ-minded believers. Through reading and studying the Scriptures. Through Scripture memorization. Through listening to God's Word being preached and explained.

(This is why I believe strongly in *expositional preaching*— preaching through entire books of the Bible, rather than preaching on topics. When a pastor preaches on topics, he is tempted to stay with his favorite themes and "safe" Scripture texts. But a pastor who preaches expositionally through entire books of the Bible is forced to deal with every theme that arises from that text—and that's good for the pastor and his people!)

In times of confusion, we need to renew our minds by listening to God's Word and allowing His thoughts to become our thoughts. Our goal is to find out what God says is true, not what everyone around us claims is true. The human-centered philosophies of this world are destroying souls, ruining families, and tearing apart the moral fabric of our nation. Only the truth of God's Word can mend souls, families, and societies.

The question that confronts us from the first two verses of Romans 12 is this: What are you going to do with the rest of your life? Are you going to spend the days you have left on self-gratification and self-worship, as this world urges you to do? Or will you invest the time God has given you for rewards that will last an eternity? When you have reached the end of your life and you stand before the throne of God, what will you have to show for the years you lived on earth? Will you have wasted those years, living a life of dull conformity to this world? Or will you have lived a grand adventure of faith?

The answer depends on whether or not you heed Paul's urging in these two verses: Are you willing to offer your body to God as a willing sacrifice? Are you willing to reject the brainwashing of this world and live as a Christian non-conformist? Are you willing to be transformed by the daily renewing of your minds, so that you will view this world with the mind of Christ?

What will you do with your life?

The Sober Truth About Ourselves

From verse 3 to the end of Chapter 12, Paul talks in specific terms about what it means to be transformed by the renewing of your mind, beginning with how we view ourselves:

> For by the grace given to me I say to every one of you: Do not think of yourself more highly than you ought, but rather think of yourself with sober judgment, in accordance

with the measure of faith God has given you. (Romans 12:3)

Notice that Paul does *not* say that we should never think of ourselves. To the contrary, he *wants* us to think about ourselves—but he wants us to think with sober judgment. In other words, we should evaluate our own lives, humbly and objectively. Paul suggests the way we should examine ourselves in another letter:

Examine yourselves to see whether you are in the faith; test yourselves. Do you not realize that Christ Jesus is in you—unless, of course, you fail the test? And I trust that you will discover that we have not failed the test. (2 Corinthians 13:5–6)

It is worldly and un-Christlike to think of nothing but yourself—but it is a godly act of renewing your mind to occasionally reflect on your Christian commitment and experience. God wants us to take stock of our relationship with Him on a continual basis.

When Paul exhorts us to think of ourselves with sober judgment, he places his entire apostolic authority on the line. He says, "by the grace given to me I say to every one of you. . . ." That is a reference to the gift of apostleship. He is saying that this word of exhortation is given to us on the basis of his office as an apostle (an apostle is a messenger sent forth by God's own authority).

Paul knows our human tendency is to overrate ourselves, so he puts this warning first: "Do not think of yourself more highly than you ought." One of the most common reasons we so easily overrate ourselves is that we tend to be heavily influenced by our feelings.

If we are well-rested and the sun is shining and our hormones are in perfect balance and our lives are going well, we feel good about life and about ourselves. But if it's rainy outside and our digestion is off, if we are feeling headachy and our bills are past due, we feel blue and depressed and we get down on ourselves.

One of the most foolish things in the world is to judge ourselves on the basis of how we feel at any given moment, regardless of whether we feel up or down.

Feelings are not unimportant, of course. But feelings are an unreliable guide to the truth about our spiritual and moral state. So we need a more reliable guide to evaluating ourselves. In short, we need to see ourselves as God sees us. And what is God's perspective on our lives?

First, we are all fallen creatures. As long as we are in our physical flesh, we will have the nature of Adam in us. That means there is something in our nature that can't be trusted. We are prone to attitudes and temptations that are morally, spiritually poisonous. We must think soberly about these dangers to our souls. We must recognize that we are prone to wander from God, prone to fall into sin, and prone to forget who we are in Christ.

Second, notice that Paul says, "Think of yourself with sober judgment, *in accordance with the measure of faith God has given you.*" What does that last phrase mean? Paul is telling us that we need to remember what God has said about us: Through faith in Christ, we are no longer in Adam, but our spirit is united with Christ. He lives in us and His power is available to us. That is the sober truth about ourselves that God wants us to know, the truth that is in accordance with the faith He has given us.

Remembering who we are in Christ gives us confidence, courage, and the ability to resist temptation and sin. It is a confidence without any conceit, because that confidence is focused on God's ability, not our own. It is the confidence that truly enables us to handle life, with all its problems and temptations.

Unity in Diversity

Next, Paul deals with our life in the church, and particularly the gifts God has given to believers:

Just as each of us has one body with many members, and these members do not all have the same function, so in

Christ we who are many form one body, and each member
belongs to all the others. (Romans 12:4-5)

In these verses, Paul gives us God's view of what the church
ought to be. If this is not your view of the church, then this is an
area where you need to be transformed through the renewing of
your mind. The church, God says, is like a human body. If you
want a good course in ecclesiology (the study and doctrine of the
church), just look at your body and all of its many functioning
parts. That is what the church is like.

Paul says that in Christ we form one body. Not two, not hundreds, not thousands of bodies—just one body. There is only one
church in all the world. All genuine Christians belong to it, and
it has nothing to do with denominations or church buildings or
church membership. If you have been born of the Spirit of God,
you are a member of that one body Paul speaks of. Within that
one body, all of us who are born of the Spirit of God are members
of one another—we belong to each other. There is one body, but
many members.

Just as every member of the human body has a purpose, every
member of the church body has a purpose. Hands are for grasping
and performing work. Feet are for standing and walking. Eyes are
for seeing. Ears are for hearing. Teeth are for chewing. A human
body is not just a featureless trunk, but a complex organism with
many parts and interesting protuberances, and each of those parts
and protuberances has a meaningful purpose. So it is with the
body of Christ, the church. The church, like the human body, is
beautiful in its diversity, complexity, and functionality.

So we must be careful to treat the members of the church as
individuals, not a series of copies. Christians don't all come from
the same economic class, race, generation, or background. They
don't have the same gifts of the Holy Spirit. Each Christian is as
unique as a snowflake or a fingerprint—no two are ever alike.

Ron Ritchie, a former pastor at Peninsula Bible Church (now a
pastor at Fellowship Bible Church in Colorado Springs, Colorado)

used to use a visual aid to illustrate the importance of diversity in the body of Christ. He painted a football so that it looked like a huge human eye with a big staring pupil. He wrapped it in a blanket and carried it as if it were a baby in his arms. He'd show it to people and say, "What do you think of my baby?" People would look at it and grimace. "Oh, gross!" they would say. And Ron would reply, "You mean you don't think the whole body should be one big eyeball?" And his point was made.

If a human body was one big eyeball or hand or foot or tongue, it would be "gross," it would be disgusting. Yet some people seem determined to build a church that has just one kind of member. They seek uniformity instead of diversity. God says we are not just one member; we are many. His goal for the church is not uniformity, but unity in diversity. The only sameness there should be in the church is that we should all have the same love and caring for one another. If we love each other the same, then we will have a glorious unity in the midst of our beautiful diversity in the body of Christ.

The Gifts of the Spirit

Paul goes on to point out that our function in the body is determined by the gifts we have been given:

> We have different gifts, according to the grace given us. If a man's gift is prophesying, let him use it in proportion to his faith. If it is serving, let him serve; if it is teaching, let him teach; if it is encouraging, let him encourage; if it is contributing to the needs of others, let him give generously; if it is leadership, let him govern diligently; if it is showing mercy, let him do it cheerfully. (Romans 12:6–8)

That is only a partial list of gifts; a more complete list can be found in 1 Corinthians 12, Ephesians 4, and 1 Peter 4. Paul's point is this: God has given gifts to the church, and all Christians have different combinations of gifts. In fact, Paul's word that is translated "gifts" literally means "graces." Something graceful is a delight to watch in action, and this is true of the gifts of the Spirit. A spiritual gift is an ability God gives you because He wants you to function effectively and gracefully in His body.

When we use our spiritual gifts, we experience a sense of fulfillment, because we are functioning as God intended us to. If we fail to discover and exercise our gifts, we miss out on the excitement and satisfaction of accomplishing our purpose in life. A Christian who doesn't use his spiritual gifts is like a child who receives a wonderful gift at Christmas but never bothers to unwrap it. Imagine how God, our heavenly Father, would feel if you turned your back on the wonderful gifts He has given you!

The first gift Paul mentions is *prophesying*. In 1 Corinthians 14:1 and 3, Paul tells us that this is one of the best gifts of all. The gift of prophecy is primarily the gift of expounding Scripture, of making the meaning of God's Word come alive. The Greek word for prophecy comes from a root word that means "to cause to shine," and it refers to the Spirit-given ability to make God's Word shine for all to understand. Peter says, "So we have the prophetic word made more sure, to which you do well to pay attention as to a lamp shining in a dark place" (see 2 Peter 1:19 NASB).

Paul says that if you have the gift of prophecy (and this gift is not just for people who go to seminary), then you should use it. But use it according to the proportion of your faith. In other words, stay within the limits of what you know. As you grow in your understanding of Scripture, you will grow in your ability to make it shine, so that others may apply it to their lives.

Next, Paul speaks of the gift of *serving*, which is probably the same as the gift of helping others listed in 1 Corinthians 12:28. The Greek word translated "serving" is *diakonia*, from which we get our word "deacon." Serving can take many forms, from serving as a deacon or usher in the church to making coffee in the fellowship hall to setting up folding chairs. The gift of serving is the ability to help others with such a cheerful spirit that both the servant and the served are blessed by it.

Next, there is the gift of *teaching*. This is the ability to impart knowledge and instruct the mind. The difference between prophesying and teaching is that prophesying instructs the heart and moves the will, whereas teaching instructs the mind. If you have the gift of teaching, don't wait for someone to ask you to teach. Find a place to use your God-given gift and put it to work.

Next, there is the gift of *encouragement*. One person in the New Testament who had this gift was Barnabas, whose name means "the son of encouragement." His given name was Joseph, but his fellow Christians apparently recognized his gift for encouraging others, so they gave him a new name to fit his character and his gift. In the book of Acts, you always find him with his arm around people, encouraging, comforting, and urging them on.

Next, there is the gift of *giving*, what Paul calls "contributing to the needs of others." Did you know that giving is a spiritual gift? God gives some people a generous heart that is always giving, giving, giving, without any thought of being repaid. If that is your gift, use it! The more you use the gift of giving, the more God will give you to distribute to others.

The New International Version renders Paul's words this way: "If it is contributing to the needs of others, let him give generously." A more literal translation would be, "Let him give with simplicity." That means to give without flourish or ostentation, without calling people's attention to the gift or the giver. I once heard of a man who stood up in a meeting and said, "I want to give a hundred dollars—anonymously." Giving with simplicity means giving with *true* anonymity. People with the gift of giving do not want to be recognized, they do not want their name on a brass plaque; they just want to give for the good of others and in gratitude to God.

Next, there is the gift of *leadership*. The original Greek word here means "leading meetings," and it comes from a root that means "to stand up before others." If you have this gift, there are all kinds of meetings that are waiting to be led. But when you use this gift, Paul says, use it with diligence. In other words, conduct your meetings in a thoughtful, well-planned, orderly way. The gift of leadership is a great gift that is much in need in the body of Christ.

Finally, there is the gift of *showing mercy*. The gift of showing mercy is a marvelous gift, and there are many ways to use this gift: in ministry to abused children, to handicapped people, to the aged, to prisoners, to shut-ins, to AIDS patients, to widows and orphans, and on and on. All across our society, there are people with needs and hurts, people who need mercy.

Christians do not have just one gift, but a number of gifts in unique combinations. I encourage you to study the spiritual gifts, discover which gifts you possess, and start putting your gifts to good use in service to God and His church. The apostle Peter tells us that there are actually two different classes of gifts:

> Each one should use whatever gift he has received to serve others, faithfully administering God's grace in its various forms. If anyone speaks, he should do it as one speaking the very words of God. If anyone serves, he should do it with the strength God provides, so that in all things God may be praised through Jesus Christ. (1 Peter 4:10–11)

The two divisions Peter identifies are speaking and serving. In Romans 12, Paul lists four gifts that have to do with speaking (prophesying, teaching, encouragement, and leadership) and three that have to do with serving (serving, giving, and mercy). There are two basic functions that believers in the body of Christ are expected to fill: Either you speak or you serve. Of course, some do both (a leader and encourager, for example, may also be a giver). The point is that everybody is expected to be involved, using the gifts God has given. If you are not speaking or serving, you are not using your gifts.

Sincere Christian Love

After talking about how the gifts of the spirit should be manifested in the body of Christ, Paul then talks about the need for Christian love to also be manifested. He writes:

Love must be sincere. Hate what is evil; cling to what is good. Be devoted to one another in brotherly love. Honor one another above yourselves. Never be lacking in zeal, but keep your spiritual fervor, serving the Lord. Be joyful in hope, patient in affliction, faithful in prayer. Share with God's people who are in need. Practice hospitality. (Romans 12:9–13)

In Paul's day as in our own, it was apparently not uncommon for people to pretend to love, using loving-sounding words, but without sincerity. Pretending to love is hypocrisy. Paul says, in effect, "Don't be hypocritical, don't just make a show of love. Demonstrate genuine love to one another in the body of Christ."

Sham love, phony love, comes from the flesh. It comes from that pretender inside of us who wants to have a good public image but is neither genuine nor sincere. Authentic love comes from the Holy Spirit. "God has poured out his love into our hearts by the Holy Spirit, whom he has given us," Paul writes (see Romans 5:5). Paul suggests six ways to authentically love one another in the body of Christ:

(1) "Hate what is evil; cling to what is good." This means that we should hate the evil that people do, but don't reject the people themselves because of that evil. God loves every human being, and so can we. Why? Because every human being is stamped with the image of God, and that is a good image. So cling to the good, to the image of God in every person, even while you hate the evil things that people do.

This is not easy to do. People who do evil things are hard to love. But if we are honest with ourselves, we have to recognize that we all do evil, and it is only by God's grace that any of us are saved. So, for the sake of the One who loved us and saved us, we must love one another. That's what genuine Christian love does.

Hypocritical, sham love rejects people who don't measure up to our standards. That is one reason may people reject the church: They hear us talk about love, peace, and joy, but they don't see us living it out. When people sin, we don't forgive and restore them; we reject them. The world observes the phoniness of our so-called "love," and sees us for the hypocrites we are.

Sometimes it is necessary to hold other people accountable for their actions, to confront them out of a genuine love and concern for their eternal well-being. Paul puts it this way:

> Brothers, if someone is caught in a sin, you who are spiritual should restore him gently. But watch yourself, or you also may be tempted. (Galatians 6:1)

That last statement is the key: Watch yourself! If you are called upon to hold a fellow Christian accountable, be aware of your own potential for sin. Correct and restore your brother or sister *gently* and *humbly*—not as if you were morally superior, but with an awareness that you yourself may need to be corrected someday.

(2) "Be devoted to one another in brotherly love." Your fellow Christians are your brothers and sisters. In Christ, you have a deep and bonded relationship with them. So be devoted to them. Be concerned about their welfare, their joys and sorrows and needs. When they hurt, be there to comfort them. When they have troubles, be there to meet their needs.

(3) "Honor one another above yourselves." The Phillips translation says, "Be willing to let other men have the credit." If that is your attitude, it doesn't matter if nobody notices what you did, or if no one bothers to thank you. The flesh demands attention and recognition, but a person who genuinely loves God and others will do good deeds for an audience of One.

(4) "Never be lacking in zeal, but keep your spiritual fervor, serving the Lord." Real love remains enthusiastic despite obstacles and setbacks. A Christian who walks in the Spirit is always rejoicing, always full of enthusiasm for God. One thing the Lord cannot put up with is a lukewarm spirit (see Revelation 3:16). He wants Christians who are on fire, not Christians who are indifferent. So

maintain your fire, your zeal, your spiritual fervor as you continue serving the Lord.

(5) "Be joyful in hope, patient in affliction, faithful in prayer." Authentic Christian love rejoices in hope. The Christian hope, our confident expectation of our future redemption and glory, enables us to be patient in our afflictions and faithful in our prayers. In fact, it is prayer that enables us to remain patient. If you are faithful in prayer, you will be patient in affliction.

(6) "Share with God's people who are in need. Practice hospitality." Authentic Christian love sees a need and meets it. Sometimes, in this day of Social Security, Medicare, and welfare, we forget that God calls us to help people in need. We think that helping people is the government's job. But governments cannot show real compassion and caring—that's what God put Christians on earth to do.

True Christian Love

Paul has been talking primarily about how we are to love one another in the church, the body of Christ. Now he tells us how to exhibit Christian love in a non-Christian world:

> Bless those who persecute you; bless and do not curse. Rejoice with those who rejoice; mourn with those who mourn. Live in harmony with one another. Do not be proud, but be willing to associate with people of low position. Do not be conceited.
>
> Do not repay anyone evil for evil. Be careful to do what is right in the eyes of everybody. If it is possible, as far as it depends on you, live at peace with everyone. Do not take revenge, my friends, but leave room for God's wrath, for it is written: "It is mine to avenge; I will repay," says the Lord. On the contrary:
>
> > "If your enemy is hungry, feed him;
> > if he is thirsty, give him something to drink.
> > In doing this, you will heap burning coals on his head."

Do not be overcome by evil, but overcome evil with good.
(Romans 12:14–21)

First, true Christian love speaks well of its persecutors. That's
what Paul means when he writes, "Bless those who persecute you;
bless and do not curse." Instead of cursing and complaining about
people who mistreat us, we are to speak well of them and pray that
God will do good in their lives.

This is a difficult command for us all—myself included. When
someone hurts us, it is not natural to respond with blessing. When
somebody persecutes me, I want to persecute back! But God calls
us to a level of behavior that goes beyond a natural reaction. In
fact, He calls us to a *supernatural* reaction. When someone cuts
us off in traffic (an act of automotive persecution!), we should
respond with a blessing, not a curse. When the boss shouts at us,
when the neighbor rattles his trash cans and wakes us up at mid-
night, when the store clerk is rude to us, when someone is angry
and abusive to us because we have just tried to share the gospel,
we should respond with a blessing, not a curse.

Second, true Christian love is sensitive to the emotional needs
of others. "Rejoice with those who rejoice," says Paul, "mourn
with those who mourn." Suppose a co-worker comes into your
office and says, "My spouse is divorcing me. My kids are rebelling
against me. I wrecked my car this morning. I'm depressed." You
could say, "Hey, why be such a gloomy Gus? Come on, the sun is
shining, the birds are singing! Smile!" This sounds cheery—but
it's actually a terribly unloving thing to say! Why? Because when
you're feeling down, there's nothing worse than a person who is
obnoxiously cheerful!

Paul says, in effect, "Adjust yourself to the emotional needs of
others. Rejoice with those who rejoice and mourn with those who
mourn." He puts the word "rejoice" first, because that is often the
hardest thing for us to do. It is easier to comfort someone who
is sorrowing than to be genuinely happy for someone who has
just won the Irish Sweepstakes. When others rejoice, we naturally

envy them. Genuine love, however, doesn't respond naturally, but *supernaturally*. Love says to the rejoicing person, "I'm happy for you!"—and *means* it.

Third, true Christian love does not show partiality or prejudice. Paul says, "Live in harmony with one another. Do not be proud, but be willing to associate with people of low position. Do not be conceited." Christian love does not treat anyone as superior or inferior. That goes against human nature. There is a natural human tendency to roll out the red carpet for people of high position, while shoving lowly people off to the side. Why? Because highly placed people can do things for us; lowly people can do nothing for us.

Paul says we must stop regarding some as Important People and others as Unimportant People. Everyone's important to God—and that should be our viewpoint as well. So he tells us: Get along with others, treat everyone as an equal, and don't be conceited. You're no better than anyone else, so be willing to get to know and enjoy ordinary people.

Fourth, true Christian love is not sneaky or underhanded. "Do not repay anyone evil for evil. Be careful to do what is right in the eyes of everybody." In other words, if someone does evil to you, don't plot some sneaky, subtle, crafty way to get even. Instead, if someone mistreats you, do good to that person, openly and for everyone to see.

Fifth, true Christian love seeks to live at peace with everyone: "If it is possible, as far as it depends on you, live at peace with everyone." Here Paul recognizes that there are some people who simply will not let you live in peace. So he adds the clause, "as far as it depends on you." In other words, even if you find yourself in conflict with someone, make sure that everything you do is focused on harmony and peacemaking. You're not responsible for what others do, but make sure that everything *you* do is loving, righteous, and Christlike.

Sixth, true Christian love does not try to get even with others. "Do not take revenge, my friends," Paul writes, "but leave room for God's wrath, for it is written: 'It is mine to avenge; I will repay,' says the Lord." Revenge is one of the most natural of human responses when we are injured or mistreated. We naturally feel that if we treat others as they have treated us, then we are getting justice, we are getting what is fair. But how many times have you done evil to others without getting caught? Are you in a moral position to judge others? No. Only God has the right and the knowledge to judge another human heart.

Taking revenge usually sets in motion a cycle of getting even that quickly spirals out of control. When I was a farmboy in Montana, I often watched cows in the corral. They would stand peacefully for a long time—then one cow would kick another. The injured cow would kick back. The first cow would kick back harder and miss, hitting a third. The third cow would kick back. Soon the whole herd was stirred up, kicking and milling about and mooing at one another, as angry as could be. Unfortunately, I've seen almost identical behavior in churches!

Paul gives two reasons why you should not avenge yourself: (1) "Leave room for God's wrath," says Paul. God is in control and His wrath is in operation. He knows you've been hurt or insulted, and He will see that justice is done. (2) "'It is mine to avenge; I will repay,' says the Lord." God alone claims the right to vengeance, because only He can dispense justice in a way that is redemptive and loving. His goal is not to injure, but to bring about repentance and restoration. If we avenge ourselves, we don't give God a chance to work.

Of course, we generally don't want the people who have hurt us to be redeemed and restored. We want them to be hurt. We are like the prophet Jonah, who became angry with God when the wicked city of Nineveh repented. Jonah didn't want Nineveh to repent and respond to God. He wanted God to wipe Nineveh off the map! And we identify with Jonah, don't we?

You may think, "Well, what am I supposed to do if someone abuses me? Should I just sit there and take it? Should I do nothing?" No. Paul does not say you should do nothing. There is definitely something you should do: "'If your enemy is hungry, feed him,'" he says. "'If he is thirsty, give him something to drink. In doing this, you will heap burning coals on his head.' Do not be overcome by evil, but overcome evil with good."

If you let God avenge you instead of avenging yourself, two things will happen: (1) You will act positively instead of negatively. You can be proactive instead of reactive. Paul quotes Proverbs 25:21–22, which says that acting kindly and lovingly toward your enemy heaps burning coals on his head. This doesn't mean you should get even by setting his hair on fire! This is a reference to the method of lighting fires in the days before matches. If the fire in your stove went out and you wanted to light a fire, you would borrow some smoldering coals from your neighbor. You'd take a fireproof earthen jar to your neighbor's house, your neighbor would put coals in it, then you'd put a cloth pad on top of your head, then steady the jar atop the pad and carry it home. So heaping burning coals on someone's head became a metaphor to describe a generous response to a neighbor in need. That is what God wants us to do toward our neighbors—to respond generously with true Christian love.

A young Christian in the Army had a habit of praying beside his bunk before going to sleep. Seeing this, some of the other soldiers in his barracks decided to ridicule and mock him to see if he would break under pressure. One day, after the entire platoon had been out all day on a forced march, they returned to their barracks, tired and dirty. As was his habit, the Christian soldier knelt beside his bunk and prayed. One of his tormentors, meanwhile, removed his muddy boots and threw them at the young man, hitting him in the head, spattering him with mud. The Christian said nothing in response, but simply kept praying.

The next morning, the tormentor woke up and found his boots standing next to his bed, shined and polished. The man was overcome with remorse for the way he had mistreated the Christian soldier, and he went to him and asked his forgiveness. The two men became friends, and in time the Christian led the other man to faith in Jesus Christ.

That is what Paul means when he says to overcome evil with good. As Abraham Lincoln once said, "The best way to overcome an enemy is to make him your friend." Three times in this passage, Paul has underscored the fact that we are not to return evil for evil. When mistreated, we are to respond with genuine Christian love. When we do that, we live according to the example of our Master. As Peter wrote, "Christ suffered for you, leaving you an example, that you should follow in his steps. . . . When they hurled their insults at him, he did not retaliate; when he suffered, he made no threats. Instead, he entrusted himself to him who judges justly" (1 Peter 2:21, 23).

Jesus loved His enemies even as they drove the nails into His hands and feet. So let us live as Jesus lived, love as He loved, and forgive as He forgave. What a testimony of grace it will be when we learn to love our enemies with the genuine love of Jesus.

The Key to Our Identity

It may not be immediately apparent, but the one theme that runs throughout Romans 12 is the theme of our identity in Christ. As you examine your own life in light of Romans 12, this question confronts you, and you must answer: "Who am I?" In fact, every morning, you should ask that question as you begin the activities of your day: "Who am I?" The answer to that question will determine how you live out each day—and your answer should come directly from the Scriptures:

"I am a child of God, living among the sons of men. My body is a living sacrifice, holy and pleasing to God. So I refuse to conform to the pattern of this world, and I choose to be transformed by the renewing of my mind. I am equipped by the Spirit of God to do His will today. I am gifted with special abilities to serve God and others, and I will use those gifts seven days a week—in my neighborhood, at my office, wherever I am. I will love my brothers and sisters in the church, the body of Christ, because we are members of one another and we belong to one another. And I will show genuine Christian love to the people outside the body of Christ, even to my enemies. That is my purpose in life. That is why God has redeemed me and placed me in the body of Christ. That is who I am."

As we live each day as a living sacrifice, serving God with our bodies, our transformed minds, our spiritual gifts, and our Christ-like love, we come to understand who we are and why we are here. There is no greater identity anyone can have than this:

"I am a child of the living God."

CHAPTER 15

GOD'S STRANGE SERVANTS

Romans 13:1–7

People often ask, "What is the best form of government in the world? Which form of government is the one God would ideally want people to have?"

We Americans generally consider our representative democracy to be the most God-honored form of government. It might surprise you to find that there is no support for such a view anywhere in Scripture. In fact, if you ask what is the ideal form of government—monarchy, oligarchy, dictatorship, republic, democracy, communism—the answer of Scripture is this: The best government for you is the government you live under.

In every place in the world, in every time in history, God has raised up various governments according to the nature of a given population, according to the degree of truth and light that population has received, and according to the moral conditions that prevail. God doesn't ordain any one form of government to continue forever. Wherever people grow toward an understanding of truth, wherever morality prevails in a community, democracy often takes root. When truth disappears, government often becomes more autocratic and totalitarian.

In any case, Paul tells us that whatever form of government you are under, God is behind it. This is true even of governments that persecute Christianity, such as Soviet-style communism or the oppressive Roman government of Paul's day. There is no government that can overturn God's plan for human history. God's purposes will be accomplished even in the most godless and repressive regimes imaginable. Why? Because, as Paul tells us in Romans 13, all governmental authority originates with God:

> Everyone must submit himself to the governing authorities, for there is no authority except that which God has established. The authorities that exist have been established by God. (Romans 13:1)

This truth did not originate in the New Testament. You find it in the Old Testament book of Daniel, where the prophet stood before Nebuchadnezzar, a great autocratic king of the ancient world. "He changes times and seasons," Daniel said. "He sets up kings and deposes them" (see Daniel 2:21). Daniel tells this king that God is not some remote figure on a distant mountain. He is involved in the affairs of humanity, and He is the one who sovereignly elevates a king—or removes a king. God is not remote from our political affairs. He is among us, involved in the pattern of our government.

When Paul wrote the letter to the Christians in Rome, they were living in the capital city of one of the most repressive regimes in human history. Nero had just begun his reign as emperor of Rome when Paul wrote this letter. It is amazing, then, that this is the background against which Paul writes, "The authorities that exist have been established by God." Paul is reminding these Christians, who live under the official persecution of Rome, that this government has been ordained by God.

Christians and the Government

When Paul refers to "governing authorities," he uses a phrase that can best be translated "the powers that be." Paul is not just talking about heads of state; he is talking about all levels of authority, from the grand emperor to the local dog-catcher. Regardless of the form of government we are under, the hand of God is in it. So when we obediently submit ourselves to the governing authorities, we are truly submitting ourselves to God Himself. Paul goes on to write:

Consequently, he who rebels against the authority is rebelling against what God has instituted, and those who do so will bring judgment on themselves. (Romans 13:2)

If God is behind governments, then those who oppose the government and seek to overthrow it are opposing God. Understand, this is not to say that everything a government does is good and righteous. When a government acts in a way that is opposed to God's law, when a government commits acts of atrocity or injustice, then Christian citizens have a right and a duty to speak up and attempt to influence their government for good.

At the same time, we have to recognize that governments have a God-given right to punish those who would rebel or try to overthrow them. Those who try to bring down a government, or who violate its laws, bring judgment upon themselves.

A government is an agent of God, but a government is not God. The rights and powers of a government are limited. I thank God that our Congress made the enlightened decision in 1954 to add two little words to our Pledge of Allegiance: "under God." That line reflects biblical truth. Our nation, and indeed any nation, exists as a nation under God. It is God who elevates a government and it is God who deposes a government.

When Jesus said, "Give to Caesar the things that belong to Caesar and give to God the things that belong to God," He implied that there are limits to the power of government. The image of Caesar was stamped on the coin Jesus held in His hand; therefore, those things that bore the image of Caesar belonged to Caesar. At the same time, some things were off-limits even to Caesar. Governments have authority over what we do with our property and how we behave toward one another, but governments have no right to touch what God has stamped His own image on: the human spirit.

Caesar has no right to control the worship of people, nor does Caesar have the right to forbid people to obey God's Word. Rulers are under God, and governments may not oppress or enslave human beings, because humanity belongs to God. Romans 13 doesn't deal with these issues at length, but Scripture as a whole makes it clear that believers have a right to resist oppression and religious persecution by nonviolent means. But believers may not resist the legitimate functions of government.

Paul goes on to describe those legitimate functions of government:

> For rulers hold no terror for those who do right, but for those who do wrong. Do you want to be free from fear of the one in authority? Then do what is right and he will commend you. (Romans 13:3)

If you don't want to be afraid of your government, then obey the laws. If you don't rob banks, commit murder, drive over the speed limit, or break any other laws, then you will probably never need to fear your government. But people who break the law *should* be afraid of the government. That is one of the most important reasons God ordained government: To make evil-doers afraid to do evil. That is why, in the next verse, Paul calls a government authority—such as a police officer, prosecutor, or judge—"God's servant":

> For he is God's servant to do you good. But if you do wrong, be afraid, for he does not bear the sword for nothing. He is God's servant, an agent of wrath to bring punishment on the wrongdoer. Therefore, it is necessary to submit to the authorities, not only because of possible punishment but also because of conscience.
>
> This is also why you pay taxes, for the authorities are God's servants, who give their full time to governing. (Romans 13:4–6)

This passage tells us that there are two basic functions of government authorities: (1) Government authorities restrain evil and protect the population; and (2) government authorities are servants of God. The word translated "servant" in verse 4 is the same word we saw in Romans 12:7, which spoke of the spiritual gift of serving. That word is *diakonia*, from which we get the word "deacon." So Paul says that governmental authorities are the deacons or servants of God. They perform God's work among humanity.

Governmental authorities punish crimes, commend good deeds (for example, by honoring good citizens with award ceremonies), they judge disputes, and otherwise maintain a well-ordered society on behalf of God. Sometimes, governments can even dispense compassion.

On one occasion during the Great Depression, New York City's mayor, Fiorello La Guardia, presided over a Manhattan police court. A man was brought before him who was thin, trembling, and shabbily dressed. He was charged with stealing a loaf of bread. The man pled guilty to the crime, but explained that his family was starving and he was unable to find work.

"I'm sorry," said the mayor, "but the law makes no exceptions. I'm going to have to fine you ten dollars."

"But," the defendant said, "I haven't got ten dollars! I haven't even got a dime!"

"I understand," said Mayor La Guardia, reaching into his own pocket. "That's why I'm going to pay the fine myself—here, take this." He handed the money to the man. "Furthermore, I'm going to remit the fine—that means you can keep the money."

The defendant stared at the ten dollar bill in his hands. It had been a long time since he had handled that much money.

"One more thing," the mayor added. "Bailiff, take off your hat and pass it around this courtroom. I'm fining everybody in this courtroom fifty cents for living in a city where a man has to steal in order to get bread for his family." The money was collected and given to the defendant. That is an example of the compassionate side of government.

A Cheerful Taxpayer

In verse 6, Paul refers to this compassionate side of government, writing, "This is also why you pay taxes, for the authorities are God's servants, who give their full time to governing." The word Paul uses for "servants" in this verse is different from the word that is translated "servants" in verse 4. In verse 4, the word meant "deacon." In verse 6, Paul uses a word that means "priest." Paul is saying that we pay taxes to support God's ministering priests in the government.

The purpose of government is not only to provide for our defense and security, but also to provide services we all need. Government servants function as priests in our society, helping to meet our needs for schools, relief agencies, postal service, roads and transportation, and other functions of government.

To make these services possible, God has given governments two powers. One is the power of force, which Paul describes by saying that the government servant "does not bear the sword for nothing." The sword symbolizes the right to use force, even the right to take life in extreme cases. This right includes deadly force in policing situations, lethal force in times of war and national self-defense, and capital punishment by the criminal justice system. Though I respect the views of those Christians who conscientiously oppose capital punishment, I think this passage and others make it clear that the Scriptures affirm the right of the government to impose the death penalty.

The second power that God has given to governments is the power to collect taxes. You may not like the level of taxation imposed on you, but you cannot object to the principle of taxation—at least, not from a biblical basis. Citizens have a duty to support the government with their taxes, and Paul makes it clear that Christians should pay their taxes.

Next, Paul deals with the Christian's motivation in obeying the government:

> Therefore, it is necessary to submit to the authorities, not only because of possible punishment but also because of conscience.
>
> This is also why you pay taxes, for the authorities are God's servants, who give their full time to governing. Give

everyone what you owe him: If you owe taxes, pay taxes;
if revenue, then revenue; if respect, then respect; if honor,
then honor. (Romans 13:5–6)

Here, Paul makes it clear that our motivation in obeying the
authorities is not primarily that we are afraid of getting caught.
Our true motivation is our Christian conscience. That means that
we should obey the speed laws whether there is a police car nearby
or not. We should pay the taxes the government says we owe, and
should not "fudge" our tax return, even if we would never get
caught. As Christians, we are to be people of integrity, obeying the
government just as we would obey God—with a clean conscience,
not out of fear of punishment.

We have no right to withhold taxes just because we disagree
with how they are being spent. We are accountable to pay what we
owe; people in government are accountable for how the money is
used. Governments are made up of fallible men and women just
like us, and there will be mistakes, waste, and fraud. That does not
relieve us of the responsibility to pay our taxes.

Moreover, Paul tells us that we should maintain a good attitude toward our government. Many people around us gripe and
groan about paying taxes, but Christians should be different from
everyone around them. We must not resent government's powers,
but respect the government because it is ordained by God.

I have had to learn these lessons myself. I remember the first
time I had to pay income taxes. I felt that it was an unfair imposi-
tion—especially since I felt I was making little enough money as
it was! I resented having to fill out the Form 1040, and when I
sent it in, I addressed the envelope to "The Infernal Revenue Service." The IRS never wrote back, but they did accept my money.
The following year, my attitude improved a bit, so I addressed
the envelope to "The Eternal Revenue Service." Since then, I
have repented of those sins and I now pay my taxes cheerfully
and with thanksgiving to God for the government I live under.

As we pay our taxes, let us do so cheerfully and respectfully. Remember, Paul said that we not only should pay our taxes, but if we owe respect, we should pay respect; if we owe honor, we should pay honor. The American government is undoubtedly the most benevolent form of government ever devised. But even the worst of governments is better than anarchy, and all governments serve a function that God Himself has ordained.

We serve a God who is neither Republican nor Democrat, neither communist nor capitalist. He transcends all political labels and ideologies. Not only are governments ordained by God, but the people in office are placed there by God. They are God's servants, whether they know it or not, whether they love God or not. Even wicked men—from Pharaoh to Nebuchadnezzar to Caesar—have unwittingly served to further God's eternal plan in history.

It is strange to realize that government officials who hate God, blaspheme His name, and persecute His people are actually His servants, but that is exactly who they are: God's *strange* servants, His reluctant and unwitting servants.

Regardless of the form of government we live under, the hand of God is in it. So let us give to Caesar what is Caesar's. Let us humbly submit ourselves to the governing authorities, knowing that as we do so, we are obediently submitting our lives to God Himself.

CHAPTER 16

LOVE, FOR THE NIGHT IS ENDING

Romans 13:8–14

Whenever I meet someone I owe money to, the first thing that comes to mind is the debt I owe—and I wonder if he is thinking about it too! This is how Paul wants us to think about Christian love. He wants us to remember that we have an obligation to every human being we meet—an obligation of love. So Paul's first word to us in this section is this: "Let no debt remain outstanding, except the continuing debt to love one another. . . ."

Love is the greatest need in the world today. When Paul wrote this letter to the Christians living in Rome, love was surely the thing most lacking in their society. The Christians in Rome suffered cruel persecution under the Roman emperor, Nero. They desperately needed to know how to authentically love one another amid the pressures and terrors of that regime.

We also need to learn the secret of authentic Christian love. So Paul writes:

> Let no debt remain outstanding, except the continuing debt to love one another, for he who loves his fellowman has fulfilled the law. The commandments, "Do not commit adultery," "Do not murder," "Do not steal," "Do not covet," and whatever other commandment there may be, are summed up in this one rule: "Love your neighbor as yourself." Love does no harm to its neighbor. Therefore love is the fulfillment of the law. (Romans 13:8–10)

Here, Paul says, in effect, "Have you ever struggled to obey the Ten Commandments? Look, keeping the Ten Commandments is not hard at all, because they are all summed up in a single command: Love one another. If you genuinely love others, you will automatically keep the commandments!"

Isn't that a beautiful, practical statement? Paul has distilled ten commandments down to one commandment: Love everyone! If you authentically love others, you will never cause any harm. Imagine how the world would be changed if everyone obeyed this one command.

If you love others with authentic Christian love, you would never harm your own family or another family by committing adultery. You would not murder your neighbor or poison his dog or throw your trash over the fence into his back yard. You would not let your own dog soil the neighbor's lawn, nor would you thoughtlessly toss a paper cup out of the window of your car. You wouldn't covet your neighbor's new car. You wouldn't envy anyone else's prosperity and success, because you would be genuinely happy for that person. You wouldn't tell lies about other people, because you would never want to injure anyone's reputation.

If everyone followed this one simple commandment, there would be no more divorces, because a divorce is nothing more or less than a failure to love one another. If there were no more divorces, if couples loved each other with Christlike love, children would grow up happy, confident, and secure in homes that are bound together by genuine love.

If everyone followed this one simple commandment, there would be no more wars. The nations of the world could disarm without fear. We could dismantle the thousands of nuclear weapons that threaten all life on the planet.

If everyone followed this one simple commandment, there would be no more crime. Our streets and parks would be safe to walk at night. People would no longer have to protect their homes with iron bars, deadbolts, and electronic alarm systems. Our tax burden would plummet, because governments would not need to spend money on prisons, police, and courts.

We could go on and on, but these few examples are all we need to catch a glimpse of the utopian heaven-on-earth that would result if people would just follow this one simple commandment. The ability to love is the radical force that Jesus Christ has turned loose on the world by His death and resurrection. The love of Jesus is the power to change the world.

Night Is Nearly Over

By urging us to love one another, Paul tells us that this revolution of love must begin with us. If we are in Christ, we have the power to love. You don't have to ask for the power to love; you have the power already. In your flesh, you may be tempted to hate, but in your spirit which is in Christ, you have the power to love as Jesus loved. Imagine how your own little corner of the world would change if you viewed everyone around you this way: "I owe this person a debt of love. Lord, help me to repay that debt. How can I show Your love to this person right now?"

Paul goes on to say:

> And do this, understanding the present time. The hour has come for you to wake up from your slumber, because our salvation is nearer now than when we first believed. The night is nearly over; the day is almost here. So let us put aside the deeds of darkness and put on the armor of light. Let us behave decently, as in the daytime, not in orgies and drunkenness, not in sexual immorality and debauchery, not in dissension and jealousy. Rather, clothe yourselves with the Lord Jesus Christ, and do not think about how to gratify the desires of the sinful nature. (Romans 13:11–14)

The opening words of this paragraph impress upon us a sense of urgency about love: We are to love, Paul says, "understanding the present time." If you truly understand the age in which we live, Paul says, you will be compelled, motivated, and driven to love your neighbor. Paul points out three important features about the times in which we live.

First, he says it is time to get going, time to spring into action: "The hour has come for you to wake up from your slumber." It is time to wake up and see all the opportunities for showing God's love to others. I am amazed at how many times in my own life I have missed opportunities to love. Sometimes I am so focused on looking for opportunities to love people in the world around me, I miss opportunities to show love to my own family! I am surrounded by opportunities to love, yet I so easily bypass them.

One much-overlooked opportunity to show love is a time of conflict or strained relations. We tend to think of Christian love as something warm and fuzzy that we dispense on Sunday mornings or at holidays with a hug and a kind word. But Jesus demonstrated for us that authentic Christian love is something we live out when we are being mistreated, mocked, beaten, and crucified.

"But," you may say, "how can I love people when they are hurting me and insulting me? I don't *feel* like loving people who are doing harm to me."

That is the problem most people have in understanding Christian love. People hear the word "love" and misunderstand what Christian love is all about. We are conditioned by our culture to think of love as a feeling. But Christlike love is not a feeling. It is a *decision*—and the decision to love is especially important at times when we don't *feel* like loving.

The ancient Greeks had various words for feeling-based forms of love. The Greeks called the feeling of affection we have for a good friend *phileo*. The romantic feeling that lovers experience when they are attracted to one another was called *eros*. But there was another word the Greeks reserved for the highest form of love, a love that is not a feeling, but a *choice*, a decision of the will. The Greeks called this form of love *agape*, and that is the kind of love Paul tells us we should have for one another.

The reason *agape*-love is so powerful is that it has nothing to do with our feelings. If someone mistreats you, then you naturally feel angry and resentful. But even though your emotions are churning, you can still make a decision in reliance upon God to *agape*-love the person who was hurtful to you. Authentic Christian love is not based on emotions; it is based on obedience. When a person is unlovely and unlovable, you can pray, "Lord, give me the strength to obey You. Give me the ability to do good to this person even though I don't feel good toward this person. Help me to express Your love in this situation."

Martin Niemoller was a leading pastor in the Evangelical Lutheran Church in Germany during World War II. A leading opponent of Hitler's militarism and hatred of the Jews, Niemoller courageously opposed the Nazis until his arrest by the Gestapo in 1937. For eight years, he was imprisoned in concentration camps, first at Sachsenhausen and later at Dachau. As the war was ending, the Nazis slaughtered hundreds of inmates in the concentration camps, trying to leave no witnesses of their atrocities. Niemoller was one of the few who escaped execution.

Niemoller died in 1984 at the age of ninety-two. Shortly before his death, he told some of his friends of a disturbing, recurring dream he had. In this dream, it was the day of God's judgment of humanity, and Niemoller saw Adolf Hitler standing before the Lord Jesus. Jesus came down from His throne, put his arm around Hitler, and said, "Adolf, why? Why did you do so much evil? Why were you so cruel?"

In the dream, Hitler hung his head sadly and said, "Because nobody ever told me how much You love me."

Niemoller said that at this point in the dream, he would awaken in a cold sweat, shaking with guilt and grief. Why did he feel guilty? Because he remembered that in the years before the war began, he had numerous meetings with Adolf Hitler. In his role as a leader of the Lutheran church, Niemoller had sat across a table from Hitler and had spoken with him face to face—not once, but many times. And in all of those meetings, Niemoller recalled, he had never once said, "Jesus loves you, Herr Hitler. He loves you so much that He came and died for you."

Martin Niemoller couldn't help wondering how the world might have been changed, how history might have been rewritten, if he had dared to obediently express the *agape*-love of Jesus to a man named Adolf Hitler.

The second important feature Paul observes about the times in which we live: Time is short. He says, "Our salvation is nearer now than when we first believed." When Paul talks about the nearness of our salvation, he is saying that Christ is returning. When He does, we will be delivered from this body of sin and from the perils and pain of this world. Paul pictures our present age as a time of darkness, a time of night. "The night is nearly over," Paul says, "the day is almost here."

Jesus once told His disciples, "As long as it is day, we must do the work of him who sent me. Night is coming, when no one can work" (see John 9:4). Jesus was aware of the brevity of His own earthly life and the urgency of His mission on earth. While He was present on earth, it was daytime. But His death and burial would bring a nightfall. We live in that period of darkness today. As Paul tells us in Philippians 2:15, Christians are like bright stars shining in the darkness of the night sky. The night of this world is all around us, but the day is fast approaching.

We don't know how much time remains to us. Christ may return today or a thousand years from now. What seems like a long span of time from our perspective is a mere eye-blink from God's point of view. The important thing for us to remember is that life is brief, time is short, Christ is coming, and we have only limited time in which to love one another. If we are going to pay the debt of love we owe, we must begin now. The night is nearly over; the day is almost here.

The third important feature Paul observes about the times in which we live: It is time to give up sin and put on God's armor of righteousness. "So let us put aside the deeds of darkness and put on the armor of light," Paul says. And he goes on to list the deeds of darkness: orgies and drunkenness, sexual immorality and debauchery, dissension and jealousy. If we are going to live in true

Christian love, then we must shed those deeds that are incompatible with love.

Clothe Yourself with Jesus

Paul tells us that we must not live for meaningless pleasure, for self-indulgence and amusements that merely waste our lives away. Every human being gets only a finite number of heartbeats, and when they are used up, life is over. The time we have on earth is precious and irreplaceable, and our time should be used to show love to others, not to merely gratify the self.

Also, we must not live for sex. Our natural human sex drive is a powerful force that is highly exploited today. God created us as sexual creatures and intended that we should enjoy sex within the secure boundaries of a committed marriage relationship. The world around us tries to arouse our sex drive in order to sell us a lot of useless products. Our entertainment media shout to us: "Do you want to be fulfilled? You need a new love affair, the excitement of a new romance! What are you waiting for? Come on! Indulge yourself!"

You can't love with Christlike love while living for sex and pleasure. Even though the act of sex is often called "making love," the immoral pursuit of sexual gratification is not about authentic love at all. It is about *using* people, not *loving* them. Paul lists a wide range of immoral behavior, because he knows that people are quick to rationalize sin, and he doesn't want to leave any loopholes. The list he gives us applies to such behavior as fornication, adultery, homosexuality, and pornography. You can't indulge in these things and still love people with a Christlike love. Such behavior cheapens God's gift of sex and brings harm to oneself and others.

Also, we must not live for strife, dissension, and jealousy. Paul's counsel in this passage acknowledges the fact that there are many people who seem to enjoy stirring up dissension—and many of those people are in the church! Jesus once said, "He who is not with me is against me, and he who does not gather with me

scatters" (see Matthew 12:30; Luke 11:23). Here, Paul suggests a
way to measure your life: What is your effect upon people? Do you
harmonize with people? Do you gather people together? Do you
create peace and joy wherever you go? Or do you generate strife,
division, and separation? Do you gather or scatter? Your answer to
this question tells you whether you are with Jesus or against Him.

Finally, Paul tells us, "Clothe yourselves with the Lord Jesus
Christ, and do not think about how to gratify the desires of your
sinful nature." When you get up every morning, you put on your
clothes. Your clothes cover you and make you presentable. In the
same way, Paul says, we must clothe ourselves with Jesus Christ
every morning. We must make Him a part of our lives each day, so
that He is with us, acting through us, demonstrating His love in us.

Notice how Paul refers to Jesus when he says, "Clothe yourselves with the Lord Jesus Christ." He uses the full name and title
of Jesus—"the Lord Jesus Christ." I think Paul does this deliberately, because each name has a special meaning. "The Lord"
stands for His authority, His power to rule over the events of history. The name "Jesus" literally means "Jehovah our Savior." Jesus
is the expression of God's infinite love for us, in that while we
were sinners and enemies of God, He sent His Son to save us.
This name speaks of the amazing love of God. "Christ" means
"anointed" (the Hebrew word for *Christ* or *anointed* is *Mashiach*,
from which we get the word *Messiah*). The title Christ or Messiah
speaks of the fact that Jesus was anointed and commissioned by
God to deliver His people, to set us free.

So when Paul tells us to clothe ourselves with the Lord Jesus
Christ, he is telling us that we have the authority of the Lord; that
we are to carry on His ministry of loving others; and that we are
to continue His messianic mission of delivering people and setting
people free.

I love the way J. B. Phillips translated this verse: "Let us be
Christ's men from head to foot, and give no chance to the flesh
to have its fling" (Romans 13:14 PHILLIPS). So put on the Lord

Jesus Christ from head to foot. Rely on His power to give you the strength to love, and let Him love the world through you.

I once had a conversation with Eldridge Cleaver, who had been a leader in the Black Panthers, a group of violent left-wing militants during the 1960s. He told me that, during his days in the Black Panther movement, he was filled with a terrible, roiling hatred toward the police. The sight of a police uniform filled him with an intense loathing, murderous rage, and an urge to do violence.

In the early 1970s, Cleaver was in the south of France, standing on a balcony overlooking the Mediterranean Sea. Suddenly, he had a vision of the face of Jesus Christ. That powerful vision drove him to open a Bible and read the 23rd Psalm. Those words spoke a strange and powerful peace to his heart. So he read the psalm again, and again, and again.

"Since the day I stood on that balcony and had that vision of the Lord Jesus," he told me, "I have never felt hatred again. The rage and the violence left me that day, and it has never come back. I even looked for it and expected to find it—but it's just not there anymore. In its place, I just have a love for everyone I meet."

That is what Jesus Christ does. He gives us the power to love others, even our enemies. If we exercise this power in all the situations of our lives, with all the people we meet, we will unleash a radical force upon the world. That force will change our lives, our homes, our communities, our nation, and our world. That is the only way to live.

CHAPTER 17

THE WEAK AND THE STRONG

Romans 14:1–15:13

During the 1950s and '60s, a flamboyant and fiery radio preacher became famous for his attacks on everything he considered evil: movies, racetracks, labor unions, sex education, socialized medicine, drinking, smoking, dancing, and fluoride in the water supply. He was a vehement anti-Communist who once claimed that the United States had a moral responsibility to launch a nuclear attack against the Soviet Union. Some of his fiercest criticism was directed at Christians who disagreed with him on any issue. He once denounced American Christians for failing to rise up and take a stand against attempts to switch temperature measurements from Fahrenheit to Celsius! He claimed that it was nothing but a sneaky Communist plot to take over the world by degrees!

There are many areas of doctrine and Scripture interpretation over which faithful, sincere believers may honestly differ. Tragically, there have always been Christians who insist on dividing with other Christians over trivial and peripheral issues.

As we examine Romans 14, we will see Paul addressing an age-old problem that is still very much in evidence today: Christians who disagree with each other and who doggedly, dogmatically try to change each other. The problem is an attitude that says, "God is clearly pleased with my beliefs and my lifestyle—but those Christians over there are wrong! This one has the wrong view of spiritual gifts! And that one drinks beer and plays cards! And that one wears lipstick and goes out dancing!" And on it goes, an endless list of taboos and no-no's.

Here Paul confronts the issue of how much fellowship we can have with professing Christians who believe, live, and behave in ways we do not approve of. This is the problem of Christian ethics, the issue of legalism versus liberty. When we place Paul's discussion of these issues in context with what he has said before, it is clear that this entire section is an extension of his commentary of Christian love that began in Romans 13.

Weak in the Faith

As we begin Romans 14, we learn that love must be patient and tolerant of other people's views, including the views of those who are less enlightened or spiritually mature than ourselves. Paul writes:

> Accept him whose faith is weak, without passing judgment on disputable matters. (Romans 14:1)

The New International Version mistranslates this verse. The meaning here should not be, "Accept him whose faith is weak," but, "Accept him who is weak in the faith." The distinction may seem minor, but it is actually an important difference. Paul is not talking about people whose individual faith is weak, people who are troubled by doubts or questions. He is talking about someone who is weak in the faith—that is, someone who does not have the maturity or experience in the Christian faith to adequately understand God's truth.

Jesus Himself said, "If you hold to my teaching, you are really my disciples. Then you will know the truth, and the truth will set you free" (see John 8:31–32). In other words, a person must hold to Jesus' teaching over time, growing in knowledge and experience of the truth. Until a believer reaches a level of mature knowledge of Jesus' teaching, that believer is considered "weak in the faith," even if he or she has a very strong and vibrant personal faith. Once that person becomes strong in the faith, he or she will understand Christian liberty and be set free.

Paul says that when we encounter someone who is weak in the faith, we should accept him without passing judgment on disputable matters. We do not reject or ignore him; we do not treat him as a second-class Christian. We do not get into a debate with him in order to set him straight. We simply accept him in Christian love. Regardless of any differences you have with each other, you are brothers and sisters in the family of God. It was God Himself who placed you in one family together.

So accept the brother or sister who is weak in the faith—not to straighten out your fellow Christian, but simply to show him or her the same accepting love that God has shown you through Jesus Christ. The first word exchanged between you and your brother or sister should not be a word of dispute, but a recognition that you belong to one another in the body of Christ.

Next, Paul begins to define the specific areas of dispute and debate he has in mind:

One man's faith allows him to eat everything, but another man, whose faith is weak, eats only vegetables. (Romans 14:2)

Paul is not talking about disputes with vegetarians. This concern arises over a moral and spiritual issue arising from the Jewish character of the early church. The Jews observed certain restrictions regarding the eating of certain kinds of meat. According to the dietary laws found in Leviticus, Jews could not eat pork. Even beef and lamb had to be killed and prepared in very specific ways. So a Jewish Christian naturally had great emotional difficulty in eating meat.

In Rome and other Greek and Roman cities, the issue of eating meat was complicated by the fact that most of the meat had been offered to pagan idols before it was sold to the public. The best meat was sold in a marketplace next to the temple; the sacrificed meat went from the temple to the butcher in the marketplace, and the people bought it from the butcher.

Some Christians believed, then, that eating meat was the equivalent of participating in idol worship. Other Christians said,

"No, meat is meat, and the fact that someone else offered this meat to an idol doesn't mean that I am an idolater. My Christian liberty allows me to eat meat with a clear conscience."

Here are two viewpoints: a narrow view and a broad view, a strict view and a liberal view. Christians don't deal with the issue of meat sacrificed to idols anymore, but that is beside the point. The principle Paul urges us to adopt is valid for all time and in an endless variety of situations. Whenever two believers find themselves on opposite sides of an issue that is not clearly addressed in Scripture, then Christian love must prevail. In our own culture, the issue may have to do with whether or not it is right for Christians to drink wine or beer; whether Christians should support military action or be pacifists; or whether Christians should adopt this or that position on baptism or eschatology. You can certainly think of issues from your own experience.

Of course, some issues are not debatable at all, because they are clearly addressed in Scripture. Whether or not it is permissible for Christians to drink beer or wine, it is always wrong to be drunk, because the Scriptures tell us so in no uncertain terms. It is always wrong to commit sins of adultery or fornication. It is always wrong to hold a doctrinal view that violates Scripture, such as a belief that the Bible is not the inspired Word of God or that Jesus was not born of a virgin or that He was not raised from the dead.

But there are many areas that Scripture leaves open and unaddressed. If Paul wanted to, he could give firm "yes" or "no" answers to those issues right here in this passage. He could settle these issues for all time—but he doesn't do so. Why? Because God Himself does not do so. There are areas that God deliberately leaves to individual discretion. He expects believers to thoughtfully consider the issue, weigh the moral pros and cons, then act in accordance with their individual convictions.

Do Not Sit in Judgment

Now, it is clear that Paul considers people holding the broad, liberal view to be strong in the faith, while those with the narrow, strict view are regarded as weak in the faith. So the mark of understanding truth is freedom and liberty. Those who do not understand Christian liberty are weak in the Christian faith because they do not understand how truth delivers us from bondage.

Those who are weak in the faith have a legalistic view of the faith. They see Christianity as a network of rules and regulations. They find it comforting to have their lives marked out and categorized by laws and rules; the idea of Christian liberty is threatening to them. In a real sense, those who are weak in the faith have not liberated themselves from a belief in salvation by works. Even though they may intellectually understand that salvation is by grace through faith, they still try to earn a righteous standing before God by keeping a set of rules.

Every church has people who are weak in the faith. Paul tells us how we must respond to them:

> The man who eats everything must not look down on him who does not, and the man who does not eat everything must not condemn the man who does, for God has accepted him. (Romans 14:3)

The strong must not reject the one who is struggling, who is still weak. The phrase translated "look down on him" literally means "push him out." The strong must not push the weak out or exclude them. There must not be a trace of contempt or disdain in our dealings with the weak.

We have all seen this tendency among those who feel great Christian freedom in certain areas. They tend to regard those who are not yet free as second-class Christians. Sometimes they even ridicule those who are weak in the faith for being "strait-laced," "narrow-minded," "hide-bound," or "puritanical." That is exactly the attitude Paul says we must not have. In fact, he implies that any so-called "strong" brothers who look down upon the "weak" brothers are showing that they, too, are weak in the faith! Someone who is strong in the faith treats everyone in the church with Christlike love, not ridicule or disdain.

At the same time, Paul makes it clear that those who are legalistic must not look down on those who are free. In other words, those who think it is morally wrong to drink wine or beer must not look down on those who feel free to do so. They must not sit in judgment of them or criticize them. They must not say, "How can you be a Christian and do such things?"

What often happens in the church is that the weak in the faith—the legalists who do not understand their freedom in Christ—make up the majority in the church. So they set artificial, man-made standards for Christian conduct and impose those standards on everybody. They imply (or state outright) that you cannot be a Christian unless you obey the rules and conform to the standards that have been set.

The legalists are largely responsible for the fact that many people in the world see Christianity as a religion of rules and regulations. The simple message of Christian liberty has been lost amid the babble of voices demanding that Christians obey the rules. Legalism—which Jesus continually battled throughout His earthly ministry—has tragically triumphed over grace in many evangelical churches.

Don't Judge God's Servant

Paul goes on to state the reason we must not judge the weak or condemn the strong: It is not our responsibility to change our brothers' beliefs and behavior. Paul writes:

> Who are you to judge someone else's servant? To his own master he stands or falls. And he will stand, for the Lord is able to make him stand. (Romans 14:4)

Every believer is a servant of the Lord. A servant is accountable to his Master, not to you or me. We have no right to judge the Lord's servant. The Lord chose him, and if the Lord's servant needs to be changed in any way, it is up to the Lord to change him. "He will stand," Paul says, "for the Lord is able to make him stand." In other words, it is not up to you to decide if the Lord's servant is standing on firm ground or has fallen flat on his face. That's God's job, and you can trust Him to do the right thing.

Sometimes the reason our brothers and sisters in Christ take the positions they do is that they don't adequately understand the truth. If that is the case, the solution is to teach the truth more plainly. As people hear it and understand it, they will become stronger in the faith. It is useless to try to force someone to comply with rules or doctrines they don't understand. So be patient and teach the truth of God's Word. As people are exposed to the truth, they will change.

It is important to keep in mind the fact that God knows every human heart; you and I do not. This, Paul says, is why we need to show patience toward those with whom we disagree:

> One man considers one day more sacred than another; another man considers every day alike. Each one should be fully convinced in his own mind. He who regards one day as special, does so to the Lord. He who eats meat, eats to the Lord, for he gives thanks to God; and he who abstains, does so to the Lord and gives thanks to God. For none of us lives to himself alone and none of us dies to himself alone. If we live, we live to the Lord; and if we die, we die to the Lord. So, whether we live or die, we belong to the Lord. (Romans 14:5–8)

Christians may have differing views of these issues, but they have the same intention: to honor God with their conduct. God knows the heart; you and I do not. We are so quick to judge our fellow Christians and find fault with their choices—but if we actually knew the honest conviction that underlies those choices, we would be ashamed of our judgmental attitudes.

We often think that we are the only people with genuine convictions, but Paul says that we must be tolerant of the convictions of others. The important thing is that whatever we do, we do unto the Lord. Our convictions must be rooted in our desire to please God, and we should live by those convictions. As Paul says, "Each one should be fully convinced in his own mind."

Don't just do what you do because of tradition, because you've always done it that way. Don't just do what you do because "it feels like the right thing to do." Search the Scriptures and justify your decisions on the basis of Scripture. In the process of exploring the issue, your mind and your convictions may change—and God may straighten *you* out!

Paul uses the example of honoring certain days to show that two completely opposite viewpoints can both be pleasing to God. One Christian may treat Sunday as "the Lord's Day," keeping that day holy in much the same way that the Jews kept the Sabbath. Another Christian may say, "To me, all days are alike. I don't feel that God wants me to set one day aside for any special purpose. I want to honor the Lord seven days a week." Neither of these two Christians should feel offended by the other. Each makes a choice from the deep conviction of his heart.

Some years ago, a nightclub singer gave her life to Jesus Christ and began attending church. When her pastor invited her to sing at a church meeting, she instantly agreed—she was eager to use her talent for God. She stood up, dressed in the kind of shimmering, stunning gown she always performed in, and sang in the only style she knew—the sultry style of a nightclub singer. It was a beautiful song about Jesus—but no one in the church had ever heard it sung *that* way before!

After the meeting, one of the strait-laced women of the church approached the singer and ripped into her. "How dare you come to church dressed like that! And how can you sing that way and call yourself a Christian!" The young singer was so stunned and shaken that she broke into tears and ran out of the church.

Was her performance inappropriate? Of course it was—and if the young women wasn't such a new Christian, young in the faith, she would have known it. Being a new Christian, she simply didn't know any better. But her heart was right and God was surely pleased with her expression of love for Him. What could *not* have pleased God was when one of the older women of the church took it upon herself to set this young women straight—and to do so with harsh, hurtful words.

Our relationship to one another is more important than any issue or disagreement. "For none of us lives to himself alone," Paul writes, "and none of us dies to himself alone. If we live, we live to the Lord; and if we die, we die to the Lord. So, whether we live or die, we belong to the Lord." The fact that we belong to the Lord is even more important than whether we live or die. Since all of us as believers belong to the Lord, we need to remember our relationship with one another.

Paul goes on to tell us that Christ alone has the right to judge people—a right he won upon the cross:

> For this very reason, Christ died and returned to life so that he might be the Lord of both the dead and the living. You, then, why do you judge your brother? Or why do you look down on your brother? For we will all stand before God's judgment seat. It is written:
>
> "'As surely I live,' says the Lord,
> 'every knee will bow before me;
>   every tongue will confess to God.'"
>
> So then, each of us will give an account of himself to God. (Romans 14:9–12)

When we judge or condemn other people, we are putting ourselves in the place of Christ. Hebrews 10:12 tells us that after Jesus offered the sacrifice for our sins upon the cross, He "sat down at the right hand of God," the seat of judgment. And in 2 Timothy 4:1, Paul says that Jesus "will judge the living and the dead." He is the Lord of the living and the dead, and He is the only one who has a right to judge any human being. The strong must not judge

the weak, nor the weak judge the strong. Each of us must indi-
vidually stand before God's judgment seat.

This is true in both a present tense and a future sense. Every
day, hour by hour, we are accountable to the Lord for our conduct—and especially for the way we treat each other and love
each other. There is also a day coming when we shall give an
account to the Lord and to Him alone. Paul speaks of this day
when he writes:

> Therefore judge nothing before the appointed time; wait till
> the Lord comes. He will bring to light what is hidden in dark-
> ness and will expose the motives of men's hearts. At that time
> each will receive his praise from God. (1 Corinthians 4:5)

On that day, all the things we thought were buried in secret
will be exposed to the light. Then we must give an account to
the Lord. Meanwhile, all believers are serving Him, struggling to
understand and do His will, learning and growing and changing,
daily coming into a deeper and deeper understanding of the truth.
Instead of judging one another, let's love one another and encourage one another along that journey—a journey that takes us from
weakness to a place of strength in the faith.

Love Limits Liberty

Paul goes on to summarize:

> Therefore let us stop passing judgment on one another.
> Instead, make up your mind not to put any stumbling block
> or obstacle in your brother's way. As one who is in the Lord
> Jesus, I am fully convinced that no food is unclean in itself.
> But if anyone regards something as unclean, then for him it
> is unclean. (Romans 14:13–14)

Notice that Paul does not stop with a merely negative command. He doesn't simply say, "Stop passing judgment on one

another." He also gives us something positive and proactive to do, telling us, in effect, "Instead, judge yourself." He urges us to inspect our own conscience. We should ask ourselves, "Have I asserted my Christian liberty in a selfish way, insisting on my own 'rights' while thoughtlessly offending the conscience of someone else?" Paul urges us to consider the effect our own conduct has on other Christians.

Next, we read, "As one who is in the Lord Jesus, I am fully convinced that no food is unclean in itself." It may seem as though Paul is saying that he is speaking on his authority as a Christian, as "one who is in the Lord Jesus." Actually, in the original language, his statement is much stronger, as reflected in the King James Version: "I know, and am persuaded by the Lord Jesus, that there is nothing unclean of itself." Paul is referring to the fact that he was taught this truth by Jesus Himself. Indeed, Jesus did declare all foods clean (see Mark 7:14–19).

Understand, this is not to say that all foods are good for you. If you are overweight, allergic, or diabetic, some foods are clearly not good for you. They are not morally wrong or unclean, but they would not be good for your body. But that's a matter of health, not conscience.

Paul is addressing the conscience of the believer. He says that our conscience needs to be trained to accept our Christian liberty. One person's conscience may take longer to grasp this concept than another person's conscience. And if your conscience troubles you and tells you that a certain food (or other issue) is "unclean," then obey your conscience. If your conscience holds you back, then for you, it *is* unclean.

Think of Christian liberty as a swinging bridge suspended by ropes over a mountain stream. The bridge is perfectly safe, and there are some people who can run across a swinging bridge without hesitation, even though it has no handrails. Others cannot cross it so easily. They look down at the river below, their hearts race, their breathing comes in gasps, they shake and tremble. You might think that they would never cross the bridge—but if you give them time, if you are patient and encouraging and let them go at their own speed, they will inch across on hands and knees. Eventually, they'll make it to the other side. After a few more crossings, their confidence will increase and they, too, will be running across.

In the same way, some people can't imagine using their Christian freedom because they were raised to think that certain forms of conduct are wrong. Intellectually, they realize that there is nothing in the Bible that forbids this or that behavior, but they have been psychologically conditioned by years of legalistic training. It would be just as cruel to force them into accepting their Christian freedom as it would be to shove someone out onto that swinging bridge against his will. That is why Paul writes:

> If your brother is distressed because of what you eat, you are no longer acting in love. Do not by your eating destroy your brother for whom Christ died. (Romans 14:15)

You have enormous freedom as a Christian, and you should use that freedom in a spirit of thankfulness to God. But if by using your Christian liberty you cause harm or offense to your Christian brother, then love demands that you limit your conduct for the sake of your brother. Love limits liberty.

There are some issues we stand firm on. We refuse to yield an inch on clear biblical truth. But on matters where reasonable Christians differ, we yield to one another in love. The apostle writes:

> Do not allow what you consider as good to be spoken of as evil. For the kingdom of God is not a matter of eating and drinking, but of righteousness, peace and joy in the Holy Spirit, because anyone who serves Christ in this way is pleasing to God and approved by men. (Romans 14:16–18)

Here Paul warns those who are strong in the faith and free in Christ not to become contentious with others over that freedom.

If we flaunt our liberty in the faces of those who disagree, we will actually cause our liberty—and the gospel itself—to be spoken of as evil. In fact, when Paul says, "what you consider as good to be spoken of as evil," he uses a specific word that means "blaspheme." By exercising our liberty in an unloving way, Paul says, we will be causing the gospel itself, the good news of Jesus Christ, to be blasphemed.

So we must not make a major issue over a minor matter. We must not cause division over secondary issues; we must seek unity in love. Our love for one another will show the watching world that the Christian faith is about acceptance, forgiveness, and peace—not legalism and rules.

Some years ago, the members of a church got into disagreement over whether to have a Christmas tree at the Christmas program. Some members wanted to have the beautiful symbolism of a tree; others believed that the tradition of the Christmas tree had its origins in pagan practices, so a Christmas tree had no place in the church sanctuary. The disagreement turned into an unholy argument; the argument escalated into a brawl. A fistfight broke out on the church grounds. One group dragged the tree outside; the other group dragged it back in.

Before long, the two groups were in municipal court, suing each other. The whole sorry episode was splashed across the front page of the newspaper. The entire community was talking about it. The church became a laughingstock. The gospel of Jesus Christ was blasphemed in that community.

Paul reminds us that the Christian faith is not about eating or drinking or Christmas trees or any of the assorted and sundry issues that cause us to square off against our brothers and sisters. The Christian faith is about righteousness, peace, and joy in the Holy Spirit. A non-Christian, looking at a Christian, ought to see love, a righteous spirit, and a peaceful, joyful disposition. All too often, non-Christians look at the church and see nothing but a lot of stubborn, contentious, self-centered people who insist on getting their way.

Righteousness, Peace, and Joy

Let's take a closer look at this phrase Paul uses: "righteousness, peace and joy in the Holy Spirit." We have seen the word *righteousness* many times before in Romans, and we know what it means: God's gift of a sense of worth. It means that, because of the death of Jesus on our behalf, we are loved and accepted by God, and we have right standing in His sight. He delights in calling us His beloved children. Righteousness is not something that we accomplish; it is a free gift that comes from God through faith in Jesus Christ. With the gift of righteousness, we receive a sense of dignity and self-respect.

That is what the world ought to see: Christians who are secure in their righteous standing before God, Christians who are confident without being conceited, Christians who demonstrate self-acceptance that is based on the grace and love of God.

The word *peace* means a calm, poised demeanor that is undisturbed by the minor irritations of the moment. It is that quiet assurance that God is present in every situation, and we do not need to become upset or angry. When we demonstrate peace in trying circumstances (such as a difference of opinion about an issue of conduct), we manifest our confidence that God is in control.

The word *joy* is a delight in life that remains stable and durable even amid trials, pain, and uncertainty. Joy is not a result of comfortable circumstances. It's the ability to find life worth living when circumstances are harsh and even nearly unbearable. Joy is a result of a secure and trusting faith in God.

Righteousness, peace, and joy are gifts from God. They always go together, and they do not come from us; they come from God.

Paul is saying that if you are experiencing the righteousness, peace, and joy that come from God, then you can easily yield to your brother and forego some momentary privilege or pleasure that your Christian freedom would otherwise bring you. If your Christian freedom would cause offense to another Christian, then give in for the moment and demonstrate your Christlike love and your obedience to God.

The apostle goes on to say:

> Let us therefore make every effort to do what leads to peace and to mutual edification. Do not destroy the work of God for the sake of food. All food is clean, but it is wrong for a man to eat anything that causes someone else to stumble. It is better not to eat meat or drink wine or to do anything else that will cause your brother to fall. (Romans 14:19–21)

The guidelines are simple: Enjoy your Christian liberty, so long as you do not destroy the peace of the church, offend the conscience of your brother, or retard his spiritual growth. You who are strong, bear that burden. Do not insist on your rights.

Peace is the work of God. Nothing can produce lasting peace among people—especially among people who come from different cultures, backgrounds, temperaments, and generations—except the Spirit of God. If you destroy the peace of God's church for the sake of some "right" you claim on the basis of Christian liberty, then you are destroying God's work.

The phrase "mutual edification" means "the building up of one another." *Edification* means "building up;" it comes from the same root word as *edifice*, meaning "a building." The kind of building up that Paul speaks of here refers to the learning and growth process that God wants us all to undergo. We are being edified as we learn more and more truth from God's Word, and as we apply that truth to our lives.

If we abuse our liberty and offend other Christians, we will cause them to become resistant to new insights and knowledge about the faith. We will interfere with the process of edification, of spiritual learning and growth. This, says Paul, we must not do.

Should the strong Christian always forsake his Christian liberty in order to keep the peace? No. It is healthy and edifying for strong Christians to gently and courteously exchange views on these issues. If the strong Christian never speaks up to talk about his Christian liberty, then every question in the church will be decided by the views of the weak in the faith, those who are the most narrow, legalistic, and prejudiced. That is not healthy for any church, and it would result in the gospel becoming identified with legalism. Strong Christians should raise questions and lovingly state their views, then wisely yield if the righteousness, peace, and joy of the church might be undermined.

Paul says, "It is wrong for a man to eat anything that causes someone else to stumble." In other words, it is wrong to do anything that would cause another person to violate his own conscience. But it is not wrong to discuss these issues so that everyone in the church can reexamine his or her own assumptions and convictions. We never want to cause a fellow Christian to violate his convictions, but we all, as brothers and sisters in the family of God, want to continually refine our beliefs so that we can grow more and more like Christ.

Paul's next statement is not well translated by the New International Version:

> So whatever you believe about these things keep between yourself and God. (Romans 14:22)

This translation suggests that we should keep quiet about our liberties, that we should never voice our beliefs about our Christian freedom to anyone else. That is *not* what Paul is saying. This passage would be better translated in this way:

> If you have faith, have it between yourself and God. (Romans 14:22, author's translation)

In other words, let God and His Word be the basis for your faith—and nothing else. Be sure that your conduct is based not on pride, nor on the desire to show off your freedom before others, but on your relationship to God and your understanding of His Word. If you do that, you will be affirmed and blessed, as Paul writes:

Blessed is the man who does not condemn himself by what he approves. (Romans 14:22)

If you have based your faith solely on God and His Word, then you will live in such a way that your conscience is clear and free of condemnation. You will be free, happy, and blessed. But if you have not based your beliefs on the firm foundation of God's Word, then your conscience will condemn you. Even if you are doing something that God permits, the fact that you are acting out of self-indulgence rather than faith will mean that you are sinning.

"Without faith," Hebrews says, "it is impossible to please God" (see Hebrews 11:6). Faith means believing what God has said. So if you want to please God, then act in faith, basing your conduct on the Word of God.

If we heed the words of Paul, we will resolve differences, heal divisions, and bring honor to God and to the gospel of Jesus Christ.

You Can't Please Everybody

In the opening verses of Romans 15, Paul summarizes what he has said in Romans 14:

We who are strong ought to bear with the failings of the weak, and not to please ourselves. Each of us should please his neighbor for his good, to build him up. (Romans 15:1–2)

Here, Paul gives us two simple rules of thumb about exercising our Christian liberty:

First rule: *Seek to please your neighbor rather than yourself.* Do not insist on getting your way; be quick to yield. Love adjusts and adapts in order to please others. The Phillips translation puts it this way: "We who have strong faith ought to shoulder the burden of the doubts and qualms of others, and not just to go our own sweet way" (Romans 15:1 PHILLIPS).

Second rule: *Focus on building each other up.* If you yield to your brother, do so to build him up. But if you see that yielding would only confirm him in his weakness, then discuss the issue with him to build him up. There may be times when you need to tell your brother, "You want me to change my conduct, but I believe God gives me freedom in this area. Let's look at the Scriptures and see what God really says about this matter. Maybe one of us should rethink his position on this issue."

These decisions can be difficult. If both Christians are not careful to remain focused on love instead of on the issue, they run a risk of dividing from each other. Paul encourages us to keep focused on love for one another and on the goal of building each other up. He writes:

> For even Christ did not please himself but, as it is written: "The insults of those who insult you have fallen on me." For everything that was written in the past was written to teach us that through endurance and the encouragement of the Scriptures, we might have hope. (Romans 15:3–4)

Paul sets before us the example of Jesus Himself. Throughout His ministry, Jesus never asserted His own rights; He always sought to please God the Father and to lovingly edify others. In the process of obeying and pleasing God, He was subjected to abuse and insult. Paul describes the attitude of Jesus by quoting Psalm 69:9: "The insults of those who insult you have fallen on me." The opponents of God took out their evil and hate against His Son—and Jesus endured their indignities and insults without complaint.

We look at the example of Jesus and we see that He said that it's impossible to please everybody. Confronting his opponents, the scribes and Pharisees, He said in effect, "John the Baptist came neither eating bread nor drinking wine, and you said, 'He has a demon!' I came eating and drinking, and you said, 'He's a glutton and a drunkard!' There's no pleasing you people! You criticize and find fault, no matter what anyone does!" (see Luke 7:33–34).

Jesus personified our Christian freedom—and He found Himself under attack by strait-laced legalists! Jesus understood that you can't please everybody. You can't adjust to all the legalistic demands people place on you. Sometimes you must simply move forward, seeking to please God and do His will, leaving it to God to heal the difficulties that remain.

This, I believe, is the principle Paul has in mind in this passage: You can't please everybody. If you can please your brother, you should. But sometimes, trying to please people will hinder their spiritual growth, so you should do whatever will edify them.

Paul continues:

> May the God who gives endurance and encouragement give you a spirit of unity among yourselves as you follow Christ Jesus, so that with one heart and mouth you may glorify the God and Father of our Lord Jesus Christ. (Romans 15:5–6)

Here Paul reminds us that God gives us the power to live together in Christian unity. This passage suggests two actions we can take whenever we encounter disagreements in the church:

First, *pray for unity*. These two verses are, in fact, Paul's own prayer that the Christians in Rome would be unified in Christ. In Luke 11:13, Jesus says, "If you then, though you are evil, know how to give good gifts to your children, how much more will your Father in heaven give the Holy Spirit to those that ask him!" Jesus says that when problems arise, we should pray. In response to our prayers, God the Father will send the Holy Spirit to aid us in solving our problems while preserving a spirit of unity.

Second, *praise God for Christian relationships*. Paul prays that God would give the Roman Christians a spirit of unity "so that with one heart and mouth you may glorify the God and Father of our Lord Jesus Christ." In other words, when you find yourself in a disagreement with a Christian brother, remember the wonderful relationship God has given you. With one heart and mouth, thank God together for the things that unite you—especially the grace you have both received through faith in Jesus Christ. Giving thanks for the things that unite you helps minimize the things that divide you.

Hope, Joy, Peace, Trust, and Power

Next, Paul encourages us by reminding us of God's promises for the future (the Scripture references in brackets refer to the Old Testament passages Paul quotes):

> Accept one another, then, just as Christ accepted you, in order to bring praise to God. For I tell you that Christ has become a servant of the Jews on behalf of God's truth, to confirm the promises made to the patriarchs so that the Gentiles may glorify God for his mercy, as it is written:
>
> "Therefore I will praise you among the Gentiles;
>   I will sing hymns to your name." [Psalm 18:49]
>
> Again, it says,
>   "Rejoice, O Gentiles, with his people."
>   [Deuteronomy 32:43]
>
> And again,
>   "Praise the Lord, all you Gentiles,
>   and sing praises to him, all you peoples."
>   [Psalm 117:1]
>
> And again, Isaiah says,
>   "The Root of Jesse will spring up,
>   one who will arise to rule over the nations;
>   the Gentiles will hope in him." [Isaiah 11:10]
>
>   (Romans 15:7–12)

Paul refers to the fact that God is working out a great program in history to reconcile the Jews and the Gentiles. Throughout the

Old Testament, God announced that He would do that, and He is already bringing it to pass. It began when Jesus reached out in ministry to both the Jews and Gentiles, and it is continuing to this day.

Church fights, feuds, and divisions can be rancorous. Yet I have never heard of a modern church fight that was any worse than the divisions that sometimes split the church in Paul's day. Those divisions usually centered on differences between Jewish and Gentile Christians.

In that culture, the Jews held the Gentiles in contempt, to the point of calling them "dogs." The Jews considered it a defiling sin to enter the house of a Gentile; they would never dream of eating with a Gentile. The Gentiles, of course, hated the Jews in return, calling them horrible names and looking down on them. Modern anti-Semitism dates back to those days when the Jews were living under Roman oppression. Vestiges of these old hatreds remained even after people came to Christ, and those tensions had to be dealt with.

Paul wants us to know that Jesus Christ is the key to healing divisions. "For I tell you," he says, "that Christ has become a servant of the Jews." In the original language, he writes, "Christ has become a minister of the circumcision." The word *circumcision* refers not merely to the Jews as a people, but to the Jewish traditions and rituals. Paul says that Jesus has healed the breach between Jews and Gentiles by limiting His own liberty. God created the human body in absolute perfection—then God's Son obediently consented to have His own body mutilated by the act of circumcision. He became a circumcised Jew—yet He was a Jew who declared that all foods are clean.

We know that God uses "clean" and "unclean foods" as symbols of the Jews and the Gentiles. In the book of Acts, when God wanted the apostle Peter to go share the gospel with Cornelius, a Roman centurion, He first prepared Peter with a vision of "unclean foods." During the vision, Peter refused to partake of the "unclean foods," saying, "I have never eaten anything impure or unclean." But God replied, "Do not call anything impure that God has made clean." Ultimately, God revealed to Peter that the "unclean foods" symbolized the Gentiles, whom God was bringing into the previously all-Jewish church (see Acts 10).

So when Jesus declared that all foods are clean, He threw the doors of the church wide open to the Gentiles. Jesus shattered the wall of division between Jew and Gentile by fulfilling the Old Testament promises that God would be praised among the Gentiles because of Jesus. The Lord accepted both Jews and Gentiles into the church so that they could become one people, one family, just as the Scriptures promised.

Notice that Paul quotes from the Psalms, the section of the Old Testament called the Writings; then he quotes from Deuteronomy, the Law; then he quotes from Isaiah, the Prophets. So the Law, the Prophets, and the Writings all agree that God is involved in the work of unifying Christians. If He can unify Jews and Gentiles in one church body, then He can resolve whatever divisions and issues we may face in the church today.

Next comes Paul's magnificent benediction:

> May the God of hope fill you with great joy and peace
> as you trust in him, so that you may overflow with hope by
> the power of the Holy Spirit. (Romans 15:13)

This is one of the most beautiful verses in the Bible, and one I like to inscribe in cards and books as a message of blessing. All the great words of the Christian faith appear here: hope (*overflowing* hope!), joy, peace, trust, and power—the power of the Holy Spirit, who opens doors and no man shuts them, and shuts doors and no man opens them. Here Paul urges us to unite on the great positive ideas of our faith—the affirmation of all that is ours as Christians, as members together of the family of God. When we reflect on everything those words mean to us, all of our trifling divisions and petty arguments fade into insignificance.

Hope, joy, peace, trust, and the power of the Holy Spirit—may the God of hope fill our hearts with love for one another so that we will manifest these characteristics before a watching world.

CHAPTER 18

PAUL'S POSTSCRIPT

Romans 15:14–16:24

I once visited the Natural Bridge of Virginia—a stone bridge carved by nature that stands twenty-three stories high over Cedar Creek. Thomas Jefferson purchased that bridge from King George III on July 4, 1774, so that he could save it for future generations. One of the features that impressed me about the Natural Bridge is the thousands and thousands of names and initials that have been scratched into the rocks. In fact, if you look high up the side of the bridge, you will see the name "George Washington" carved into the stone. It's true. The father of our country couldn't resist leaving his name for future generations to see. As a young man, Washington carved his name into the stone while working as a surveyor in the area.

There is something in all of us that wants to see our names preserved for posterity. In the last chapter and a half of Romans, we come to a final, personal postscript that Paul appends to this great letter—a section that includes the names of many of Paul's close friends, names that have been carved into this letter and preserved for the past two thousand years.

Paul has brought the themes of this letter to a close, capping it off with the great benediction of Romans 15:13. Now, in this concluding section, we catch a glimpse of the human heart of this flesh-and-blood man, the apostle Paul. Here, he talks in an affectionate way of his longing to visit the Christians in Rome, "so that by God's will I may come to you with joy and together with you be refreshed" (Romans 15:32). Here, he sends greetings to dozens of his close friends and partners in the ministry, securing for them a place of undying fame in the pages of Scripture.

Three Things They Had; Three Things They Lacked

The letter closes much as it began, with a personal word from Paul about himself and about the believers in Rome. Paul writes:

> I myself am convinced, my brothers, that you your-
> selves are full of goodness, complete in knowledge and
> competent to instruct one another. (Romans 15:14)

Paul describes three qualities the Roman Christians possessed.

First, the Roman Christians were "full of goodness." In other words, their motives were right and pure. They were motivated by a compassion to reach out to people in need. They were motivated by Christian love to share with one another and carry each other's burdens.

Second, they were "complete in knowledge." Paul did not mean, of course, that they knew all there is to know about the Christian faith. No matter how much a person (or a church) knows about God, there is always more to learn. The riches of God's truth are inexhaustible. Even so, the Christians in Rome were diligent students of God's Word, and they were intensely committed to understanding God's will. So Paul affirmed them and said, "You are complete in knowledge."

Third, Paul says they were "competent to instruct one another." A more literal translation would be, "You are compe-tent to counsel one another." In today's churches, a great burden is placed on most pastors to be a counselor—the listening ear and problem-solver of the congregation. That was never God's plan for the church.

God intended that the entire congregation should be involved in the work of counseling. In the body of Christ, there should be many counselors, helping people to find sound, biblically based solutions to their problems and spiritual comfort for their sorrows and hurts. The Christians in Rome lived out God's plan for the church as a place of healing. They were competent to counsel and instruct one another.

But Paul also notes three things the Christians in Rome lacked:

> I have written you quite boldly on some points, as if to remind you of them again, because of the grace God gave me to be a minister of Christ Jesus to the Gentiles with the priestly duty of proclaiming the gospel of God, so that the Gentiles might become an offering acceptable to God, sanctified by the Holy Spirit. (Romans 15:15–16)

You would think a church that was full of goodness, complete in knowledge, and competent to counsel would need no word of reminder. Yet Paul says there are three things that the Roman Christians need to be reminded of.

First, they needed a *bold reminder of the truth*. "I have written you quite boldly on some points, as if to remind you of them again." We need to be reminded again and again of the great themes of the gospel. That is why we need to gather in our churches for worship and instruction every Sunday. Living our everyday lives, we easily get drawn into the mindset of the world around us. We need to be continually brought back to the great truths of our faith. We need to be continually transformed by the renewing of our minds, as Paul told us in Romans 12:2.

Second, the Christians at Rome needed a *priestly ministry*. Paul says he has written to them "because of the grace God gave me to be a minister of Christ Jesus to the Gentiles with the priestly duty of proclaiming the gospel of God." Paul is telling them, in effect, "God has given me the privilege of being the Lord's minister to the Gentiles. My special calling is like that of a temple priest, working to awaken a sense of worship among you, a realization of the greatness of God." Sometimes our spiritual lives become drab and lifeless, and we need to be reminded of who God is. Throughout Romans, Paul reminds us of such wonders as "the depths of the riches of the wisdom and knowledge of God" (Romans 11:33).

Third, they needed to become *sanctified*. Paul says he has written to them "so that the Gentiles might become an offering acceptable to God, sanctified by the Holy Spirit." Every congregation needs to experience sanctification. Sanctification is the process by which the righteousness we have received from God begins to gradually change our attitudes, habits, speech, and conduct. As we become sanctified in Christ, people notice that we are becoming more like Christ. A church that is not sanctified by the Holy Spirit is just a religious organization; but a sanctified church is the living body of Jesus Christ! When the divine wind of the Spirit blows upon the dead, dry bones of a church, and those bones spring to life, that's sanctification!

The Five Principles of Paul's Ministry

Next Paul talks about his own ministry in service to God. The apostle gives us a fascinating insight into his own life and work.

Do you realize the influence the apostle Paul has had on this world, and upon your own life? He lived two thousand years ago, yet your life, my life, and the lives of virtually everyone we know have been profoundly affected by this man. The course of history has been altered by the truths he taught. In fact, it would not be an exaggeration to say that history itself has been built around the letters and teachings of the apostle Paul. His teachings profoundly influenced the thinking of our founding fathers on such matters as liberty, justice, and fairness, so America itself would not exist as it does if Paul had never lived. The vitality of his spirit, the greatness of his mind, and the fullness of his heart still echo through the ages and touch our lives.

Paul describes three features of his own ministry in next passage:

> Therefore, I glory in Christ Jesus in my service to God. I will not venture to speak of anything except what Christ has accomplished through me in leading the Gentiles to obey God by what I have said and done—by the power of signs and miracles, through the power of the Spirit. So from Jerusalem all the way around to Illyricum, I have fully

proclaimed the gospel of Christ. It has always been my ambition to preach the gospel where Christ was not known, so that I would not be building on someone else's foundation. (Romans 15:17–20)

The three features of Paul's ministry that we find here are: (1) the five principles he embraced in his ministry; (2) the means by which he carried out those principles; and (3) the power he relied on. First, let's look at Paul's five principles of ministry.

Principle 1: Paul rejoiced wherever he went. When he writes, "I glory in Christ Jesus in my service to God," he is speaking of rejoicing. Despite the hardships and difficulties he faced, Paul continually rejoiced. Why? Because wherever he went, he found villages, towns, and cities in the iron grip of Roman authority. The people in those communities were deep in despair and emptiness, longing for something they could not find, trembling in superstitious fear. That meant that Paul always found people who were open to the gospel and hungry for God. Paul rejoiced because his preaching gave these people a light in their darkness, and he had the privilege of seeing many lives changed as people heard about Jesus for the very first time.

Principle 2: Paul allowed God to work through him. He said, "I will not venture to speak of anything except what Christ has accomplished through me." That is one of the great secrets God wants to teach us—that we don't do great things for God, but He does great things through us. Sometimes we get the idea that God couldn't get along without us. We feel self-important as we think back over our successes in ministry. You never hear that attitude from Paul. He always talks about what God has done through him. That is the secret of a truly effective ministry, and when Paul learned that secret, God used him to change the history of the world.

Principle 3: Paul relied upon the power of the Holy Spirit. He writes that what he accomplished, he did "by the power of signs and miracles, through the power of the Spirit." The signs and miracles he mentions are the signs of an apostle. Paul wrote elsewhere, "The things that mark an apostle—signs, wonders and miracles—were done among you with great perseverance" (2 Corinthians 12:12). If you want to know why God has never performed signs and wonders through you, it is because only apostles can do these things. Today we do not need any more apostles, because the original apostles are available to us through their writings. Though we do not have any new apostles, we do have the power that Paul mentions—the power of the Holy Spirit. The power of the Spirit is available to you and me, just as it was available to Paul.

Principle 4: Paul willingly went anyplace God led him. He describes how far-flung his ministry has been: "So from Jerusalem all the way around to Illyricum, I have fully proclaimed the gospel of Christ." If you look at a map, you will see how far Paul has traveled. Jerusalem is down in the southern part of Israel; Illyricum is the region we now know as Yugoslavia, in the Balkan region of eastern Europe. Looking at a modern map, we see that Paul has traveled up the Mediterranean coast, through Israel, Lebanon, Syria, Turkey, across the Dardanelles, into Greece, Macedonia, and Yugoslavia. He did most of his traveling on foot, and he endured hardship wherever he went. He obediently went wherever his Lord sent him.

Principle 5: Paul was a pioneer. "It has always been my ambition," he wrote, "to preach the gospel where Christ was not known, so that I would not be building on someone else's foundation." Someone has suggested that there are only two kinds of Christian ministry: there is "Settler ministry" and "Pioneer ministry." Some Christians want to be Settlers. They have no desire to reach out, risk, and explore. They just want to move into town and let the mayor run everything. Others want to be Pioneers. They have a spirit of adventure. They seek to advance the gospel in new and unreached places. The Pioneer spirit is characteristic of the Spirit of God. Our Lord loves to break new ground and perform new, creative works.

The Means of Ministry

Next, Paul discusses the means of carrying out his ministry:

> This is why I have often been hindered from coming to you.
>
> But now that there is no more place for me to work in these regions, and since I have been longing for many years to see you, I plan to do so when I go to Spain. I hope to visit you while passing through and to have you assist me on my journey there, after I have enjoyed your company for a while. (Romans 15:22–24)

Here we see Paul's practical approach to ministry, which involved three practical considerations. The first consideration, which we see in these verses, is *planning*. Many Christians do not believe that we should plan our ministry. They think we should let God guide us from moment to moment, and that we should never look ahead to the future. But Paul didn't live that way. He says he has spent years laying plans for a journey to Rome and Spain. Paul was practical and he was a planner.

Next, we see the second practical consideration in his ministry for Christ:

> Now, however, I am on my way to Jerusalem in the service of the saints there. For Macedonia and Achaia [Greece] were pleased to make a contribution for the poor among the saints in Jerusalem. They were pleased to do it, and indeed they owe it to them. For if the Gentiles have shared in the Jews' spiritual blessings, they owe it to the Jews to share with them their material blessings. So after I have completed this task and have made sure that they have received this fruit, I will go to Spain and visit you on the way. I know that when I come to you, I will come in the full measure of the blessing of Christ. (Romans 15:25–29)

Paul's second consideration, which we see in these verses, is *completion*. Some Christians continually jump into new ministry efforts before old ones are finished. But Paul didn't work that way. He said, "*After I have completed this task* and have made sure that they have received this fruit, I will go to Spain and visit you on the way." Paul had a practical, methodical approach to ministry: He worked steadily toward a goal, he achieved that goal, then he went on to the next goal.

The specific ministry task he talks about involves taking up a collection for the needy Christians in Jerusalem. He points out that the spiritually needy Gentiles have received great spiritual blessings from the Jews, so it is only fair that the Gentiles share their material blessings with the materially needy Jews. That is God's program: spiritual blessings can be exchanged for material blessings so that everyone is blessed and no one is in want.

Paul has taken up an offering in every city he has visited, and he will deliver it personally to the suffering saints in Jerusalem when he returns there. This is a demonstration of the practical side of the gospel: Christianity is concerned with physical needs as well as spiritual needs.

Next, we see the third practical consideration in Paul's ministry for Christ:

> I urge you, brothers, by our Lord Jesus Christ and by the love of the Spirit, to join me in my struggle by praying to God for me. Pray that I may be rescued from the unbelievers in Judea and that my service in Jerusalem may be acceptable to the saints there, so that by God's will I may come to you with joy and together with you be refreshed. The God of peace be with you all. Amen. (Romans 15:30–33)

Paul's third consideration, which we see in these verses, is *prayer*. What was behind this mighty apostle's ministry? Prayer! Why has it lasted and expanded for two thousand years? Prayer! What opened doors and gave Paul access even to Caesar's household and the throne of the emperor himself? Prayer! Paul's ministry was empowered, energized, and protected by the power of prayer. There is no more practical consideration in any ministry than the power of prayer.

Prayer, says Paul, is our most potent spiritual weapon: "I urge you, brothers . . . to join me in my struggle by praying to God for me." When we are engaged in ministry, there is nothing more critical to ministry success than prayer.

Prayer also helps to protect God's frontline servants from harm: "Pray that I may be rescued from the unbelievers in Judea." We mistakenly assume that Satan only attacks us spiritually, through temptation or discouragement. We forget that Satan sometimes attacks God's servants directly and physically, by undermining their health or stirring up enemies to acts of violence.

Paul was wise to ask the Roman Christians to pray for him. Later, when he arrived in Jerusalem, he was attacked by a mob in the Temple courts. The rioters beat him and would have stoned him to death, but the commander of the Roman legion saw the riot from the walls of the Antonia fortress. He led a band of soldiers down to rescue Paul from the mob. So the prayers for Paul's safety were answered (see Acts 21).

Prayer is the key to resolving disputes, disagreements, and misunderstandings so that ministry can go forth without hindrance. Paul asked the Roman Christians, "Pray . . . that my service in Jerusalem may be acceptable to the saints there." During Paul's absence, a misunderstanding had arisen. Because Paul was taking the gospel to the Gentiles, a rumor had arisen that Paul was urging Jewish Christians to turn away from the teachings of Moses, and to ignore Jewish traditions and rites, such as circumcision. Though the rumor was false, many Jewish Christians were stirred up against Paul. When Paul arrived in Jerusalem, the apostle James suggested that Paul demonstrate his regard for the Jewish rites and traditions by undergoing certain rites himself. Paul agreed, and this turned opinion in Paul's favor. His ministry was warmly accepted—again, as an answer to prayer.

Next, Paul writes, "by God's will I may come to you with joy and together with you be refreshed." This hope of Paul's was realized three years after the writing of the book of Romans. The last chapter of Acts describes how Paul—having been arrested by the Roman government, having survived shipwreck and other arduous perils—finally arrives in Rome:

> And so we came to Rome. The brothers there had heard that we were coming, and they traveled as far as the Forum of Appius and the Three Taverns to meet us. At the sight of these men Paul thanked God and was encouraged. (Acts 28:14–15)

Imagine the great feeling of encouragement Paul felt when these Roman Christians came out to meet him. The very sight of them caused Paul to thank God. Even though he came as a prisoner, though he was chained to a Roman guard and destined to stand trial for his life, Paul felt a surge of joy and a refreshment of his spirit.

Two Thousand Years of Fame

Who were these Christians in Rome? The final chapter of Romans gives us an insight into some of the people who were among the first in history to hear this great letter. Many people skip over Romans 16, thinking that it is nothing but a list of dead, anonymous saints. At first glance, Paul's postscript to Romans looks about as interesting as a page from the phone book. To me, however, this is one of the most fascinating chapters in the book.

In Romans 16, Paul lists thirty-three men and women who had no idea that they were going to be famous—not for fifteen minutes, as artist Andy Warhol once said, but for two thousand years. These thirty-three people were Paul's personal friends. Twenty-four of them (seventeen men and seven women) were in Rome. Nine of them (eight men and one woman) were with Paul in Corinth, where he was staying when he wrote the letter. There were two households mentioned and two unnamed women—the mother of Rufus and the sister of Nereus. There were also references to some unnamed brethren.

Though Paul had not yet visited Rome, he had personal connections to quite a number of people there. We tend to think of those ancient days as a time of limited travel—and it is true that it took weeks to reach places we can now fly to in an hour. But many people did travel extensively, and this chapter bears witness to that fact.

Romans 16 divides into three sections: (1) Paul's greetings to the brothers and sisters at Rome, verses 1–16; (2) a warning about false "Christians," verse 17–20; and (3) greetings from the brothers who were with Paul in Corinth, verses 21–27. This letter was carried to Rome by a traveling businesswoman, Phoebe, who is introduced in the opening verses:

> I commend to you our sister Phoebe, a servant of the church in Cenchrea. I ask you to receive her in the Lord in a way worthy of the saints and to give her any help she may need from you, for she has been a great help to many people, including me. (Romans 16:1–2)

The whole church can be grateful to Phoebe for her courage and faithfulness in carrying this great letter on that hazardous journey from Corinth to Rome. She is called by the apostle "a servant of the church in Cenchrea," which was the port town nine miles east of Corinth. Phoebe was a servant (or *deacon*) in the church in Cenchrea (*deacon* is the correct term rather than *deaconess*, since the original Greek language makes no distinction between deacons of either gender). The fact that she was a servant or deacon doesn't necessarily mean that she held an office in the church. Rather, it means that she had a ministry of servanthood within the church. She was also a servant to Paul, who noted, "She has been a great help to many people, including me."

Phoebe is the first of many women listed in this postscript. Women occupy a prominent place in the New Testament. Romans 16 affirms the fact that Christianity has done more to elevate the status and dignity of women than any other movement or social force in history.

Next, Paul greets a well-known husband-and-wife ministry team:

> Greet Priscilla and Aquila, my fellow workers in Christ Jesus. They risked their lives for me. Not only I but all the churches of the Gentiles are grateful to them. Greet also the church that meets at their house. (Romans 16:3–5)

We meet this couple in other letters of Paul. We encounter them first in Acts 18, where Luke tells us they were Jewish tent-makers who were driven out of Rome by a decree of the Emperor Claudius. They went to Corinth, where another tentmaker named Saul of Tarsus (later known as the apostle Paul) moved in with them and led them to Christ. Their home was probably the first church in Corinth. Luke tells us that Paul spent two years in Corinth, then he went to Ephesus, and Priscilla and Aquila went with him.

Now Priscilla and Aquila are back in Rome, and Paul greets them, reminding the church that they risked their lives for him. Paul probably refers to the incident in Acts 19, when a riot broke out in Ephesus. This couple may have helped save him from the mob.

Paul continues:

> Greet my dear friend Epenetus, who was the first con-vert to Christ in the province of Asia. Greet Mary, who worked very hard for you. Greet Andronicus and Junias, my relatives who have been in prison with me. They are outstanding among the apostles, and they were in Christ before I was. Greet Ampliatus, whom I love in the Lord. Greet Urbanus, our fellow worker in Christ, and my dear friend Stachys. (Romans 16:5–9)

We do not know why Epenetus was in Rome, but he was cher-ished because he was Paul's first convert in the province of Asia. You never forget the first person you lead to Christ.

Next, Paul greets Mary, an anonymous servant who had the spiritual gift of helps. She could not teach or preach or evangelize, but she was a hard worker. Paul is careful to affirm those who exercise the gift of helps.

Andronicus and Junias were relatives of Paul. He says "they were in Christ before me," which tells us that they were among the earliest believers in the first-century church. They had probably feared their zealous relative, Saul of Tarsus, when he was persecuting the church. They must have been thrilled to learn of his miraculous conversion! Paul's encounter with the Lord on the Damascus Road was undoubtedly an answer to the prayers of Andronicus and Junias.

It is not clear if these two people are husband and wife or two brothers. There is some confusion in the early manuscripts as to whether the second name is Junia or Junias. Early church fathers, such as John Chrysostom and Origen of Alexandria took it to be Junia, a woman's name, though many modern scholars read it as Junias, a man's name.

Andronicus and Junias were such dedicated Christians that even the twelve apostles in Jerusalem held them in high regard. Paul also notes with fondness and gratitude that they were fellow prisoners with him at one time, and he undoubtedly appreciated their company while he was in prison for the sake of the gospel.

Ampliatus is an interesting name. In the catacombs of Domitilla, there is a highly decorated tomb bearing the single name Ampliatus. A single name usually suggests that the man was a slave; the ornate decorations on the tomb, however, indicate that Ampliatus was well-liked by the leading citizens of Rome. We don't know if the Ampliatus who is entombed in the catacombs is the same person mentioned by Paul, but it is likely. This man, who was greatly loved by Paul, had a significant ministry among the Christians in Rome.

Of Urbanus and Stachys we know only what Paul says here: Urbanus had served on Paul's ministry team, and Stachys was a dear friend.

Servants in the Corridors of Power

Paul continues his greetings:

> Greet Apelles, tested and approved in Christ. Greet
> those who belong to the household of Aristobulus. Greet
> Herodion, my relative. Greet those in the household of Nar-
> cissus who are in the Lord. (Romans 16:10–11)

I have always been fascinated by this man Apelles, whom Paul
says has been "tested and approved in Christ." He will forever be
known as one who endured the testing of his faith and emerged
with the approval of his Lord. The name Apelles means "called,"
and he proved himself to be one whom God had called.

Bible commentator William Barclay suggests that Aristobulus
may have been the grandson of King Herod the Great. Aristobulus was a close friend of Emperor Claudius. When Aristobulus
died, his household (that is, his servants) became the property
of the emperor (by this time Nero had succeeded Claudius, who
had been murdered). Though the servants legally belonged to the
emperor, they were still known as "the household of Aristobulus."
These facts suggest that there were a number of Christian servants
and slaves who may have had opportunities to witness to the leaders of Rome.

Paul mentions his relative, Herodion, in connection with these
servants. The name Herodion indicates a connection with the family of Herod, so Paul may have been related to the ruling family
of the Jews. Herodion had become a Christian and was living in
Rome as part of the household of either Aristobulus or Narcissus.

Paul greets "the household of Narcissus," which is probably
a reference to the servants of the former slave Narcissus, who
became the personal secretary of Emperor Claudius. The personal secretary decided whether or not a letter would reach the
emperor's attention—and no letter got past the personal secretary
unless accompanied by a bribe. So Narcissus gained wealth and
prestige in that position. When Nero succeeded Claudius, the new

emperor forced Narcissus to commit suicide. Though Narcissus was not a Christian, there were Christians among his servants, and it is the Christian servants of Narcissus that Paul greets. From this brief statement, we can see that God had established a Christian witness in the very corridors of Roman power.

Next, Paul greets some hard-working women in the church:

> Greet Tryphena and Tryphosa, those women who work hard in the Lord. Greet my dear friend Persis, another woman who has worked very hard in the Lord. Greet Rufus, chosen in the Lord, and his mother, who has been a mother to me, too. Greet Asyncritus, Phlegon, Hermes, Patrobas, Hermas and the brothers with them. Greet Philologus, Julia, Nereus and his sister, and Olympas and all the saints with them. Greet one another with a holy kiss. All the churches of Christ send greetings. (Romans 16:12–16)

There is an irony in those names, Tryphaena and Tryphosa; the names mean "dainty" and "delicate"—yet these women were hard workers, and probably not nearly as delicate and dainty as their names suggest. They were probably so-named because they came from the aristocratic class. Though they did not have to work as the lower classes did, these women worked hard out of love for the Lord Jesus.

We know nothing of Paul's dear friend Persis except that she had worked with him somewhere; perhaps she had traveled in his company of missionary evangelists.

Paul greets Rufus and his mother. This is probably the same Rufus who is mentioned (along with his brother Alexander) in Mark 15:21. It is the scene where Jesus, beaten and weakened, staggers under the weight of the cross as He is being led out of Jerusalem to be crucified. Mark writes: "A certain man from Cyrene, Simon, the father of Alexander and Rufus, was passing by on his way in from the country, and they forced him to carry the cross." Simon was a Jew from North Africa who was in Jerusalem for the Passover. As an eyewitness to the crucifixion, Simon was probably one of the first Christians, and he may well have been present in Jerusalem on the day of Pentecost. He doubtless raised his sons, Rufus and Alexander, in the Christian faith, and they became outstanding men in the Christian community.

Asyncritus, Phlegon, Hermes, Patrobas, and Hermas are all Greek names. They were Greek Christians, probably business-men, who lived and worshiped in Rome.

Philologus means "a lover of the word"; it was probably a nickname describing the fact that he sincerely loved the Word of God. Gathered with him (perhaps they were all members of the same local house church) were Julia, Nereus, the sister of Nereus, and Olympas.

Nereus is another fascinating name. Dr. Barclay suggests that he may have been the housekeeper of a prominent Roman citizen, Flavius Clemens. History records that Flavius Clemens became Consul of Rome, the highest political office in the city. He was executed for his Christian faith by Emperor Domitian in AD 95. His wife, Domatilla, was banished for her Christian faith. It may well be that this housekeeper, Nereus, led this prominent Roman couple to Christ.

In this list of names we find a strong hint that Roman society was being steadily infiltrated, from top to bottom, by the gospel of Jesus Christ. The church is at its best when it quietly penetrates all levels of society and brings them together in the church of Jesus Christ.

Finally, Paul concludes with a general greeting from all the churches that he has visited or helped plant in Palestine, Asia Minor, Greece, and Macedonia. This is a reminder that churches (plural) are really *one* church, *one* body of Christ, unified in love and in the Holy Spirit.

A Word of Warning

Next, Paul offers this warning against false "Christians" who preach a false and divisive doctrine:

> Greet one another with a holy kiss. All the churches of Christ send greetings.
>
> I urge you, brothers, to watch out for those who cause divisions and put obstacles in your way that are contrary to the teaching you have learned. Keep away from them. For such people are not serving our Lord Christ, but their own appetites. By smooth talk and flattery they deceive the minds of naive people. Everyone has heard about your obedience, so I am full of joy over you; but I want you to be wise about what is good, and innocent about what is evil.
>
> The God of peace will soon crush Satan under your feet.
>
> The grace of our Lord Jesus be with you. (Romans 16:16–20)

Paul warns of people in the church who profess to be Christians, but who stir up discord by elevating one particular point of doctrine at the expense of the full counsel of God's Word. Throughout church history, one of the greatest dangers has been the presence of false teachers who emphasize one spiritual gift or some other teaching, claiming that *this and this alone* is the mark of a true believer. These false teachers sometimes introduce practices or rituals that they insist are the marks of true Christianity. They seduce the unwary into a sense of spiritual arrogance that says, "We have this doctrine that marks us as *superior* Christians, *genuine* Christians."

Despite their smooth words, these false teachers do not seek to serve Christ; they only seek to advance themselves and gain a following. They create division and factions, using biblical-sounding language and flattering words to entice the unwary.

What does Paul recommend? Should they be censured, denounced from the pulpit, excommunicated and tossed out of the church? No. Paul's advice is to simply avoid them. "Keep away from them," he says. If you do this, the God of peace will preserve the peace of the church. He will crush Satan under your feet. Eventually, the eyes of the people will be opened and the false teachers will lose their following.

Final Greetings

Paul adds the greetings of those who are in Corinth with him:

> Timothy, my fellow worker, sends his greetings to you,
> as do Lucius, Jason and Sosipater, my relatives.
> I, Tertius, who wrote down this letter, greet you in the
> Lord.
> Gaius, whose hospitality I and the whole church here
> enjoy, sends you his greetings.
> Erastus, who is the city's director of public works, and
> our brother Quartus send you their greetings.
> Now to him who is able to establish you by my gospel
> and the proclamation of Jesus Christ, according to the rev-
> elation of the mystery hidden for long ages past, but now
> revealed and made known through the prophetic writings
> by the command of the eternal God, so that all nations
> might believe and obey him—to the only wise God be glory
> forever through Jesus Christ! Amen. (Romans 16:21–27)

First, Paul sends greetings from Timothy, one of his closest
friends. Timothy was the son of a Greek father and a Jewish Christian mother, Eunice. Paul spoke of Timothy as his son in the Lord
(1 Corinthians 4:17), and Timothy was associated with Paul in the
writing of five of his letters (1 and 2 Thessalonians, 2 Corinthians,
Colossians, and Philippians). Timothy traveled extensively with
Paul, was eventually imprisoned with Paul in Rome, and remained
Paul's faithful friend and companion to the end. If you have spent
much time with Paul's two letters to Timothy, then you probably
feel you know Timothy well. Second Timothy was, in fact, the last
letter Paul wrote from prison before his death.

Paul also sends greetings from Lucius (mentioned in Acts 13
as one the teachers in the city of Antioch), Jason (Paul's host in
the city of Thessalonica), and Sosipater (who may be "Sopater" of
Berea, mentioned in Acts 20).

Next, Tertius, who transcribed this letter as Paul dictated it, sends his own greeting. The name Tertius indicates that he was born a slave. The name means "Third." In slave families, it was common to number the children instead of naming them, so the children would be named First, Second, Third, Fourth, and so forth. Quartus, who is named in verse 23, was probably the younger brother of Tertius (Quartus means "Fourth").

Paul is probably staying in the home of the next man he names: "Gaius, whose hospitality I and the whole church here enjoy." Gaius has opened his house to the entire Christian community at Corinth. There may have been a whole group of Corinthian Christians in the house of Gaius, listening to Paul as he dictated. If so, they were the very first hearers of the truths we have studied in this book.

Finally, Paul sends greetings from Erastus, the director of public works in the city of Corinth. Here again we see that the gospel has penetrated all levels of society, so that slaves, civil servants, and leading officials of the empire are all sharing together an equal ground of fellowship in the church of Jesus Christ. All class distinctions disappear within the church—for that is what happens whenever the church is functioning as God intended.

Clearly, this final chapter of Romans is not just a list of names. Looking down this list, we have caught a glimpse of flesh-and-blood people who lived the rugged adventure of the Christian life. Paul commended the Roman Christians for their authentic love, their proven commitment, and their faithfulness to the gospel.

The Roman believers lived in the capital of the very empire that had, in fact, nailed their Lord and Savior to a cross. They did not live by the values and philosophies of this dying world. They did not live for pleasure, status, or fame. They lived at the bloody crossroads of history, and they were involved in the eternal struggle between good and evil, life and death. They trusted God to take them through the battle and bring them safely home, even if the way led through persecution, imprisonment, torture, and death.

God expects no less of us. The battle is still raging, our ancient enemy is still on the attack, and God has called not called us to a picnic ground but a battleground. Are you ready for the battle?

The Revelation of the Mystery

The last paragraph of this letter was probably written in Paul's own hand. In 2 Thessalonians 3:17, he wrote, "I, Paul, write this greeting in my own hand, which is the distinguishing mark in all my letters. This is how I write." It was Paul's custom to dictate his letters (probably because he suffered from a vision problem), then write the last paragraph himself. He did this to protect his letters from forgery. In Galatians 6:11, he wrote, "See what large letters I use as I write to you with my own hand." So at the end of this letter, Paul writes these marvelous words in large letters, bringing the book of Romans to a triumphant close:

> Now to him who is able to establish you by my gospel and the proclamation of Jesus Christ, according to the revelation of the mystery hidden for long ages past, but now revealed and made known through the prophetic writings by the command of the eternal God, so that all nations might believe and obey him—to the only wise God be glory forever through Jesus Christ! Amen. (Romans 16:25–27)

Here, Paul states his goal for all who read this letter: that they be *established*. What does it mean to be established? Many people who think they are established are merely stuck in the mud! Some of us think that being established means that we become rooted in one place, and we no longer need to make progress toward a goal.

But when Paul speaks of being established, he means that we are on solid, stable ground. Have you ever tried to eat a meal at a table with a wobbly leg? It's annoying and maddening, because the table keeps rocking. It is not established and stable. Christians who are not established are like that table—unstable, undependable, and wobbly.

Paul wants to bring us to a place where we are secure and unshakable. He wants us to be so mature that we do not get frustrated by circumstances or question God's goodness every time things don't go our way. It is God Himself who establishes us. We willingly cooperate with Him in this process, but we are not ultimately responsible for our own maturity and stability. That's God's job.

God took an idol worshiper named Abraham and established him as the father of our faith. God took a runaway named Moses and established him as the deliverer of the Hebrew nation. God took a murderer and adulterer named David and established him as a man after God's own heart. God took a hardened Pharisee, a persecutor of the church named Saul, and established him as Paul the apostle, author of nearly half of the New Testament and the greatest missionary evangelist of all time.

Paul says that God is able to establish the Roman Christians "by my gospel and the proclamation of Jesus Christ." When God establishes His people, He does so by means of the truth of the gospel and the proclaiming of a Person—Jesus Christ. Here, Paul opens to us the heart of the gospel. Though Paul was a mighty theologian, his primary goal in Romans is not to communicate theology, but to reveal Jesus Himself. Everything centers on Christ. Any so-called "gospel" that minimizes or marginalizes Christ is a perversion of the true gospel. Jesus Christ is the central figure of all history, of all time, of all faith.

Next, Paul says that his revelation of Christ is "according to the revelation of the mystery hidden for long ages past." Here is the ultimate test of any Christian message: Does it proclaim "the mystery"? There are many churches that have all the right biblical doctrines, yet they seem lifeless and do not reach out and touch the community. Why not? Because the mystery is not being proclaimed. What is this mystery that Paul talks about?

He referred to it earlier in Romans: "I do not want you to be ignorant of this mystery, brothers, so that you may not be conceited: Israel has experienced a hardening in part until the full number of the Gentiles has come in. And so all Israel will be saved. . . ." (see Romans 11:25–26; see also Ephesians 3:2–6). That is part of the mystery—the fact that God intends to unite both Jews and Gentiles into one body.

This is not to say that the mystery is made up of a number of separate and distinct parts or smaller mysteries. The mystery is all one mystery, and the heart of the mystery is revealed to us in the opening chapter of Colossians:

> Now I rejoice in what was suffered for you, and I fill up in my flesh what is still lacking in regard to Christ's afflictions, for the sake of his body, which is the church. I have become its servant by the commission God gave me to present to you the word of God in its fullness—the mystery that has been kept hidden for ages and generations, but is now disclosed to the saints. To them God has chosen to make known among the Gentiles the glorious riches of this mystery, which is Christ in you, the hope of glory. (Colossians 1:24–27)

That is the mystery of mysteries: Christ in you, the hope of glory! Everything that God is has been poured into human form and given to us, sacrificed for us, implanted in us, and made available to us. Through Him, we have a certain hope of future glory, intended for us from before the foundation of the world. This great mystery was sung in a hymn of the early church, which Paul includes for us in a letter to Timothy:

> Beyond all question, the mystery of godliness is great:
>> He appeared in a body,
>>> was vindicated by the Spirit,
>> was seen by angels,
>>> was preached among the nations,
>> was believed on in the world,
>>> was taken up in glory. (1 Timothy 3:16)

Jesus Himself is the mystery. By means of His virgin birth, His holy and sinless life, His sacrifice upon the cross, His startling breakout from the prison of death, and His gift of the Holy Spirit on the day of Pentecost, God has given Jesus to you and me. He lives His life through us. That is the radical, mysterious secret of authentic Christianity—Christ in you, the hope of glory.

Do you know the mystery? Do you live it? If you do, then your life is a thrilling adventure! The authentic Christian life may be risky, it may be scary, but it is never boring! If you are filled with the indwelling Christ, then it makes no difference if you are a Jew or a Gentile. All divisions of class, gender, race, and ethnicity are obliterated by the mystery, because we are all one in Christ.

When you read the Old Testament, you see why this truth is called "the mystery." Down through the centuries before Jesus, you see that the wisest Jewish leaders, prophets, and scribes puzzled over how God would tie together all the promises of the Old Testament. There is the promise of Israel's restoration, the promise of the forgiveness of sin, the promise of a suffering Messiah, the promise of a triumphant king, and the promise of the healing of nations and the end of war and sorrow. How could all of these unrelated promises come true?

Then Jesus came, and the mystery began to unfold! He was the secret! He would tie all of these promises together in Himself. All of the great themes of the Old Testament, from Genesis to Malachi, converged on Him. This mystery was hidden for centuries, but was revealed in Jesus by the command of God.

So Paul closes with this great doxology: "To the only wise God be glory forever through Jesus Christ! Amen."

The same wisdom and power that spoke the universe into being now flows through us. We are channels for the gifts of His Spirit. Through Him, we can dare the unthinkable and achieve the impossible. God is at work in us—that is the mystery! He gives His glory to us, and so we give glory to Him: To the only wise God be glory forever and ever through His Son, Jesus the Lord!

Amen and amen!

NOTES

Editors' Preface

1. Edior James Denney has provided a few updated examples to the author's writing when appropriate.

Chapter 2. The Divine Diagnosis

1. C. S. Lewis, *Mere Christianity*, (San Francisco: HarperSan-Francisco, 2001), 102–103.

Chapter 3. Sinful Morality

1. Ibid., 475.
2. Don Richardson, *Peace Child* (Ventura, CA: Gospel Light/Regal Books, 1974), 10.

Chapter 6. Rejoicing in God

1. Ray Stedman, *Authentic Christianity* (Grand Rapids, Discovery House, 1996), 26.

Chapter 10. If God Be for Us

1. C. S. Lewis, *The Weight of Glory* (San Francisco: HarperSan-Francisco, 2001), 41,42.

NOTE TO THE READER

The publisher invites you to share your response to the message of this book by writing Discovery House Publishers, Box 3566, Grand Rapids, MI 49501, USA. For information about other Discovery House books, music, or videos, contact us at the same address or call 1-800-653-8333. Find us on the Internet at http://www.dhp.org/ or send e-mail to books@dhp.org.